THE EX

0222954

KT-549-208

This reader is one part of an Open University integrated teaching system and the selection is therefore related to other material available to students. It is designed to evoke the critical understanding of students. Opinions expressed in it are not necessarily those of the course team or of the University.

THE EXPERIENCE OF WORK

Edited by
Craig R. Littler

Gower
in association with The Open University

For Dene

Published by
Gower Publishing Company Limited,
Gower House,
Croft Road,
Aldershot,
Hampshire GU11 3HR,
England

British Library Cataloguing in Publication Data

The Experience of work.
   1. Work—Social aspects
   I. Litfler, Craig, R.
   306'.36   HD6955
   ISBN 0–566–00856–4
   ISBN 0–566–00857–2 Pbk

Phototypesetting by Inforum Ltd, Portsmouth
Printed in Great Britain by
Biddles Ltd, Guildford, Surrey.

Contents

Acknowledgements

The editor and the publishers would like to thank the following for permission to reproduce the articles contained within (page numbers in this book shown in brackets): George Allen & Unwin, Hemel Hempstead (262–270); Allison & Busby, London (183–189); The Association of Social Anthropologists, Canterbury (23–33); B.T. Batsford Ltd, London (85–104); Basil Blackwell Ltd, Oxford (50–71, 190–206); John Calder (Publishers) Ltd, London (117–131); Cambridge University Press, Cambridge (13–22); Free Association Books, London (172–182); Mrs Janet Gouldner, St Louis (141–150); The Institute of Electrical and Electronics Engineers Inc., New York (161–171); New Society, London (247–251); Oxford University Press Australia, Melbourne (151–160); Penguin Books Ltd, London (75–84, 209–215); Pluto Press, London (132–140); Problems of Communism, Washington (252–261); Psychology Today, Washington (271–276); Routledge & Kegan Paul p.l.c., London (105–116).

1 Introduction: the Texture of Work
Craig R. Littler

> Without work all life goes rotten. But when work is soulless, life stifles and dies.
>
> *Albert Camus*

For some, hard work is the path to salvation; for others it is a means to money, whilst for the cynic it is merely the best way to fill up a lot of time before death. Work, then, carries many individual significances, but more generally work has three levels of meaning: an economic, social and personal meaning.

At the economic level, work is the means whereby the vast majority of people earn their livelihood and it provides, through cooperative efforts, the goods and services needed by people and by society generally. Chapter 2 ('The Primitive Economics of the Trobriand Islanders') portrays a situation where the economic meaning of work in terms of food production is transparent and obvious to all: 'man with no food' is one of the greatest social insults (p. 19). In complex industrial societies the immanent connection between work and survival has become obscure, and such societies tend to become racked by debates about 'production for what?' Nevertheless, the economic interpretation of work activity remains predominant.

Even in small-scale, non-complex societies, such as that of the Trobriand Islanders, work activity takes on ritualistic and religious significance. Generally, work has always been invested with moral qualities, and the economic meaning of work becomes intertwined with the social meaning. On an individual plane, the nature of the work performed has usually conferred a social status on the worker and the worker's family. This is conveyed most powerfully in Chapter 3, where the work of the Indian sweepers is linked up to a hierarchy of purity and impurity.

A consequence of work organisation is that it enforces on those who participate in it certain categories of experience – it imposes a time structure on the waking day; it demands participation in cooperative relationships and regular activity; and it clarifies personal identity and creates some sense of personal worth. (Jahoda, 1982). These are the personal dimensions of work. Indeed, one's success or failure in the work world is often translated into a measure of being a valuable or worthless human being. Such a measure, of course, pushes to the social margins all work activity which is unpaid – not only voluntary or community work but housework and mothering (see Chapter 15).

For most people the first experience of the world of work is not the job itself, but seeking work. It is in the labour market – that nexus of employment exchange, newspaper job column and grapevine – that sellers and buyers of labour meet. In many societies the pressures of the unemployed and underemployed are so great that there is a continual surge of poor peasants from the country to the towns in search of work. To take one example, in Mexico it is estimated that between 25–50 per cent of the labour force is under or unemployed. (Thompson, 1983, p.65.) Under these circumstances, the relations of buying labour are naked and overt. In Mexico City – a city swollen with job-seekers – the labour market for building workers consists of a pavement line of under-nourished men each with a card proclaiming 'carpenter', 'brick-layer' or 'labourer'. Every day they stand, hoping to be purchased and put to work.

In European societies, labour markets are not usually so overt or casualized, but for many the insecurities remain – a continual tinge of anxiety or a burning pressure of worry – and are reflected most in the conditions of the unemployed. Here are three voices of the unemployed:

I really feel so lost without a regular daily activity. It's all bits and pieces now. My work provided a long, absorbing day. I now lack a focal point in life. How long can I stand this?

It's like being in limbo or stateless. I feel disoriented. I *hated* taking unemployment benefit. Felt 'unearned', 'money for nothing', 'gained under false pretences'. I couldn't relax at home. Felt conversation becoming dull and house-bound, centred around daily chores. To others I looked a normal married woman 'at home'.

Being out of work is dreadful, running from interview to interview. You're manhandled like a shoe in a jumble sale. I got so fed up with false promises and false expectations.

(Quoted in Fineman, 1983, pp.57 and 113)

For many people (though certainly not all), paid employment acts as a psychic glue; it holds an individual together in terms of aim, purpose and identity. Unemployment does not just mean the absence of work, but that people are *in* the labour market, subject to its insecurities, and aware of themselves as commodities, like shoes or sausages.

At the time of writing (1984), there were nineteen million people unemployed in Western Europe. But even the dimensions of this vast army does not tell the whole story: in Britain, for example, 22 per cent of all British households had experienced unemployment at some time during a twelve-month period (CSO, 1984). So a significant slice of the population must be aware of themselves as insecurely positioned within a labour market, rather than tied to a work organisation.

One group particularly affected by the labour market situation of the 1980s is the new recruits to the army of job-seekers. For young people paid employment is not just a way to make money, but is the main route to adulthood and an identity in society. Long-term unemployment of the young tends to create a deep culture of unemployment in which young people become increasingly isolated, with a loss of dignity and self-respect. One study (Unemployment Unit, 1983) indicates that men out of work for more than a year are more than eighteen times more likely to attempt suicide than those with a job.

Many people seek shelter from the fears of unemployment, erecting walls of job security around themselves if they can. And some can, with the help of employers. Even in the labour market conditions of Mexico there is a difference between the permanent workers (*de planta*) and the *eventuales* – temporary workers suitable for any eventuality of shifts in demand and whom the employer can lay off almost at will. Similarly, in Japan there is an entrenched distinction between the standard permanent workers and the casual temporary workers. In Britain there has long been a culture of casualism for manual work, especially in industries such as construction, quarry work, docks, and so on. Many factory-based trades were also subject to seasonal fluctuations and in these trades a minority of workers were favoured with regular employment, as employers sought to retain a number of particularly adept or docile workers.

These differences in labour market status help to create (or reinforce) different orientations to work. For example, women's domestic work shapes many women's conceptions of themselves as workers. 'The home and its responsibilities persistently invade women's thoughts, fragmenting and diluting their consciousness of themselves as wage workers' (Herzog, 1980, p. 31.) But such work orientations are reinforced by the location of women's work in the production process as secondary and temporary. Work orientations, then, represent a meshing together of workers' biographies, within which age and family position play an important part, and the forces of the labour market. Older women may fit their working lives around their families, whilst many young women regard work as temporary – an unpleasant interlude before marriage and children – which means that they treat one tedious unskilled job as being as good as another. When the myths of romance and ultimate escape dissolve, for many, into the realities of continued work, it is too late. Life has gone by, the chances missed (Pollert, 1981).

Not that there is much escape or romance in housebound domestic work, as is vividly shown in the reading from Gail (Chapter 15). Most mothers soon discover that young children constitute an enormous, never-ending set of demands – 'a baby demands the whole of you' – which can thrust the housebound childminder into a mental prison. Gail recalls that she freed the surface of her mind from thoughts altogether, 'leaving it swimming aimlessly so that it can be called into action by an alarming sound' (p. 187 of this volume). The account by Gail suggests that even young couples who are initially determined to avoid a traditional household division of labour, find themselves propelled by children into the pattern of preceding generations. Many women adjust: many do not, and feel with Gail that 'Office or factory work seems more annihilating because even less of me would be involved, but if I were given the choice between that or housework I would rather be out working *in any conditions.*' (p. 186, my emphasis). Such are the social and psychological sources which create the temporary labour feedstock for factories and offices.

Work organisation, then, consists of various labour market 'slots' – a division of security and insecurity reinforced by attitudes to work. But what of the actual work experiences in the job? In no modern society is all people's work the same or even similar. There is no simple community of situation, so that the nature, content and texture of other people's working lives is something strange. The major function of the following readings is to convert some of this strangeness into an understanding.

The book begins with a society (the Trobriand Islanders) where there *was* a common community of work experience: nearly all the islanders were involved in gardening and growing food. Nevertheless, simple traditional societies did not represent clusters of closed family-based economies. As Malinowski makes clear, there were patterns of communal work, on various scales, beyond the family, and the society, in part, constituted a means for summoning and maintaining communal labour. Indeed, the whole community was enmeshed in a network of reciprocal obligations and dues, a constant flow of gifts and counter-gifts, such that 'Everybody is working for somebody else.' (p. 18).

In large-scale, more complex societies there are clearer developments of 'occupations', so that work can become a major determinant of identity and status. Indeed, the Indian caste system is a hierarchy of purity which fills certain occupations with ritualistic significance, such as those of the Benares sweepers who handle human excrement.

Both Malinowski and Chatterjee make clear that we should not romanticise the work experiences of traditional societies. This has been a tendency in some recent literature (such as Braverman), and is partly true of the influential work of E.P. Thompson, who assumes that traditional agricultural work involves little division between 'work' and life and 'work' and the family, such that the day's tasks disclose themselves by a logic of need and a logic of nature. Chapter 5 ('The Household at Work') indicates that under certain circumstances, such as that of independent peasant farming, there may be some truth in such notions, but, more generally, productive labour was not confined to the social terrain of the family or kinship group. However, it is true that the widespread development of wage-labour implies a shift to timed labour, the development of a time orientation, and different work patterns: time becomes currency. This transition, discussed in Chapter 4, is the most fundamental change in the quality of work experience associated with industrialism.

The reading by Littler and Salaman ('The Design of Jobs') attempts to provide an overall view of some of the main dynamics within modern industrial work. It shows that though the assembly line has had a restricted diffusion, nevertheless it retains an importance as an *ideal* of work organisation for many employers. An ideal involving routinised, compartmentalised work. The force of such work design is well caught by a Finnish worker at a large Swedish telecommunications firm (L.M. Ericsson):

Things are arranged so that the worker is easy to replace, easy to move, easy to fire, and his work is broken down into small operations. . . . So it gets like that in industry that they get more and more workers who easily forget what is important . . . if speed is the only thing that counts, then you get fast workers, quick-fingered workers, careless workers. And if you have a lot of moving, turnover, idiot work, scheming, everything, then you get drifters and robots and schemers and bloody foreigners.

(Quoted in Palm, 1977, pp. 107–8)

Some of the realities of working on assembly lines are captured in the extracts from Cavendish (Chapter 8) and Linhart (Chapter 9). Both writers describe the endless pressure and the continual fear of slipping behind. But there is something deeper than just moans and groans about one's job. The vast majority of people want to work and even like to work, but such desires turn upon a sense that people are doing a 'good job'. However, many modern work systems, especially those involving piecework or payment-by-results, encourage a more or less systematic carelessness in quality. The Finnish sheet-metal worker quoted above expresses this tension well:

When you're not young and crazy any more . . . You want to be more responsible. You want to do a good job, take care of your tools, protect yourself too, check every component you produce, things like that. I want to feel the metal sheet with my hand, to see that it is even. But that is not allowed . . . It's not supposed to be a good job, only a fast job, a quick job . . . If I make them perfect, I don't make any money. And no praise, never. Only more, that I am slow and stop things. . . . Like I was being too fussy. Those blanks should only *just* pass through the inspection, that is the best. Maybe I think they are awful. But they do not think so, the management, they reckon with carelessness.

(Quoted in Palm, 1977, pp. 100–1)

This quotation illustrates that much assembly line and machine minding work becomes narrowed down such that it is an unattainable ideal to expect work that demands involvement or the use of actual or potential skills. Instead, the control system and the payment system hook one into a manic concern for throughput and little else.

In a different context, that of a Soviet-type society, Harastzi charts out an almost identical set of individual responses. He describes the way in which he becomes obsessed about 'making out', that is about making a regular rate of pay (see Chapter 17, 'A Worker in a Worker's State'). The machine-minder on a piecework system has an illusion of independence, and the reality of chasing himself driven by insecurity.

If there are few intrinsic satisfactions in assembly line work or most machine minding, and if the work becomes a daily struggle to keep pace with machine cycles and conveyors, then why are not reactions of severe distress more apparent? One answer is that people become resigned to a daily drudge, going on from day to day, week to week, year to year, and before they know where they are they are drawing their pension. But work experience is partly shaped by previous experience; and for many people, especially in developing societies, factory jobs are not (as they tend to be regarded in Britain) the lowest of the low, but represent a form of promotion. Factory jobs can offer, or appear to offer, money, security, and a better work environment than the arduous conditions of peasant life. Cavendish (see Chapter 8) makes clear that nearly all of the women on her assembly line were Irish or West Indian immigrants. In France (see Chapter 9) and in West Germany, a large majority of workers in the car industry are either foreign migrants or recruits from agriculture, and it is they who bear the brunt of assembly line work and of fluctuations in employment levels. In China factory work in the state sector, which includes all of the large, mass production factories, is highly regarded and sought after as secure and well-paid employment (see Chapter 18). That this is not peculiar to China as a socialist society is indicated by India where the pattern is similar (see Holmstrom, 1976).

Some analysts have suggested that tedious work is accompanied by compensating psychological mechanisms – a sense of 'traction' ('the feeling of being pulled along by the inertia inherent in a particular activity. The experience is pleasant, and may . . . function as a relief from tedium.') or an internal escape into the land of day-dreams (see Baldamus, 1961, p.59). However, the evidence for this is slight: most machine tasks require a fitful concentration such that any dream processes are constantly interrupted (Lane, 1969). More plausibly, the oppressiveness of repetitive, pressurised work activities may not result in any dramatic symptoms, only in a slow death of hope in a sea of headaches, backaches and tranquillisers.

Perhaps the greatest relief from the tedium and oppressiveness of repetitive machine-paced work is humour. Here is the text of one notice I saw pinned to the workshop wall by the workers:

The Management regret that it has come to their attention that employees dying on the job are failing to fall down.

This practice must cease, as it becomes impossible to distinguish between the dead and the natural movements of the staff.

Any employee found dead in an upright position will be dropped from the payroll immediately.

The Management

Only a minority of the labour force are involved in assembly line work or in machine minding. One avenue of avoidance, especially for men, is the traditional one – learning a trade. Perhaps the most prestigious working-class trade is that of printer. The reading by Cockburn (Chapter 10) deals with the skills and situation of this occupational group – the epitome of craftsmen. It shows that technological changes have and are threatening residual ideas of craftsmanship, leading to a loss of occupational identity: the printers 'have gone up a ladder of learning, alluringly set before them, and dropped off the top', to descend to the status of the common man, and, even more fearfully for the printers, to the common woman. The printers' case illustrates a frequent occurrence: that as workers slip down the skill hierarchy, they often cling, at least for a time, to the old identity; '*I* am skilled, even if the *job* is not.' (p. 134).

The world of the printer, as Cockburn makes clear, is being transformed from manual work dealing with hot metal to a form of clerical work; an occupational transition which echoes the overall trends in the labour force. One crucial white-collar group is the professional occupations, and the readings from Rosenbrock (Chapter 13) and Hales (Chapter 14) indicate some of the nature and meaning of professional work. In particular, the two chapters show that an important segment of professional work is concerned with designing the work lives of others.

Hales emphasises the extreme separation of design and daily operations: all the human effort embodied in a chemical plant 'took place at some other time, in some other place, involved some other workers: effectively a different world' (p. 182). The older, traditional professions were permeated by an ethic of 'service', but the newer professions of engineers and designers are permeated by a different ethos – one of 'efficiency', 'reliability' and 'quality control' – which carries a certain interpretation; namely that as far as possible manual functions and operator control should be automated out of the productive process. Rosenbrock (Chapter 13) calls this ethos a 'paradigm' – a process of seeing or re-shaping problems so that they are amenable to the existing professional techniques. And these techniques involve a particular conception of man/machine relationships which tend to undervalue or diminish human skills, so that, paradoxically, if the engineers 'had been able to consider people as though they were robots, they would have tried to provide them with less trivial and more human work'. (p. 165). The force of such paradigms assails not just traditional crafts like printers, but even the traditional professions themselves; solicitors, for example, will have to confront computerised house transfer and conveyancing whilst doctors will have to cope with computerised diagnosis. All the professional occupations will have to confront the mechanisation of knowledge in the dying years of the twentieth century.

Rationalisation, mechanisation and automation are long words and long-drawn out processes, but they all imply and have meant more output with less human effort. Fine for some, but what happens to the redundant and the unemployed in the slimmed down world of slim machines and slim organisations? One answer is working outside the official economy. The last set of readings (Chapters 19, 20, 21 and 22) illustrates the attention given to these processes in recent years, as both tax inspectors and academics catch up with the realities of the labour market.

Working outside the official economy, whether it be extended working in the domestic economy (chickens and goats in the back garden) or in the underground economy, may be an avenue for some, but is hardly a solution for nineteen million unemployed in Western Europe. Some observers argue that the combined economic and technological impacts of the last decades of the twentieth century are creating the 'collapse of work', so that there will have to be a drastic redistribution of working opportunities and that fairly soon unemployment will not carry the same social implications which it now does. The details of these arguments, which seem to me to be a peculiar mixture of hope and wishful thinking, are examined in the concluding chapter, 'The Future of Work'.

This book, along with its companion volume (*Work, Employment and Unemployment*, edited by Kenneth Thompson and published by the Open University Press), form part of the teaching materials of the Open University course *Work and Society* DE 325). Nevertheless, we have designed both volumes so that they are of interest and value to the general reader and those on other courses concerned with the sociology of work.

References

Baldamus, W. (1961), *Efficiency and Effort*, Tavistock.

Braverman, H. (1974), *Labor and Monopoly Capital*, Monthly Review Press.

CSO (Central Statistical Office) (1984), *Social Trends*.

Fineman, S. (1983), *White Collar Unemployment: Impact and Stress*, Wiley.

Holmstrom, M. (1976), *South Indian Factory Workers*, Cambridge University Press.

Herzog, M. (1980), *From Hand to Mouth: Woman and Piecework*, Penguin.

Jahoda, M. (1982), *Employment and Unemployment: A Social-Psychological Analysis*, Cambridge University Press.

Lane, A.D. (1969), 'The Machine Minders', in *New Society*, 30 January pp. 45–6.

Palm, G. (1977), *The Flight From Work*, Cambridge University Press.

Pollert, A. (1981), *Girls, Wives, Factory Lives*, Macmillan.

Thompson, M. (1983), 'The Permanent Employment System: Japan and Mexico', International Industrial Relations Association, 6th World Congress, *Proceedings* Vol. 4. mimeo.

Truss, B. (1976), 'My Life as a Screwdriver' in *New Society*, 15 January p. 93.

Unemployment Unit (1983), *Bulletin No. 10*.

Work in Non-industrial Societies

2 The Primitive Economics of the Trobriand Islanders*

Bronislaw Malinowski

Editor's Introduction: This chapter consists of a classic paper written over half a century ago by the influential anthropologist Malinowski. As such, it shares the vocabulary and outlook of its times (e.g. the then acceptable usage of terms such as 'savage' and 'natives'). Despite this, the paper provides valuable insights based on lengthy first-hand field work into thè nature of work in a pre-industrial traditional culture. In a small-scale, horticultural society, such as that of the Trobriand islanders, what was the nature of work and work organisation? Malinowski's paper seeks to answer this question.

In this article I shall try to present some data referring to the economic life of the Trobriand Islanders, a community living on a coral archipelago off the north-east coast of New Guinea. These natives, typical South Sea Islanders of the Melanesian stock, with a developed institution of chieftainship, great ability in various crafts and a fine decorative art, certainly are not at the lower end of savagery. In their general level of culture, however, they may be taken as representative of the majority of the savage races now in existence, and they are less developed culturally than the Polynesians, the bulk of North American Indians, of Africans, and of Indonesians. If we find, therefore, distinct forms of economic organisation among them, we are safe in assuming that even among the lowest savages we might expect to find more facts of economic interest than have been hitherto recorded.

I shall first give an outline of the natural resources of the Trobrianders and a broad survey of the manner in which these are utilised. The natives live on flat coral islands, covered with rich, heavy soil, very well suited for the cultivation of yams and taro, and they also enjoy a good regular rainfall. The coast is surrounded in parts with a fringing reef, in parts it encloses a big, shallow lagoon, teeming with fish. Having such excellent natural inducements, the natives are splendid tillers of the soil

---

* Abridged from *The Economic Journal*, March, 1921, pp. 1–16.

and first-rate fishermen, efficient and hard-working in both pursuits. These in turn reward them with a perennial abundance of food, sufficient to support a population very dense, as compared with other tribes of that part of the world. In gardening the natives obtain their fine results in spite of using only the most primitive implement – a pointed stick, made and discarded every time they go to work. In fishing they use big nets, also traps, fish-hooks and poison. As manufacturers they excel in wood-carving, basket-weaving, and the production of highly-valued shell ornaments. On the other hand, through lack of material, they have to rely on the importation from other tribes of stone implements and pottery, as, of course, neither hard stone nor clay are obtainable on a coral island. I have begun by giving this general outline of their resources, pursuits and crafts, in order to indicate the narrow frame within which the current accounts of economics are encompassed. The data would there, no doubt, be given with a much greater wealth of detail – especially in the technological aspect – but it would be mainly the successive description of the various activities, connected with the quest for food and the manufacture of objects, without any attempt being made at a discussion of the more complex problems, referring to organisation of production, apportionment, and to the mechanism of tribal life in its economic aspect.

This will be done here, beginning with production, and taking agriculture as an example.

The questions before us are, first, the important problem of land tenure; next, the less obvious problems of the organisation of production. Is the work in the gardens carried out by each family, or each person individually and independently? Or is there any general co-ordination of this work, any social organisation of their efforts, and, if so, how is it done, and by whom? Are the successive stages of the work integrated into any organic whole, by any supervision, by any personal guidance, or any social or psychological force?

Land tenure among the Trobriand natives is rather complex, and it shows well the difficulties of solving ethnographic field problems of this type and the dangers of being misled into some inadequate approximation. When I began to inquire into this subject, I first received from my native informant a series of general statements, such as that the chief is the owner of all land, or that each garden plot has its owner, or that all the men of a village community own the land jointly. Then I tried to answer the question by the method of concrete investigation: taking a definite plot, I inquired successively, from several independent informants, who was the owner of it. In some cases I had mentioned to me successively as many as five different 'owners' to one plot – each answer, as I found out later on, containing part of the truth, but none being correct by itself. It was only after I had drawn up complete plans

of the garden land of several village communities, and inquired successively into the details, not only of each separate garden unit, but also
into the details of each of the alleged forms of 'ownership,' that I was
able to reach a satisfactory conclusion. The main difficulty in this, as in
ever so many similar questions, lies in our giving our own meaning of
'ownership' to the corresponding native word. In doing this we over-
look the fact that to the natives the word 'ownership' not only has a
different significance, but that they use one word to denote several legal
and economic relationships, between which it is absolutely necessary
for us to distinguish.

The chief (*Guya'u*) has in the Trobriands a definite over-right over all
the garden land within the district. This consists in the title of 'master'
or 'owner' (*Toli*), and in the exercise of certain ceremonial rights and
privileges, such as the decision on which lands the gardens are to be
made, arbitration in garden disputes, and several minor privileges. The
garden magician (*Towosi*) also calls himself the 'master of the garden'
and is considered as such, in virtue of his complex magical and other
functions, fulfilled in the course of gardening. Again, in certain cases,
and over certain portions of the land, the same title is given to notables
or sub-chiefs, who carry out certain minor offices in connection with it.
Finally, each garden plot belongs to some individual or other in the
village community, and, when the gardens are made on this particular
land, this owner either uses his plot himself or leases it to someone else
under a rather complicated system of payment. The chief, the magician
and the notables also own individually a number of garden plots each,
independently of their general over-rights.

Now the reason why an economist cannot ignore such over-rights
and complications is that the natives value them extremely, and, what is
more important, that such over-rights carry with them definite functions and wield definite influences of economic importance.

Thus the complex conditions of land tenure, the not infrequent
quarrels about gardening, and the need for summoning and maintaining communal labour require a social authority, and this is supplied
by the chief with the assistance of the notables. On the other hand, the
Towosi, the hereditary garden magician of each village community, has
to a great extent the control over the initiative in the more detailed
proceedings of the work. Each stage of gardening is inaugurated by a
magical rite performed by him. He also orders the work to be done,
looks after the way in which it is carried out, and imposes the periods of
taboo, which punctuate it.

The proceedings of gardening are opened by a conference, summoned
by the chief and held in front of the magician's house, at which all
arrangements and the allotment of garden plots are decided upon.
Immediately after that, the members of the village community bring a

gift of selected food to the garden magician, who at night sacrificially offers a portion of it to the ancestral spirits, with an invocation, and at the same time utters a lengthy spell over some special leaves. Next morning, the magician repairs to the garden, accompanied by the men of the village, each of whom carries an axe with the charmed leaves wrapped around its blade. While the villagers stand around, the *Towosi* (magician) strikes the ground with a ceremonial staff, uttering a formula. This he does on each garden plot successively, and on each the men cut a few saplings with their axes. After that, for a month or so, the scrub is cut in the prospective gardens by men only, and communal labour is often resorted to. The *Towosi* has to decide when the next stage, the burning of scrub and the clearing of soil, has to begin. When he thinks that the cut scrub is sufficiently dry, he imposes a taboo on garden work, so that any belated cutting has to be suspended. In a series of rites, lasting, as a rule, for about three days, he inaugurates the work of clearing the garden plot; this afterwards is carried on by men and women jointly, working in families, each on its own plot, without the help of communal labour. The planting of yams is inaugurated by a very elaborate ceremony, also extending over a few days, during which no further garden work is done at all. A magical rite of its own inaugurates each further stage, the erection of supports for the yam vine; the weeding of the gardens, done by female communal labour: the cleaning of the yam roots and tubers; the preliminary harvest of early yams; and finally the main harvest of late yams.

When the plants begin to grow a series of magical rites, parallel with the inaugural ones, is performed, in which the magician is supposed to give an impulse to the growth and development of the plant at each of its successive stages. Thus, one rite is performed to make the seed tuber sprout; another drives up the sprouting shoot; another lifts it out of the ground; yet another makes it twine round the support; then, with yet other rites, the leaves are made to bud, to open, to expand, respectively.

Besides the indirect influence which the *Towosi* exercises on garden work by giving the initiative and inaugurating the successive stages, by imposing taboos, and by setting the standard by means of the *Leywota* plots, he also directly supervises certain activities of general importance to all the gardens. Thus, for example, he keeps his eye on the work done in fencing round the garden. All the plots are placed within a common enclosing fence, of which everyone has to make his share, corresponding to his plot or plots. Thus, the neglect of one careless individual might result in a damage to all, for bush pigs or wallabies might find their way in and destroy the new crops. If this happens, the garden magician gets up in front of his house in the evening and harangues the village, often mentioning the culprit by name and heaping blame on him – a proceeding which seldom fails to take effect.

It is easy to see that the magician performs manifold and complex functions, and that his claim to be the 'master of the garden' is not an empty one! What is now the economic importance of his function? The natives believe deeply that through his magic the *Towosi* controls the forces of Nature, and they also believe that he ought to control the work of man. To start a new stage of gardening without a magical inauguration is, for them, unthinkable. Thus, his magical power, exercised side by side with their work, his magical co-operation, so to speak, inspires them with confidence in success and gives them a powerful impulse to work. Their implicit belief in magic also supplies them with a leader, whose initiative and command they are ready to accept in all matters, where it is needed. It is obvious that the series of magical rites – punctuating the progress of activities at regular intervals, imposing a series of rest periods, and, in the institution of standard plots (*Leywota*), establishing a model to the whole community – is of extreme importance. It acts as a psychological force, making for a more highly organised system of work, than it would be possible to achieve at this stage of culture by an appeal to force or to reason.

Thus, we can answer the questions, referring to the organisation of production, by summing up our results, and saying that the authority of the chief, the belief in magic, and the prestige of the magician are the social and psychological forces which regulate and organise production; that this latter, far from being just the sum of uncorrelated individual efforts, is a complex and organically united tribal enterprise.

Finally, a few words must be said about the character of native labour in the Trobriands. We would see their economic activities in an entirely wrong perspective, if we were to imagine that these natives are temperamentally lazy and can work only under some outside pressure. They have a keen interest in their gardens, work with spirit, and can do sustained and efficient work, both when they do it individually and communally. There are different systems of communal work on various scales; sometimes the several village communities join together, sometimes the whole community, sometimes a few households. Distinctive native names are given to the various kinds of communal work, and payment in food also differs. In the more extensive kinds of work, it is the chief's duty to feed the workers.

An interesting institution of ceremonial enterprise deserves special attention. This is known as the *Kayasa*, and might be described as a period when all activities, whether gardening, fishing, industrial or even merely tribal sports and merrymaking, are carried out with special intensity. When the season is good, and the time is felt by the whole community to be propitious, the chief announces the *Kayasa*, and inaugurates it by giving a big feast. The whole period of the *Kayasa* is punctuated by other feasts, also provided for by the chief, and everyone who takes part is under an implicit obligation to do his best, and work his hardest, so that the *Kayasa* may be a success.

We have discussed their production on the example of gardening. The same conclusions, however, could have been drawn from a discussion of fishing, building of houses or canoes, of from a description of their big trading expeditions. All these activities are dependent upon the social power of the chief and the influence of the respective magicians. In all of them the quantity of the produce, the nature of the work and the manner in which it is carried out – all of which are essentially economic features – are highly modified by the social organisation of the tribe and by their magical belief. Customary and legal norms, magical and mythological ideas, introduce system into their economic efforts and organise them on a social basis. On the other hand, it is clear that if an ethnologist proposes to describe any aspect of tribal life, without approaching it also from the economic point of view, his account would be bound to be a failure.

This will be still more evident after a description of the manner in which they apportion the produce and utilise it in what could be called the financing of tribal enterprise. Here, again, I shall speak, for simplicity's sake, mainly of the garden produce. As each man has allotted to him for each season one or several garden plots, we might expect that, following the principle of 'closed household economy,' each family would by themselves consume the results of their labour. As a matter of fact, the apportionment or distribution, far from following such a simple scheme, is again full of intricacies and presents many economically interesting features. Of these the two most important are: the obligations, imposed by rules of kinship and relationship-in-law, and the dues and tributes paid to the chief.

The first-named obligations involve a very complex redistribution of garden produce, resulting in a state of things in which everybody is working for somebody else. The main rule is that a man is obliged to distribute almost all his garden produce among his sisters; in fact, to maintain his sisters and their families. I must pass over all the complications and consequences implied by this system, and only notice that it means an enormous amount of additional labour in handling and transporting the produce, and that it enmeshes the whole community into a network of reciprocal obligations and dues, one constant flow of gift and counter-gift.

This constant economic undertow to all public and private activities – this materialistic streak which runs through all their doings – gives a special and unexpected colour to the existence of the natives, and shows the immense importance to them of the economic aspect of everything. Economic considerations pervade their social life, economic difficulties constantly face them. Whenever the native moves – to a feast, to an expedition, or in warfare – he will have to deal with the problems of giving and counter-giving. The detailed analysis of this state of affairs would lead us to interesting results, but it would be a side issue from our main theme – the public economy of the tribe.

To return to this, we must first consider, what part of the whole tribal income is apportioned to the chief. By various channels, by dues and tributes, and especially through the effect of polygamy, with its resulting obligations of his relatives-in-law, about 30 per cent. of the whole food production of his district finds its way into the large, finely-decorated yam houses of the chief. Now to the natives the possession and display of food are of immense value and importance in themselves. Pride in possessing abundant food is one of their leading characteristics. One of the greatest insults that can be uttered is to call someone 'Man with no food,' and it would be bitterly resented, and probably a quarrel would ensue. To be able to boast of having food, is one of their chief glories and ambitions. Their whole conduct, in the matter of eating in public, is guided by the rule that no suspicion of scarcity of food can possibly be attached to the eater. For example, to eat publicly in a strange village would be considered humiliating, and is never done.

Their ambitions in this direction are also shown by the keen interest taken in the display of food. On all possible occasions – at harvest time, when there is an interchange of gifts, or when the enormous food distributions (*Sagali*) take place – the display of the food is one of the main features of interest. And there are even special food exhibitions, in which two villages compete against each other, and which in the old days used to be taken so seriously that often war was the result.

The chief is the only person who owns a big yam house, which is made with open interstices between the beams so that all may look through and admire the yams, of which the finest are always placed to the front. The chief is, as a matter of fact, also the only person who can accumulate, and, as a matter of privilege, the only one who is allowed to own and display larger quantities. This gives him a definite status, is a sign of high rank, and satisfies his ambition. Finally, it enhances his power, broadly speaking, in the same manner as possession of wealth does with us.

Another important privilege of the chief, is his power to transform food into objects of permanent wealth. Here again, he is the only man rich enough to do it, but he also jealously guards his right, and would punish anyone who might attempt to emulate him, even on a small scale.

The possession of the beautiful yam houses, always ready to receive the crops, and often filled with them; the acquisition of a large amount of *Vaygua* (tokens of wealth), and of the greater part of the pigs, coconuts and betel nuts, give the chief a static basis of power, prestige and rank. But also the control over all these classes of wealth allows him to exercise his power dynamically.

For in a society where everything has to be accompanied by gift and payment, even the chief, the highest and most powerful individual in the community, though, according to customary rule, he can command the services of all, still must pay for them. He enjoys many personal services, such as being carried about on his journeys, sending people on errands, having all forms of magic performed for him. For such services, rendered by retainers and picked specialists, a chief must pay immediately, sometimes in *Vaygua*, sometimes in food, more especially in pigs, coconuts and betel nuts.

The essential of power is, of course, the possibility of enforcing orders and commanding obedience by means of punishment. The chief has special henchmen to carry out his verdicts directly by inflicting capital punishment, and they must be paid by *Vaygua*. More often, however, the punishment is meted out by means of evil magic. How often the sorcerers in the Trobriands use poison, it would be difficult to say. But the enormous dread of them, and the deep belief in their power, renders their magic efficient enough. And if the chief were known to have given a *Vaygua* to a powerful sorcerer in order to kill a man, I should say that man was doomed.

Even more important than the exercise of personal power, is the command, already mentioned once or twice, which wealth gives the chief over the organisation of tribal enterprises. The chief has the power of initiative, the customary right to organise all big tribal affairs, and conduct them in the character of master of ceremonies. But there are two conditions incidental to the *rôle* he has to play. The leading men, such as the headmen of dependent villages, the main performers, the always indispensable magicians, the technical specialists, have all to be paid, and are, as usual, paid in objects of wealth, and the bulk of the participants have to be fed.

Both these conditions can be fulfilled by the chief in virtue of his control over a considerable portion of the consumable and condensed wealth of the tribe.

We see, therefore, that in following up the various channels through which produce flows, and in studying the transformations it undergoes, we find a new and extremely interesting field for ethnological and economic interest. The chief's economic *rôle* in public life can be pointedly described as that of 'tribal banker,' without, of course, giving this term its literal meaning. His position, his privileges, allow him to collect a considerable portion of tribal yield and to store it, also to transform part of it into permanent condensed wealth, by the accumulation of which he gives himself a still bigger fund of power. Thus, on the one hand, the chief's economic function is to create objects of wealth, and to accumulate provisions for tribal use, thus making big tribal enterprises possible. On the other hand, in doing so, he enhances his prestige and influence, which he also exercises through economic means.

It would be idle to generalise from one example, or to draw strained parallels – to speak of the chief as 'capitalist' or to use the expression 'tribal banker' in any but the most unpretentious way. If we had more accounts of native economics similar to this – that is, going more into detail and giving an economic synthesis of facts – we might be able to arrive, by comparative treatment, at some interesting results. We might be able to grasp the nature of the economic mechanism of savage life, and incidentally we might be able to answer many questions referring to the origins and development of economic institutions. Again, nothing stimulates and broadens our views so much as wide comparison and sharp contrast, and the study of extremely primitive economic institutions would no doubt prove very refreshing and fertilising to theory.

To sum up the results so far obtained, we may say that both the production and its apportionment in the native communities are by no means as simple as is usually assumed. They are both based on a special form of organisation, both are intertwined with other tribal aspects, depending and reacting on other social and psychological forces.

Through the institution of chieftainship and the belief in magic, their production is integrated into a systematic effort of the whole community. By this a considerable amount of consumable wealth is produced, a great part of which is controlled by the chief, who transforms some of it into permanent wealth and keeps the rest in store. This, again, coupled with the natives' regard for wealth, and the importance of material give-and-take in their social institutions, allows the chief to wield his power to organise and finance tribal life.

All the facts adduced in this article lead us to the conclusion that primitive economics are not by any means the simple matter we are generally led to suppose. In savage societies national economy certainly does not exist, if we mean by the term a system of free competitive exchange of goods and services, with the interplay of supply and demand determining value and regulating all economic life. But there is a long step between this and Buecher's assumption that the only alternative is a pre-economic stage, where an individual person or a single household satisfy their primary wants as best they can, without any more elaborate mechanism than division of labour according to sex, and an occasional spasmodic bit of barter. Instead, we find a state of affairs where production, exchange and consumption are socially organised and regulated by custom, and where a special system of traditional economic values governs their activities and spurs them on to efforts. This state of affairs might be called – as a new conception requires a new term – Tribal Economy.

The analysis of the natives' own economic conceptions of value, ownership, equivalence, commercial honour and morals opens a new vista of economic research, indispensable for any deeper understanding of a native community. Economic elements enter into tribal life in all its aspects – social, customary, legal and magico-religious – and are in turn controlled by these.

3   The Polluted Identity of Work*
Mary Searle-Chatterjee

Introduction
This paper is concerned with a particular group of 'Untouchables' in a
large, pre-industrial city – Benares, the holy city of North India. The
people that I studied are mostly employed by the municipal authority to
sweep the streets and clean the public lavatories. Their work requires
regular contact with substances considered to be polluting although
they are not responsible for moving and handling animal carcasses or
corpses. First, I describe the organisation of their work and the interactions in which it involves them; then I discuss the fact that the
identity given by it is one which is debased in the eyes of the larger
society and polluting.

Benares, or Varanasi, as it is now called, is a very ancient city
characterized by cottage industry. It has a settled population of about
half a million, apart from the floating population of pilgrims. Sweepers
usually live in close-knit localities separate from other castes. The
particular group studied are first and second generation migrants from
the rural areas of Kanpur, nearly 200 miles further west. In the villages
they are engaged in earth work and agricultural labour as well as being
Drummers. Sweeping, being a primarily urban activity, is of hardly
any importance.

The Concept of Work
It is useful to begin by asking how far the Sweepers conceptualise their
experience in the same way that the Anglo-Saxons do when speaking of
'work'. Sweepers use a general word for 'work', *kaam*, denoting, on the
one hand, activity which is purposeful and, on the other hand, activity
which cannot be avoided. It can, then, be applied to the performance of
ritual and social obligations as well as to earning of a livelihood,
housework etc. Work is doing (*karna*) and the deeds of 'work' one does
both cause and constitute one's fate, *karma*. It is in the nature of things
that men and women should work and the word *kaam* is generally,
though not always, used positively. Sweepers' concepts are not so
very different from English ones where there are two main categories

* Abridged version. First published in S. Wallman (ed), *Social Anthropology of Work*,
Academic Press, London 1979.

contrasted with 'work'. One is 'rest' or 'leisure', the other is 'play'. Similarly in India, common phrases make the same contrasts: *kaam* versus *aaraam* (ease, relaxation and nowadays at least, 'leisure'); and *kaam* versus *khel* (play), the former referring to the absence of activity and the latter to activity which is non-purposeful.

For the purposes of this paper I shall use the word 'work' in the sense of earning a livelihood. In fact, Sweepers are engaged in a variety of income earning activities of an informal kind, quite apart from their sweeping. They keep pigs and scavenge dung for fuel as well as rags and odd bits of wood etc. Some of them earn money from drumming in marriage processions or make and sell baskets. Within the locality a few earn money by selling various items, by letting out a bicycle or by occasional performance of ritual duties. This paper is concerned only with the work of sweeping since this is by far the most important.

Systems of Sweeping

Sweepers in Benares are involved in two quite distinct work systems, each with its characteristic ideology. One is based on municipal organisation, itself partly determined by statutory regulation. In this, Sweeper men and women, known as 'class IV employees', are paid monthly and receive fixed holidays, maternity leave and so on. There is a clear structure of authority and demarcation of work areas. In the other system, Sweepers are employed by private householders and receive payments in kind as well as in cash. They enjoy certain traditional rights to clothing, food remaining after feasts etc. Although neither Sweepers nor householders refer to this as a *jajmani* relationship, it clearly has hereditary familial aspects characteristic of what anthropologists often describe as rural *jajmani* system (Lewis 1958).

The contrast between the two systems is reminiscent of Weber's distinction between a bureaucratic framework and 'traditional', more patrimonial and personal patterns said to be characteristic of most non-industrial societies (Weber 1964). It has, of course, become a commonplace that the Weberian model was oversimplified, as, indeed, all models are. Studies of work places both in Europe and the USA as well as in areas traditionally studied by anthropologists have revealed the interplay between informal, personal and, in Weber's sense 'non-rational', patterns and bureaucratic ones (Roethlisberger and Dickson 1964; Sheth 1968; Shih Kuo-hung 1944). At first, and even as late as 1962, this was interpreted as due to the survival of older, inappropriate forms (Kerr 1962). More recently, it has even been argued that the appearance of such non-bureaucratic elements, apart from being inevitable, may even on occasion be conducive to greater efficiency (Blau 1955: 148). In the case of the Sweepers, however, the pattern of organisation of work cannot simply be classified as a mixed case any more than it can be described in terms of one or other of Weber's models: it comprises two distinct systems – i.e. both of Weber's types but in spatial and temporal separation.

I shall describe first the bureaucratic sphere – the municipal organisation of street sweeping – since in terms of hours and remuneration it is the more important. This order of presentation may be surprising: it is natural for a European to assume that the household system is the older one from which municipal sweeping evolved or on to which municipal sweeping was imposed. In fact, however, there have been systems of municipal government and hence of municipal sweeping in various periods of Indian history, in very ancient times as well as under the Moghuls and, more recently, since at least the 1914 Town Area Committee Act.

Sweepers in the Municipal Bureaucracy

The Corporation is a large organisation employing 2305 Sweepers, under the jurisdiction of the Health Officer. Conditions of work are governed by written regulation broad guidelines for which are laid down by the State Government and in the Public Health Manual and, even more generally, by the Central Government, for whom the Commissioner for Scheduled Castes acts as a watchdog in his annual reports.

The formal system is as follows: Sweepers work from 5–7 on summer mornings and from 7–11 in the winter and again for three hours in the afternoon. Each individual is attached to a sub-office in a particular ward and within that district is allocated a particular area of 1200 sq. ft. which is to be swept and have its drains and public lavatories cleaned. The rate of pay for this at the time of study (1972) was 103 rupees (£1 equalled Rs. 21) per month rising by annual increments of one rupee per year for seven years. There are three other types of cleaning work with which I shall not deal as they are generally handled by persons of other castes, i.e. underground work in the sewers, removing corpses or animal carcasses (*Doms*) and watering the gutters in the early morning (Muslims known as *Bhistis*).

Work areas are allocated to individuals, but Sweepers working in neighbouring streets may assist one another; one may push a cart and another shovel rubbish into it but there is no fixed demarcation of tasks. Unlike Sweepers in many other cities in India they do not have to remove excrement from dry latrines since these are non-existent here. This does not, however, greatly affect the nature of their work as the streets are used as latrines in the early morning by most of the poorer people. The rubbish thrown out by householders is swept up into heaps and shovelled into head baskets and then into handcarts which take the garbage from four Sweepers and are assigned to every fourth one. These are pulled along to more central places where they are unloaded into buffalo carts which in turn carry rubbish to the trucks which take it outside the city. Truck and bullock cart drivers receive an extra Rs.2 per month. Sweepers are officially supplied monthly with bristles and sticks and have to trim them and make their brooms themselves. They are also supplied with baskets and they shape their own 'shovels' from the scrap iron supplied. Tools, then, are controlled by the individuals who use them, many taking their own home at night although they are supposed to leave them in the depot.

There is a fixed hierarchy of roles relating to the work of each ward sub-office. The ordinary Sweeper, *mehter*, is under the general supervision of a *jemadar* (a word which is sometimes used honorifically for all sweepers), who, in only a couple of cases, has been promoted from the Sweeper ranks. There are only five of these in each sub-office. They are paid RS.150 per month and ride around on bicycles, scolding and swearing at the 20–25 Sweepers in their charge. In each ward there is one *daroga* or *havildar* (earning RS.250 who supervise the work at the office. No Sweepers have, as yet, been promoted to this position.

The last three of these terms resemble occupational titles in the police service and it is for this reason that children in Benares sometimes shout 'bumpolice' as Sweepers go by. Even the word *mehter* was originally an honorific title with courtly and military connotations (Russel 1975 reprint). This is, perhaps, related to the fact that sweeping has had a longer association with bureaucratic organisation than most other occupations, and that it is – after police and military service – the supreme bureaucratic occupation.

I have already referred to the rates of pay and to the fact that remuneration is not only in cash. Sweepers receive clothing supplies every winter officially worth Rs.75 and in summer to the value of Rs.36; as well as 14 days 'casual' leave, one month 'privilege' leave, two weekly half days, 12 months sickness leave in a lifetime (though not more than 1½ months at a time) and 42 days maternity leave for up to three children. Cheap accommodation is supplied or else a housing allowance per person per month. In addition, interest-free loans of up to Rs.400 are available from the Municipality Co-operative Society. Repayment is then deducted in monthly instalments. These forms of remuneration are, of course, more resistant to inflation than simple cash payments. However, as can be seen from the list of complaints published by the Sanitation Workers Union in 1972, they are not always given on time. Weekly holidays, too, are often cancelled when important political figures are expected. Moreover many Sweepers (about one fifth), admittedly mainly teenagers, are temporary employees and hence not entitled to all these benefits. Apart from the remunerations laid down in the regulations it is also customary that the people living in houses fronting the streets that a Sweeper cleans should give small sums of cash on special festival days. The municipal sphere of work, then, cannot simply be seen in impersonal bureaucratic terms nor in terms of the cash nexus.

Recruitment to sweeping, although in one sense governed simply by the universalistic requirement that an employee be willing to handle excrement, is at the same time governed by particularistic factors: in general only persons of certain castes are prepared to satisfy this requirement. Recruitment is also affected by an unwritten law (which Sweepers are trying to get written into the regulations) requiring that when a Sweeper dies or retires, preference in the allocation of the vacancy should be given to members of his family, either male or female, who are not yet employed. Municipal housing, too, is inherited, usually by the youngest son. If there is no close relative in need, another Sweeper may, by paying something to the family of the deceased man or woman, be allowed to pretend to be a relative and hence secure either the flat or the post, but this would be a rare case. For highly coveted sweeping posts such as those in the Railways or Banks, a sum of about Rs.500 could be exchanged. In most cases, however, there are family members at hand who fill the vacancy.

Again in the actual organization of the work of sweeping there is a great deal of flexibility and fluidity. Knowledge of the regulations alone gives little idea of what happens in the streets. Sweepers often unofficially stand in for one another. Payment of a small bribe to the *jemadar* enables a considerable number to be absent at any one time. Although the Municipality does not in theory employ Sweepers under the age of 15, children often stand in for their parents or help them with their work. Family members also try to exchange their areas to be closer to one another. Sweepers, like most lower level employees, are expected to be available for additional forms of unpaid work such as cleaning lavatories in the homes of their supervisors. When they work in wealthier organisations like Banks or the University, they may have to clean the drains in inner courtyards or sweep garden paths or clean roofs for their superiors.

Identity and Demeanour in the Municipal Work Sphere

A Sweeper need never fear that brooms or barrows left around will be stolen by other castes. While going about his work he may stop for tea but he will drink it in an earthen cup to be thrown away afterwards, or in a separate one reserved for his use, and he will sit or stand on the ground, not on the bench provided. Only when he is without his broom and in other parts of the city can he mingle unknown in the crowd, eating and worshipping wherever he pleases. While going about his work in a narrow lane, a Sweeper will be circumspect in his movements. In the alleys with many temples near the holy river Ganges, Sweepers call out as they move along, warning worshippers to avoid them, for if someone accidentally touches a Sweeper or his broom he will not be able to worship without a purificatory bath. Many Sweepers in fact avoid the riverside area in the early morning to avoid contact with newly purified bathers. Brooms, when not in use, are carried high over the shoulder, partly for the same reason.

In broad streets, however, Sweepers walk boldly, and confidently, even contemptuously, knowing how people fear their touch. Similarly, in their dealings with municipal officials at the Health Office they are forthright and unabashed. They deal, after all, only with low level officials, themselves not of much higher caste, and they have the strength of numbers.

Change

Changes in the organisation of municipal sweeping come partly from above in the form of technical innovation thought to be in the interests of public cleanliness as when tractors and trucks were introduced to supplement the work of bullock carts. Changes in ideas about what is acceptable or desirable also affect the rules. There is now in official circles a general feeling that carrying of garbage and excrement in head baskets should come to an end and State Governments have been asked by the Commissioner for Scheduled (or untouchable) Castes to work towards elimination of the custom. It is for this reason that the New Provincial Constitution of 1970 laid down that, on Municipality Co-operative Society Executive Committees, eleven members (i.e. about one third) must be Sweepers.

Sweeping of Private Households

Now to turn to the other system of sweeping – the daily morning cleaning of lavatories for rich or high caste households. This may be an alternative form of employment to municipal sweeping but is more commonly an unofficial supplement to it. The work is not absolutely delimited. Sweepers may clean drains in the garden or inner courtyard or do certain kinds of garden work. They do not in Benares sweep floors in the house, though they do in Delhi, and they certainly do not clean sinks. Sweepers carry a brush, but many households provide their own which they expect to be used along with their cleaning powder. Many Sweepers work in 6–10 households in addition to doing municipal work, earning a few rupees a month in each. They also receive 'gifts' of cash or clothing at major festivals and at important household ceremonies, as I mentioned earlier. Old clothing is given occasionally, as is the food remaining on plates after weddings and other feasts. Cooked food that has been spilt or contaminated by insects may also be given. On the *Kitcheree Sankranti* festival,

Sweepers may receive the raw ingredients for cooking kedgeree.

Work for private householders also provides the possibility of access to loans and of influential contacts which can provide openings to jobs sweeping in better paid institutions, or even to other types of work such as being a night watchman or artisan. The rates of remuneration change more slowly than in the municipal sphere but, because the payment in kind is often more important than the cash payment, tend to be more immune to inflation. The right to work in a private house is usually inherited by whichever son or daughter is nearest at hand and most in need, with priority being given according to age rather than sex. Only in the case of exceptionally rich or generous households might it be sold, but this is rare. House Sweepers do not generally receive any fixed holidays but often do remain at home on important festival days.

When a Sweeper cleans the lavatory in a private house the owner will pour the water for him so that he will not touch the bucket or tap himself. Many bathrooms, even in new flats, have an outer door to enable the Sweeper to enter without passing through the rest of the house. In older houses the lavatory is placed in a corner of the court-yard, well away from the main building. Modern houses are sometimes built without a courtyard and older relatives may be reluctant to stay when they find that the lavatory is incorporated into the main building. In very orthodox homes the householder may pour water on any areas where a Sweeper has walked, even on an outer verandah. If by any chance the Sweeper requires water, he may be given it in a separate glass, or it will be poured so that he can cup it in his hands. The same practice is common among higher castes – in their case to protect themselves as receivers from any possible contamination from an unknown source.

The relationship between Sweeper and householder is usually reserved and aloof on both sides. Sometimes Sweepers adopt a sub-servient and cringing manner when they enter a house, although nowadays, in homes without a separate entrance, they often walk proudly, even insolently, as they pass through the main part of the house. Sometimes a chatty, even gossipy, friendship may develop, with the housewife pumping her woman Sweeper for information about the houses and behaviour of neighbours. Only very rarely a woman Sweeper has sexual relations with the male of the house when his wife and children are away. He will ask her to bathe before she does so and will give her a couple of rupees in payment. But these relations are not easy to arrange: Sweepers normally only remain for a few minutes a day and the neighbours will soon notice any deviation from normal custom which will be more reprehensible if it involves an untouchable than any other caste. High caste men certainly like talking to Sweeper women in private, but they do not, in public, like to be seen taking much interest in them. In the obscene pamphlets published during the Saturnalian Festival of *Holi*, lewd poems refer to all low caste women except for Sweepers.

The Power of the Polluted

There are many resemblances between the two systems of work. My initial account of them has magnified the differences for analytic purposes. Threat of withdrawal of labour as a means of securing compliance is one of the most important features common to both systems. Municipal Sweepers all belong to the Sanitation Workers' Union which has several times been able to get wages raised by petitioning the Local Authority. In Benares, they have twice in living memory been on strike. The most notable of these occasions was in 1960. The Authorities called in Sweepers from outside, from Kanpur, in an attempt to break the strike. Fights broke out between the outside Kanpuris and the Benares Kanpuris as well as others, and several informants spoke of having been sent to prison for several days along with other family members. Wages were, however, raised. Sweepers can make efficient use of Trade Unionism because few castes are prepared to challenge their monopoly of a low status yet socially indispensable occupation. They continue sweeping partly because they fear to move out of the security of the known world into an alien and unsympathetic one; other castes, on the other hand, fear to move into that lowly world through taking up the economically attractive work of sweeping. The very lowness of Sweepers in this sense gives them a certain amount of power. Sweepers can make further efficient use of Trade Unionism because their occupational and residential homogeneity, again partly due to their despised status, enable rapid mobilisation.

Sweepers sometimes withdraw labour to force private householders to give them what they consider to be their due. In suburban villages of Benares it is customary for householders on certain festivals to give delicacies of cooked food to the municipal Sweepers who clean the drains fronting their homes. If due to illness, for example, the householder forgets to present the appropriate items he finds a stinking upswept drain facing him for two days.

Apart from the fact that they have a work monopoly, Sweepers are prepared to unite and use physical force if they feel that they have been wronged. The utter lowness of their position makes them unaffected by the inhibiting status concerns of higher groups.

*   *   *

I suspect that in urban situations where Sweepers are found in large numbers in compact groups, they have always had at least some advantage over other low caste groups: their extreme lowliness makes persons of higher caste likely to attempt violence only as a last resort because of the degradation involved in touching, pulling or even beating them.

Sweepers, then, are neither penniless or impotent, despite the fact that they are quite without status. Their situation lends support to Dumont's view that in India, economic and political values are clearly disjunct from religious ones. What is more, one can say that power and prosperity, relative though they may be in this case, actually rest on degradation.

Caste and Identity

The identity that a Sweeper derives from his work is one which is considered debased and polluting. Work is a major determinant of self identity and status not merely in an industrial society: the identity given by caste membership is in many cases associated with a particular traditional occupation, even if that is not the main work of the group, but simply its distinctive activity.

★　　★　　★

I have already described some of the implications of the Hindu belief that sweeping is polluting. Sweepers are not only low themselves (the word *Bhangi*, meaning Sweeper, is one of the more common swear words), they can also pollute others; they have taken the dirt of society upon themselves and hence must be avoided. Others take a variety of precautions in self-protection. Despite the new laws, Sweepers are often not allowed to worship in local temples or shrines where they are known and people avoid touching them in the street – old ladies often quite ostentatiously.

How far do Sweepers internalise attitudes which others have towards the work of sweeping? Do they feel too that they are polluted by it or do they feel alienated from their work and hence uncontaminated by it? Do they in fact identify with it in any way?

Sweepers express different attitudes and feelings at different moments so it is not possible to give a clear answer to these questions. They all consider that sweeping is dirty and unpleasant. Many, however, say that they prefer to live in a city and sweep than to live in a village and work in the fields. They also say that sweeping is essential work and requires strength. My impression is that they consider sweeping to be physically dirty rather than polluting, and that in most cases they attribute their lowliness to the power rather than the superiority of others. Some, however, say that they are low because they are uneducated and drink excessively, and many of the older Sweepers will not enter the most sacred Visvanath temple, even though they are now allowed to do so. They feel that it would show a lack of respect.

When talking to persons of high caste, Sweepers may suppress mention of customs such as eating pork and drinking. But away from a multi-caste context they express no shame about either of these customs, or about their work as Sweepers. In the language of social esteem theorists (Coopersmith 1967), it is the 'significant others' who are important – in this case the caste itself. Sweepers make only half-hearted attempts to modify their behaviour to suit the tastes of the higher castes. They show no interest at all in the grooming of their children's hair or clothing, a matter closely related to the esteem of the urban higher caste mother. I believe that in this case this is not due to fear of the 'evil eye' but to lack of involvement with higher caste concerns. Sweepers are perfectly conscious of high caste feelings; they simply do not share them.

Sweepers associate their work of sweeping with a toughness that they admire in both men and women; with drinking and eating of 'hot' substances, meat and strong liquor. Linked with this is their belief that they are hot-blooded and highly-sexed. Both men and women lay great emphasis on 'honour' and will in defence of it fight without much provocation. 'It's a matter of honour' is a very common phrase. *Dom* sweepers lay particular emphasis on readiness to fight and frequently bring out long spears. Sweepers also admire those who are spirited and can outwit the authorities, and those who are physically strong: their children play with clay body-building weights.

The Sweepers' sense of identity and self esteem comes from their style of life rather than from their work, though they see both to be part of the same complex of toughness. It would be misleading, however, to over-emphasise their self esteem as Sweepers. Individuals within the group aquire status and respect from skills in basketry, music making, story telling, literacy and also from committee membership and riches acquired in the pig trade. The work of sweeping is the major, but not the only source of a Sweeper's identity, and the meanings he attributes to that work are different from those attributed to it by the larger society.

References

Blau, P. 1955. *The dynamics of bureaucracy.* Chicago: University Press.
Coopersmith, S. 1967. *The antecedents of self esteem.* San Francisco: W.H. Freeman.
Kerr, C. 1962. *Industrialism and industrial man.* London: Heinemann.
Lewis, O. 1958. *Village life in north India.* Urbana: University of Illinois Press.
Roethlisberger, F.J. and Dickson, W.J. 1964. *Management and the worker.* Chichester: Wiley (first published in 1939).
Russell, R.V. (ed.). 1975. *The tribes and castes of the central provinces of India.*

Delhi: Cosmo Publ. (Repr. 1916 edition, London: Macmillan).

Sheth, N.R. 1968. *The social framework of an Indian factory*. Manchester: University Press.

Shih, K.-H 1944. *China enters the machine age*. Harvard and Oxford.

Weber, M. 1964. *The theory of social and economic organisation*. New York: Free Press. (First published in 1925).

4 Work in Traditional and Modern Societies
Craig R. Littler

This chapter explores some of the differences between work in traditional and modern societies. It does so by examining structures of production (economic structures) and the culture of 'work'. It is these frameworks of social organisation and social meaning that shape the nature of work experiences.

Comparing types of economy and types of work organisation is important, especially to overcome the continual tendency to take Western capitalist society as the absolute centre of reference. The purpose in comparing types of economy, however, is not to construct an evolutionary framework or to imply a simple linear evolution. Any evolution can only be indicated by examining *particular* historical developments. Instead, comparison is intended to be a typological process in order to illuminate the particular mechanisms of modern industrial societies and to construct theories which have their roots in more than the quicksand of the present and the contemporary.

Structures of Production
Production is the totality of operations and processes aimed at procuring for a society its material means of the existence. Human groups face various alternatives in relation to the environment – food gathering, hunting and fishing, or settled agriculture. Hunting and gathering are largely non-transformative; in other words, the territory is occupied and the resources of life are 'found' there. Settled agriculture and, later, industrial economies produce goods by transforming nature (Godelier 1978: 60–1). Indeed the development of settled agriculture may foreclose options by so radically altering the flora and fauna of an area as to make any return to hunting and gathering impossible. Any one society may combine different forms of production – hunting, rotational slash and burn agriculture and craft work is a typical combination which was practised by, for example, the Mayan civilisation in Central America (Coe 1971).

Stripped to formal essentials, production entails combining resources available from the environment, instruments of labour (tools etc.) and men (labour power), in accordance with certain technical rules, in order to obtain a product that can be used socially. However, this formalism should not suggest that there is a simple logic of tasks or a logic of nature. Consider, for example, the planting of rice in a peasant economy:

> Given decisions about land and timing, a variety of more subtle and complex selections must be made within the context of the agricultural cycle itself. A crucial one concerns choice of seed variety. There are about one dozen different rice strains of which the peasants are aware and to which they have access. Some of these varieties are traditional, in that they have been used in the countryside for at least a generation, while others were introduced recently by the rice mills or have spread from person to person. From the peasants' standpoint, each strain embodies certain characteristics which may or may not be useful in a given context; however, a bundle of these features is always tied together in a seed type, making it impossible to optimize every characteristic. A beginning point for seed selection is the condition of the land. In general, land is said to be low and wet or high and dry, and for each, certain rice types are considered preferable. Of course, other characteristics of the land also are noted, such as its softness and fertility, but the strains are not adapted for these conditions. In addition, the rice types differ markedly in their cooking and eating qualities. Some are softer, some harder, and some preserve better after cooking. The varieties also differ in grain size and behaviour when milled; these characteristics are important to the peasants only in that they sell a small quantity of rice each year and receive a higher or lower price for the type offered. Some varieties are hardier than others, being more resistant to disease, plagues and variable weather conditions than others. Important, also, is the growing time of the rice, which ranges from two and a half months to six months. The duration from seeding to harvesting has an effect on the state of household supplies as well as the other kinds of crops which may be planted. Lastly, all the rice types differ in the number of sprouts they throw off, the number of seeds which must be planted in each hole, and the spacing which must be given between the holes.

> (Gudeman 1978: 73)

In general, as this example indicates, all exploitation of resources presupposes a certain knowledge of the properties of objects, materials and tools. Productive activity is, thus, an activity governed by technical norms. But where do these technical norms originate? And who controls them? These are some basic questions of work and the experience of work which this chapter will approach in the second section. However, before turning along that path it is important to examine some further aspects of the structure of production.

The combining of factors of production is carried out within the setting of 'production units' – understood in an abstract sense. Such units may be the small family holding, the village community, the tribe as a collection of communities, or an industrial enterprise. (Godelier 1978: 62.)

The extent to which a 'production unit' is a work group or a work organisation in a modern, Western sense of an explicit economic organisation is highly variable. If we look at one of the simplest hunting and gathering economies – the Copper Eskimos – as an example, then this point becomes clear. The composition of the Eskimo hunting and fishing groups varies throughout the year, according to the kinds of game being hunted and the type of fishing being done. A large number of people are involved in hunting seals during the winter, and at that season the Eskimos live in large communities by the sea. In contrast, during the summer when possibilities for fresh-water fishing and hunting occur, the communities break up into smaller bands and move inland. As the season progresses, the exigencies of deer hunting demand smaller groups still and a further fragmentation occurs. The only organisational continuities are that first, most (though not all) fragmentation occurs along family lines and, second, there is a general division of labour by gender (Udy 1970: 38).

In societies with stable (or relatively stable) cultivation, horticultural and agrarian societies, work organisation is more permanent. In many such societies the production unit was based on the family and such an organisation constituted the sub-structure of most economies (see Chapter 5). Membership in familial work organisation is derived from membership in some kinship unit with participation institutionalised as an obligation of kinship. Familial work organisation suffered, and suffers, from intrinsic manpower limitations. This raises the problem of how does work which is too great a burden for one family get done? Beyond the household, the typical pattern was one of familial reciprocity. Udy (1970) distinguishes between two types: (a) non-routine work (such as building a house) where there is a diffuse quid pro quo obligation, and (b) routine work relating to peak periods (e.g. planting, harvesting) in the farming cycle. The latter form of reciprocity usually entails extensive pooled arrangements, whereby several families work for one another in successive rotation. When the rotation cycle has been completed, all work obligations have been discharged.

The above work arrangements presuppose something: namely an equal distribution of property. In the face of unequal distribution of property, they tend to break down – or be reconstructed. The typical pattern in complex traditional societies was one of family-based work organisation assisted by norms of reciprocity combined with a top-structure of forced labour (or corvée) politically imposed by larger landholders or by the state. In medieval Europe, for example, peasants were obliged to work on their lord's land for anything from one up to seven days per week throughout the year, the average being about three days (Lenski 1966: 268). The lord's claims on peasant-family labour was an essential aspect of work relations (and class relations) of the medieval manor. In practice, this link between manor and peasants was not always universal nor permanent. The peasant's obligations could differ from region to region, from village to village, and even from household to household in the same village (Postan 1975: 88).

A form of production nearer to us in time, but reflecting many of the characteristics of the feudal manorial system, is the hacienda system. This was the predominant type of agricultural work organisation in South America in the nineteenth and early twentieth centuries. The hacienda consisted of a very large agricultural estate characterised by (as with the feudal manor) the coexistence on one property of the owner's farm and a number of peasant-economy farms. The landowner let out parcels of land to peasant farmers, who paid the rent by working on his farm. The relative size of the home farm and the peasant holdings varied, but the latter normally accounted for more than half of the cultivated area and the landowner usually retained the grazing lands for himself. In this way there grew up a class of worker bound to the soil and working both on the peasant farms and on the landowner's. The main characteristic of the work relationship was that it was not clearly delimited in scope, since it affected every aspect of the life of the individual. Because the hacienda was in a position to satisfy all the basic needs of the workers and their families, their possibilities of contact with the outside world were reduced to a minimum: the school, the church and the food store were all there on the spot, turning the hacienda, like the manor, into a closed and self-sufficient economic and social system. One result of the relationship of dependency generated by the hacienda system is that the landowner acted as an intermediary between the worker and the world outside and derived profits from his role of middleman between the peasant and the market. Another characteristic of the social system prevailing on the hacienda was a low degree of division of labour, all the peasants having to perform a wide range of tasks. This fitted in with the productive role of the family. A member of the family could replace a (male) worker in his obligations to the hacienda or in his work on the family's own holding. Such work formed part of the ordinary household duties of women and the normal obligations of children, such that the concept of employment in the modern sense had little significance. Since there was neither a clear-cut division of labour nor a rigid separation of roles within the family group, 'employment' and the manifold other daily tasks that had to be performed merged into a single joint activity for all its members (Kay 1974: 69–98).

The hacienda system, then, though it had some peculiar characteristics, typifies the cluster of production relations which existed in many agrarian societies. However, in focusing on the relations of production we are ignoring the significance of the instruments of labour – of tools and technology. Tribal societies tend to be based on the use of a hoe (or digging implement) with rotating cultivation, whilst large-scale, more complex societies tend to be based on the plough, the use of which results in enhanced productivity. Moreover, some writers argue that the difference in technology implies differences in the relations of production to the extent of reaching right into the household. Hoe agriculture has often been (there are many exceptions to this) women's work, so that when the hoe is used men will try to accumulate wives because they represent labour power. Thus polygymy preponderates to an overwhelming extent in traditional African societies, prevailing in 88 per cent of a representative sample of 154 societies drawn from the entire continent (Murdock 1959: 25). In contrast, plough agriculture is largely a male activity and so it does not tend to induce polygymy (Goody 1977).

However one analyses the mutual linkages between the relations and instruments of production, the relations of production represent the immediate framework of work experience. The examples of work within traditional societies, including the hacienda system, point towards a general conclusion, spelt out by Godelier:

The work is at one and the same time an economic, political and religious act, and is experienced as such. Economic activity then appears as activity with many different meanings and functions, differing each time in accordance with the specific type of relations existing between the different structures of a given society. The economic domain is thus both external and internal to the other structures of social life, and this is the origin and basis of the different meanings assumed by exchanges, investments, money, consumption, etc., in different societies, which cannot be reduced to the functions that they assume in a capitalist commodity society and that economic science analyses.

(Godelier 1978: 63)

In other words, the notion of 'work' is one which has evolved out of the modern relations of production. This leads us on to the question: what are the basic elements of these relations?

One basic idea is that of contractual labour – an explicit agreement to perform specified work for a specified time in the future. Such ideas were not unknown in traditional societies: there were ascriptive groups available for hire under limited circumstances in many tribal societies. In addition, mutual associations set up to perform collective works, such as the construction and maintenance of irrigation works, have often appeared (Udy 1970). However, such forms of organisation are not equivalent to the development of wage labour in modern, capitalist economies. The linkage of wage labour to the modern factory system was not inevitable. During the nineteenth century many people did not relish a move into the factory; as Pollard says: 'As long as there was some measure of choice between cottage and factory, the workmen preferred the cottages.' (Pollard 1968: 191). Even when they had been recruited many 'peasant-workers' lived on the margins of the factory world with an ambition to leave as soon as possible. Frequently, the entrepreneur's answer to these problems of recruitment was to employ unfree labour. Widespread use was made of paupers and pauper-apprentices, prisoners and ex-prisoners, and lunatics. Some entre-preneurs employed agents to travel the country combing the work-houses and lunatic asylums for people. But this compounded the problem of recruitment, because the early factories became associated with workhouses and prisons in people's minds.

In the event, in every West European society entrepreneurs failed to establish factories on the basis of coerced labour. Instead, labour was deemed to be 'free' of all diffuse and general obligations to employers, hired – not to do specified work, but often to do unspecified work – for a specified time. Wage labour created a world of employers and hired hands. In so doing, these relations of production created 'work' as it is experienced today: 'Those who are employed experience a distinction between their employer's time and their own time. And the employer must *use* the time of his labour, and see it is not wasted: not the task, but the value of time when reduced to money is dominant. Time is now currency: it is not passed but spent.' (Thompson 1974: 43). Modern industrial work organisation resulted in a new economy of time, culminating in Henry Ford's moving assembly line in 1914 which chopped the average job down to task duration of 1.19 minutes (see Chapter 7). Time is also reduced to money. Traditional work patterns were often *non*-market oriented. As we have seen, they were based on domestic and familial forms of production, within which people produced for subsistence and were unaccustomed to a money economy. Gudeman notes that Panamanian villagers in a peasant, subsistence economy which is crumbling before a larger, capitalistic system, are aware of their position:

We think of working in order to eat. I want to have food to eat. We don't make sums of what we gain or lose – no one thinks of this. We think about getting food to eat, of having enough for next year. I work hard now to have enough food for next year.

(Gudeman 1978: 39)

Contrast the logic of this work situation with a modern account of assembly work:

On our line each man . . . has a different price for his job. I get threepence more than the man behind me, for example. It all depends on how clever you are at pulling the wool over the time-study man. The more you do him down, the more the group benefits as a whole. There's always a rumpus though when the time-study man comes. We always know when he's on his way because somebody in the next shop will come over and tell the first man in our shop when he sees him. At that moment we start to rehearse the speed which we want him to see as our normal one. In other words we slow down. He comes up to me finally, because I'm the last one on the bench, and he puts his stop-watch down to look at me, and so that I can see the second hand go round from the corner of my eye. He didn't used to do this, but once I thought he'd stopped his watch before putting it down, and accused him of it, so now he sets it close for me to see. Anyway, he then makes you an offer for the job. You either accept it, or you don't. You haggle. If he offers you less than your rehearsal price and time, you fetch the shop steward. Eventually the three of you sort it out!

(Fraser 1968: 102–3)

Time becomes money, and both become the battleground between those who work and those who structure the experience of work. At this point we can turn to another critical dimension of difference between traditional and modern forms of work and return to the questions of the origin and nature of the technical norms governing productive activity. These questions are taken up in the next section in a consideration of ideology and culture.

Work Procedures, Ideology and Culture

There are enormous conceptual difficulties in talking about ideology and culture, a fact recognised by many authors, whether sociologists like Abercrombie, Hill and Turner (1983) ('The analysis of ideologies and forms of knowledge and belief is in a state of disorder.'), or anthropologists like Godelier (1982) ('. . . something is wrong in the state of the human sciences when it comes to ideology.'). Analysing concepts of ideology and mentalities is a bit like trying to nail jelly to the ceiling! Nevertheless, some problems seem self-generated. It is desirable to escape from a rigid duality and attempt to understand subjective/objective, social structure/culture within one conceptual frame. Bauman has emphasised this point:

These two requirements of the specifically human condition – ordering and orientation – are as a rule subsumed under two separate headings: social structure and culture. A historical study of circumstances which led to petri-fication of two inseparable faces of one coin into two, for a long time uncon-nected, conceptual frameworks – remains to be written. . . . a dispro-portionately time-consuming effort has been invested by scholars into solving of what under closer scrutiny appears to be a sham and artificial problem. In keeping with the notorious human tendency to hypothesise purely epistemological distinctions, the two analytical concepts coined to describe the two indivisible aspects of the human ordering activity have been taken for two ontologically distinct beings.

(Bauman 1973: 78)

If we adopt this perspective, then thought ceases to be a 'level' which is separate from other levels. Instead, as Godelier argues, 'any social relation necessarily contains an element of thought that is not necessarily either "illusory" or "legitimising", and which forms part of this relation from the moment of its formation' (Godelier 1982: 17 and 19). In relation to work, the material means of existence equally imply a complex set of ideas, rules and understanding. All work activities entail cognitive routines and shared logic which accompany and surround task performances. Such cognitive routines, which may or may not accompany the activity on a conscious level, are both part of the task performance and a constraint in relation to it. It is both constitutive of the activity and stands outside of it. This argument can be clarified by a specific example. Here is how to lock up somebody:

How I Put a Prisoner in the Cells
I get the key
I go down to the cells
I unlock the outer door
I lock it behind me
I unlock the cell
I check the lavatory
I check the blanket
I go back and unlock the outer door
I lock it behind me
I get the prisoner
I unlock the outer door
I take him through, and lock it again
I put him in the cell
I unlock the outer door
I go out, and I lock it again.
(Quoted in Laurie 1972: 42)

This litany is learnt by every policeman at training school. It represents a verbal modelling and a conceptual representation of the activity sequence. Clearly, this litany constrains actions and converts them into a routine, especially if the activity is novel to the actor or if it is interrupted in any way. Moreover, cognitive routines have a certain independent momentum, a fact which most people have directly experienced – almost everyone has caught themselves, in moments of absent-mindedness, half-way down the steps of the *wrong* routine.

Cognitive routines are based on training, both formal or informal. Consciousness is socially accessible, indeed consciousness *is* social: language and training convert a person into a carrier of routines. Thus writers, such as Weber, conceived of 'rationality' not as a characteristic of individuals but, instead, as a property of a social structure. Men are more 'rational' under some circumstances than under others and societies vary in the extent to which there are structural and normative devices to isolate the organisation of work from other spheres of activity and subjectivity (Stinchcombe 1974: 33–4). But do cognitive routines, once implanted, function in the same way as a heart-pacer, inevitably regulating the flow of consciousness? Clearly not. Routine practices can be changed and modified; essentially they are capable of becoming objects of reflection such that there is a kind of functional circle in which people make culture and culture makes people. Nevertheless, at any one point culture and ideology cannot be made and re-made at will, there is a constraining influence derived from the narrowing of perception and the pre-structuring of choice such that innovation always has to flow over a barrier of mental and social rigidity. Once learnt, routines limit one's perception of the possible.

So far, we have argued that material practices have a subjective element, such as cognitive routines, which are an essential part of their *material* existence. But such routines have to be 'activated' within a framework of specific social relations 'which imposes a determinate form of division of labour by attaching a specific value to a specific task and by linking that task to a specific social category (men/women, elders/young people, master/slave, etc.)' (Godelier 1982: 20). These linkages also have a subjective aspect, whose effect is to legitimise the position and status of individuals and groups in terms of varying access to perform social activities. However, this does not mean that we can say that 'ideology' enters the picture at this juncture and not until this juncture. One reason for this caution is that the work process itself often involves symbolic elements. As Godelier points out, 'a labour process often involves symbolic acts through which one acts not upon visible nature, as with implements, but on the invisible forces which control the reproduction of nature and which are thought to be capable of granting or refusing man his wishes: a good harvest, good hunting, etc. This symbolic element in the labour process constitutes a *social* reality that is every bit as real as material actions upon nature' (1982: 32). In the rest of this chapter we will look at some of the relations between material practices (cognitive routines), culture and ideology in particular types of society.

In many simple societies, such as nomadic or horticultural societies, no clear line can be drawn between the cognitive and symbolic aspects of work. Typically, the situation is that 'purposive-rational action' (to use the jargon of Habermas) is located within the socio-cultural frame. Work is dyed with the colours of sacredness. There is no English word to express this cultural idea, but there many words in other cultures. For example, in Maori culture (the Maoris were the original inhabitants of New Zealand) the word for the holy or sacred was 'tapu'. Tapu was applicable to things, to people and to activities. The Maoris were a small dispersed society which practised a simple garden culture, of which by far the largest crop was the kumara, a kind of sweet potato. The planting of the kumara was governed by tapu:

Before new land was used, the original cover was burnt off, cleared, and broken-up with a hoe (ko) or wooden grubber (timo). This was usually finished in late autumn, before the rains clogged the soil. In spring, before the seed tubers were planted, the ground was dug over. *This was a very tapu operation, following a procedure ritually laid down in every detail.* The whole field was not dug up, but small mounds were formed in an extremely regular pattern, again using the ko. The soil in these mounds was pulverised, after which the seed tubers were distributed at the mounds and planted.

(Schwimmer 1974: 73, emphasis added)

When the kumara had been planted, the Maori would call upon Rongo, god of the kumara, for a good harvest. The actual harvesting was determined by the heliacal rising of the star Vega (ibid.: 19–20). Clearly in this case material practices and cognitive routines are located securely within the wider communal belief system.

However, it is worth noting that in Maori society 'tapu' did not apply to all activities. Some regular processes, notably cooking, were 'noa', which means devoid of tapu. This raises the point that in most cultures there will be areas of activity that are less 'tapu' and, as a consequence, will be more open to innovation. Thus the Maoris developed a varied and sophisticated cuisine based on birds and fish.

If we look at more complex agrarian societies, then the major belief-systems in such societies varied widely, such that it seems that generalisations about culture and ideology in agrarian societies are impossible. Nevertheless, some broad points can be made. The overwhelming majority of such belief-systems were (using a distinction from Carlton 1977: 36–9) 'cosmic' as opposed to 'civic'. In other words, they were religions oriented to the supernatural rather than humanistically-oriented. As religions, belief in the gods is crucial and service to the gods becomes a (or *the*) central focus of human activity. In addition, the social order was often seen as in some way dependent on the cosmic order: perhaps both orders are thought to enjoy a form of mystical congruence. Cosmic ideologies vary in terms of whether they are universalistic, such that proponents attempt to recruit others across social boundaries and eliminate other belief-systems, or whether they are introverted, such that believers are the elect, guardians of provinces of special revelation and divine force (ibid: 37). Most religions in agrarian societies have been introverted and only religions like Islam and Christianity have tended to be universalistic, though with a continual tendency to degenerate into a special preserve of the faithful.

Given the general characteristics of cosmic ideologies, what has been the relation between them and routine work activities? The answer to this varies with the institutional context of work. As we have seen, the typical pattern in complex traditional societies was one of work organisation based on the family, supplemented by reciprocal assistance amongst the lower classes, combined with a top-structure of forced labour (or corvée) in varying forms and degrees politically imposed by the ruling elite. For example, in ancient Egypt (which was only partly a slave society) the annual corvée involved a mass mobilisation of labour which would normally be used for religious or state purposes. Carlton describes the composition of an expedition under Ramesses IV to collect stone:

He mobilised 9368 men including the high priest of Amun and other high officials together with the cupboards and some 20 scribes. These were merely the headquarters staff. . . . The main body of the expedition included 91 masters of the horse, baggage train overseers, 50 police and 50 minor administrators, 5000 soldiers, 2000 temple staff, 800 foreign auxiliaries and 900 further officials of the central government. The particular craftsmen who were crucial to the entire undertaking, the draughtsmen, sculptors, stone-dressers and quarrymen, 140 in all, represented a mere fraction of the total force. . . . *A high proportion of the personnel was composed of ritual experts, and the entire operation was dedicated to the gods*, particularly Amun, without whose goodwill it was thought to be doomed to failure. . . . The whole burden of state economic activity was charged with ritual necessity.

(Carlton 1977: 133–4, emphasis added)

Clearly such forms of work organisation were highly ritualised and the state religion was directly relevant to task performance. However, as has been suggested, the majority of work in agrarian societies was performed in different circumstances by the peasants and a limited segment of artisans. And in relation to such agricultural work and craft work the predominant ideology had retreated somewhat. It no longer formed the weft and warp of work, but had become a distant clamour of angels and devils. As one writer has pointed out in the English case, 'the hold of orthodox religious views on the mass of the English people was never more than partial' (Budd 1973: 126). This view is echoed by Abercrombie, Hill and Turner (1980: 70); they conclude that it is highly unlikely that the great mass of the population in feudal England

and France were kept in subjection by incorporation into the dominant ideology of medieval Catholicism, largely because the apparatus of ideological transmission was so weak. Outside of the cultural influence of the cities, the priesthood was poor in quality, sermons were irregular and there was a low level of ritual participation. More generally, the retreat of religion from day-by-day work practices arose from the institutional divorce between state religion and that of the people. Religion became associated with a literate elite, whilst in opposition to this was a 'low intellectual tradition' consisting of magical and semi-magical beliefs and filled with practical matters of peasant technology (Lenski 1966: 208; Thomas 1971: 776–7). This situation is well exemplified by fifteenth and sixteenth century Spanish society, which became one in which agricultural work and the crafts were considered labours unworthy of a Christian.

This partial divorce of the areas of purposive-rational action from the wider cultural frame was even more marked in the case of the crafts. The earliest artisans and merchants were attached to lord's households and it was only gradually that they began to serve other clients than their lords and acquire a market autonomy. The craft guilds with their desire for autonomy and protection of traditional knowledge represents the peak of such a development. But it was a development in which craft lore separate from any religious beliefs became an integral part of craft independence. Some major belief-systems attempted to accommodate such tendencies by including occupational gods within their pantheons. For example in ancient Egypt it was the cultural norm to shave and have one's head shaven which provided a good market for itinerant barbers, who sometimes doubled as doctors. The emergence of this occupational group was accommodated by the creation of a barber-god in the Egyptian pantheon! (Carlton 1977:·273, fn. 59).

In general, then, stratification in complex agrarian societies combined with the typical contempt of the upper classes for manual labour, served to de-ritualise work to some degree, or at least it left the work routines supported by only a semi-sacred and often 'pagan' patina. This is not to say that cosmic ideologies did not attempt (successfully or otherwise) to legitimate tributes, forced labour and other forms of obligation.

So far, we have argued that in simple societies the whole of life tends to be enclosed in a network of magical techniques. In contrast complex traditional societies are characterised by the prevalence of a central worldview, such as a coherent religion, under which 'technique' retreats and becomes secondary: technical activities have little ideological place in these societies. This lack of 'place' permits a certain degree of innovation in work routines but there is no institutionalisation of innovation. In small simple communities innovation is seen as pathological behaviour. For example, in southern Mexico any members of the Oxchuc Indians who invest in new equipment or explore new techniques in order to increase crop yields, or show in any other way their ambition to become wealthy, are distrusted by their neighbours and often accused of practising witchcraft (Siverts 1969). The social environment of complex agrarian societies is not so hostile to innovation; in particular the craft tradition is one in which value is attached to product excellence, which permits the gradual evolution of techniques relatively independently of mythical and religious interpretations of the world. However, as Habermas points out, 'despite considerable differences in their level of development, civilisations, based on an economy dependent on agriculture and craft production, have tolerated technical innovation and organisational improvement only within definite limits' (1971: 94–5). Some of these limits are explored by William Golding in an hilarious story about the Roman empire: he imagines a librarian, called Phanocles, who invents a steamship, explosives and a pressure cooker! Phanocles tries to explain the advantages of his steamship to the Roman Emperor:

'When the wind falls what happens to a ship?'
Indulgently, the Emperor turned to him.
'She waits for the next one. The master invokes a wind. Sacrifices and so on.'
'But if he does not believe in a wind god?'
'Then I suppose he does not get a wind.'
'But if the wind fails at a moment of crisis for your warships?'
'The slaves row.'
'And when they tire?'
'They are beaten.'
'But if they become so tired that beating is useless?'
'Then they are thrown overboard. You have the Socratic method.'
Phanocles allowed his hands to drop to his side in a gesture of defeat. The Emperor smiled consolingly at him.

(Golding 1971: 133)

One can see in this imaginary dialogue some of the cultural and structural limits to inventions and innovations in traditional societies. It is in modern industrial societies that the practices of innovation become central and crucial.

In modern industrial societies the cultural framework becomes subservient to the development of the forces of production, which in turn are linked to the institutionalisation of scientific and technical development. Modern sciences produce knowledge which is of a form to be technically exploitable and to offer technical control (Habermas 1971: 88 and 99). Innovation as such becomes institutionalised. Indeed the very substantial effects of technical stasis in many industries even for a short period make the rate of innovation the key factor in the rationality of industrial administration. Stinchcombe argues that 'the fundamental characteristic of a rational industrial administration is that it innovates constantly', whether by invention, incremental adaption or by borrowing (1974: 35).

Cognitive routines in modern industrial societies tend to be either technical or legal. Decision-making and behaviour are subsumed under technical rules – this is part of what Weber meant by the notion of 'rationalisation'. Some writers have argued that the end result is not a process of de-ritualisation, but the development of a new ideology of technocracy. For example, Ellul argues that 'technique' has become sacred:

> The individual who lives in the technical milieu knows very well that there is nothing spiritual anywhere. But man cannot live without the sacred. He therefore transfers his sense of the sacred to the very thing which has destroyed its former object: to technique itself . . . technique has become the essential mystery.
>
> (1964: 143)

The effects of this process on human choice, according to Ellul, is a state of 'automatism':

> When everything has been measured and calculated mathematically so that the method which has been decided upon is satisfactory from the rational point of view, and when, from the practical point of view, the method is manifestly the most efficient of all those hitherto employed, or those in competition with it, then the technical movement becomes self-directing. I call this process automatism. . . . Technique itself selects among the means to be employed. The human being is no longer in any sense the agent of choice.
>
> (1964: 79–80)

This argument, whereby 'technique' becomes a reality in itself, confuses levels of analysis. It is this very view of technical cognitive routines which represents the ideological aspects and which can be labelled 'technocratic'. Technocracy creates a form of 'thought dependency' by the apotheosis of the expert and the scientific sanctification of the technique. There is no place for choice ('automatism'), because one cannot choose on the basis of ignorance; there is no place for negotiation, because one cannot negotiate about scientific facts.

Technocratic ideology can take many specific historical forms; for example Taylorism (see Chapter 7) with its view of the one scientifically determined method of performing work tasks. However, perhaps technocratic ideas were best expressed by the 'New Machine' movement in the 1920s in the United States. This was an association which sought political power and advocated scientific government by 'experts' in all spheres of society: power should pass to the priests of the machine (Maier 1970: 32–4 and 60–1). The New Machine movement failed and this failure underlines that technocratic ideology is a *tendency* in capitalist industrial societies, and not necessarily the predominant ideological framework. But it is the framework within which most work activity takes place and as such it marks a clear distinction from work within traditional societies.

References

Abercrombie, N., Hill, S. and Turner, B.S. (1980), *The Dominant Ideology Thesis*, Allen and Unwin.
Abercrombie, N., Hill, S. and Turner, B.S. (1983), 'Determinacy and indeterminacy in the theory of ideology', *New Left Review*, 142, pp. 55–66.
Bauman, Z. (1973), 'The structuralist promise', *British Journal of Sociology*, 24, pp. 67–83.
Budd, S. (1973), *Sociologists and Religion*, Collier-Macmillan.
Carlton, E. (1977), *Ideology and Social Order*, Routledge & Kegan Paul.
Coe, M.D. (1971), *The Maya*, Penguin.
Ellul, J. (1964), *The Technological Society*, Vintage Books.
Fraser, R. (1968), *Work*, Penguin.
Godelier, M. (1978), 'The object and method of economic anthropology', in D. Seddon (ed.), *Relations of Production*, Frank Cass, pp. 49–126.
Godelier, M. (1982), 'The ideal in the real', in R. Samuel and G. Stedman-Jones (eds.), *Culture, Ideology and Politics*, Routledge & Kegan Paul, pp. 12–38.
Golding, W. (1971), *The Scorpion God*, Faber & Faber.
Goody, J. (1977), *Production and Reproduction*, Cambridge University Press.
Gudeman, S. (1978), *The Demise of a Rural Economy*, Routledge & Kegan Paul.
Habermas, J. (1971), *Toward a Rational Society*, Heinemann.
Kay, C. (1974), 'Comparative development of the European manorial system and the Latin American hacienda system', *Journal of Peasant Studies*, October, pp. 69–98.
Laurie, P. (1972), *Scotland Yard*, Penguin.
Lenski, G. (1966), *Power and Privilege*, McGraw-Hill.
Maier, C.S. (1970), 'Between Taylorism and technocracy: European ideologies and the vision of industrial productivity in the 1920s', *The Journal of Contemporary History*, 5, 2.
Murdock, G.P. (1959), *Africa*, McGraw-Hill.
Pollard, S. (1968), *The Genesis of Modern Management*, Penguin.
Postan, M.M. (1975), *The Medieval Economy and Society*, Penguin.
Schwimmer, E. (1974), *The World of the Maori*, A.H. & A.W. Reed.
Siverts, H. (1969), 'Ethnic stability and boundary dynamics in Southern Mexico', in F. Barth (ed.), *Ethnic Groups and Boundaries*, Little, Brown.
Stinchcombe, A.L. (1974), *Creating Efficient Industrial Administration*, Academic Press.

Thomas, K. (1971), *Religion and the Decline of Magic*, Penguin.

Thompson, E.P. (1974), 'Time, work-discipline and industrial capitalism' in M.W. Flinn and T.C. Smout (eds.), *Essays in Social History*, Clarendon Press, pp. 39–77.

Udy, S.H. (1970), *Work in Traditional and Modern Society*, Prentice-Hall.

5 The Household at Work*
Martine Segalen

*Editor's Introduction: Britain has long ceased to be a peasant
society, but the importance of peasant, small-scale, family-based
farming has been crucial in many other economies. Segalen, drawing on historical accounts and detailed ethnographic research in
France in 1945/6, describes the peasant work situation. There is
both a rigid sexual division of labour and considerable husband-
wife cooperation.*

The solidarity of house-household–farm gives rise to a family-based
organisation of labour which plays an important role in kinship relations: The extended family, cousins, uncles and aunts, are called upon
in times of family crisis such as childbirth or sickness, and their help
may also be asked for during threshing-time or harvest, on a reciprocal
basis. But the daily life of labour rests more often on the shoulders of
the man and his wife, the parents of one of them, with the help of the
children and sometimes of servants. The narrower family unit for the
daily work which closely identifies the household and the farm; the
more extended family grouping for important social occasions: acces-
sion to political power, the handing-on of goods, and marriage strategies.

The organisation of labour also places the man and his wife within
wider solidarities which merge with or complete the kinship network.
The men or women meet and help each other on specific occasions, so
that a family organisation of labour, often based on a principle of
separation of the sexes within the house, is reinforced by the solidarity
and the sociability of men and women in a way that emphasises their
disunity.

Activities reserved to women
In the chronological succession of these daily acts, the first was to light
the fire. The woman daily gathered her supply of wood, and, every
morning she relit the fire under the cooking pot. A physical act, but an
act charged with symbolism. The woman was the guardian of the

* Extract from *Love and Power in the Peasant Family: Rural France in the Nineteenth
Century*, Basil Blackwell, Oxford, 1983. Translated by Sarah Matthews.

hearth, with all that that could mean in protective or maleficent terms for the household. Just as she is responsible for the fire, so also she is responsible for the water.

Woman Returning From the Well is a picture which Millet painted between 1855 and 1862. The way the woman is standing with arms stretched out by the weight of the water immediately gives some indication of the importance of water in the life of the family and on the farm. The painter wrote about this picture:

I have tried to paint her so that she seemed neither a water-carrier nor a servant; that she had been to draw water for her household, water to use in cooking for her husband and children; that she did not appear to be carrying a weight which was either lighter or heavier than two full buckets; that through the kind of grimace which was almost forced from her by the weight pulling at her arms, and through the way the sunlight makes her half-shut her eyes, one can make out an air of rustic goodness on her features . . . I wanted . . . her to be accomplishing with simplicity and cheerfulness, without considering it a burden, an act which, with the other household duties, is a daily task and her life's habit.

A task to be performed daily, and even several times a day. It is hard to imagine what a life without running water must have been like, and the important responsibility which this laid on the woman in looking after the precious liquid. Water is necessary to prepare and cook food for men and beasts; it provides drink for people and animals; it is used for washing and bathing. The size of the house and farm thus determines how much water will have to be fetched every day. In the nineteenth century, provision of water always posed a serious problem. 'Gutters running along the roofs of the buildings collected the precious rainwater into cisterns, troughs, sluices, or barrels; but there it either stagnated, or was quickly used up, and then it was a question of turning to the well or to a pond.' A number of farms visited between 1944 and 1946 did not have any water, and the description of the tasks which this entailed is as relevant to the nineteenth century as to the centuries before that.

In the Eure, at Vannecroq, Mme C . . . fetched water from a small pond dug near the entrance, called the *mare nette* (clear pond) or *marnette*, and protected from the sun by willows. In the Morbihan, at Thèse, water was fetched from the spring in buckets; in the Tarn-et-Garonne, in Lavit, water was still a problem of prime importance. There were two springs from which water had to be fetched in two buckets twice a day. In the Basses-Pyrénées, in Alcay, drinking water was fetched in buckets from the village well 50 metres away from the house. In the Corrèze, at Bugeat, the source of water was a 150 metres from the house and 125 metres from the byres, which meant frequent, tiring trips, since the road was uphill.

In the Haute-Vienne, at Rochechouart, the farmer's wife went to fetch water from a stone well with a winch. The water was carried back in buckets hung from a wooden 'carrier', a sort of yoke which spread the weight over the shoulders. One bucket stood permanently on the draining-board by the sink; drinking water was taken out with the help of a ladle, a sort of large spoon made of wood or metal with a hollow handle. The other bucket stood on its own shelf under the sink. This was water for doing the dishes, for washing, and for the laundry.

The emptying of used water posed a second problem. It was not always wasted. In the last house mentioned, in the Haute-Vienne, used water was emptied out of the house through a hole in the wall, under the sink, the *bassi*; a large flat slate, leading to the outside wall and gently hollowed in the centre, took the water away from the wall and emptied it into a little granite trough which the ducks and hens could dabble in. On this farm, it was also necessary to fill the water-troughs for the piglets and the fat pigs with water drawn from the well. Water which was precious and rare, and always difficult to get in the nineteenth century, and even, on some traditional farms, right up to 1946, this was one of the essential physical elements determining the shape of household tasks; devolving entirely on the woman, shaping the rhythm of her daily life, fetching the precious liquid was crucial to running the farm. It was so fundamental that it was one of those mechanical acts of which one ceases even to be aware: women, when asked about their daily tasks, forgot to mention it!

The woman went to fetch water or went to the water. The great launderings which periodically occurred were organised within the framework of mutual female help. The heavy linen – that is sheets, cloths, and work-clothes – was washed with ashes in a big wash-tub, then brushed, beaten and soaped at the spring or in the wash-house. It was a long and exhausting process which took place during April and October, and a third time, if necessary, after the harvest. Smaller and less spectacular launderings were regularly necessary to deal with the day-to-day washing; especially if there were little children.

There is a deep-seated affinity between the woman and water which appears in rituals as a symbolic element ensuring the passage from life to death. Analysing the acts of the woman who 'came in' to help at births and deaths, washing the new-born child and laying out the corpse, Yvonne Verdier remarks that 'washing appears to be an act laden with symbolic powers . . . Over and above the Christian symbolism of purification, washing offers an image of the passage from life to death, a passage of which water will be the vehicle, and the image works in two ways: to pass on, but also to come into the world, as if the child too had to pass through water . . . In this double passage, the washing-women could thus act as guide.' The woman handles the water, consumes and manipulates the liquid. She accomplishes physical tasks and production tasks; contact with the purifying liquid confers on her a symbolic power, the power to put the world back in its place, to turn back the clock of life and death.

With the water the woman cooks, boiling and stewing the meals. It is the privilege of the mistress of the house since she knows that its reputation, with neighbours and servants, depends on it. The servants only play an auxiliary role in this task. The number of meals and their composition vary according to the seasons and the length of the working day:

In summer, the peasant has five or six meals, two breakfasts, the first a snack about five in the morning, the second between about seven and seven-thirty; lunch at midday; a snack about five in the evening and supper at dusk, usually about eight or eight-thirty . . . In the winter, two meals were not taken, the snacks early in the morning and late in the afternoon. The single breakfast is then carried forward to between six and seven in the morning, and supper is at seven in the evening at the latest. The early morning snack is made up of bread and cheese; it is taken standing, a hunk of bread in the hand, after which, in the larger households, the carter goes and feeds the horses. At the second breakfast, to the cheese is added either a slice of salt lard, or a round of sausage, or a piece of liver pâté, locally called *fromage de cochon*, pig's cheese. At midday, the woman of the house will serve a fat soup followed by boiled pork with vegetables, a salad and cheese. The evening snack is taken wherever the worker happens to be employed at the time . . . Finally, the last meal of the day is made up of soup eked out with leftovers from midday's soup, an omelette or a dish of potatoes boiled with lard, and fruits in season, cherries, plums, apples or pears.

Was the preparation of meals a very time-consuming task in traditional cooking? Meals for feast-days, made at the end of the major agricultural undertakings, or for a wedding, brought a lot of guests together, and presented quite a different array of dishes from usual, dishes which took a long time to cook. Their preparation was based on cooperation between the women: it was an occasion for mutual help between neighbours and kin; but everyday meals were not so time-consuming as in nineteenth-century bourgeois society, where culinary etiquette demanded two elaborate meals a day. Meals like that demanded a lot from those working in the kitchen. By contrast, in the rural environment, the daily meals remained for a long time, during the nineteenth and twentieth centuries, monotonous menus, in which every day resembled the day before, and where all that was required was to add a piece of lard or a few potatoes to the pot which was kept constantly on the boil. Cooking was thus a very different task from what it is today, in town or in the country. It was in a very fundamental way associated with the woman, and not just any woman, not the servant, nor the daughter of the house. It was the responsibility of the mistress of the house; it was her privilege in the same way that sexual relations were her privilege, and she learned about both at the same time when she got married.

As well as cooking food for humans, food also had to be prepared for the animals, particularly the pig-swill which had to be made up and boiled twice a day before or after the men's soup.

This female cooking was based on boiling and simmering, a product of the relationship between food and water. When the men cooked, they would grill, demonstrating a contrast between day-to-day cooking and feast-day cooking, a contrast which is continued to this day in the barbecue at the end of the garden – an American custom recalling a long-standing organisation of labour. In addition, men were involved in the food process, although usually at the beginning; they supplied the grain to be made into soup or bread; they killed and salted the pig which the women were to cook.

In this rapid enumeration of the tasks reserved for women, and account devoted to feeding, some mention must be made of bread, but its preparation varies from region to region, and in any case involved the other principle of organising labour which we mentioned, that of male–female cooperation. We will thus discuss it later. To complete this treatment of tasks relating to meals, let us mention the making of preserves, in fruit-growing areas, a task which only petered out relatively recently, and partially, at the end of the nineteenth century and the beginning of the twentieth, with the takeover of this domestic production by industry.

The domain reserved for women also comprises all the jobs aimed at the upkeep of the house, and one must add to them the general list of tasks usually included under the heading of 'housework': sweeping, dusting, making the beds, etc. The amount of time spent by the mistress of the house on this sort of task depended on the number of little children in the house and the number of servants. (Although it is not clear from available descriptions, servants seem by and large to have been assigned to production tasks such as milking and working in the fields, rather then looking after the house itself.) These maintenance tasks were also related to particular cultural environments. Thus, in some regions, the interior was regarded as 'sordid' or 'dirty', although observers testified to carefully polished furniture. In Brittany, for instance, the housewife prided herself on the shine of the nails which decorated her cupboards and enclosed beds, and a sort of local competition enforced cleanliness. In a novel situated in the Bigouden region, the heroine, Thumette, polished every Saturday in anticipation of the visits of the morrow 'all the copper on the cupboards, all the locks, nails and hinges; and Saturday night, her forehead shining with sweat and her cheeks ablaze, she gazed with pride at her clean and shining house, with its pleasant smell of wax.'

Nevertheless, the upkeep of the house and the housework did not make up a substantial part of the mistress's tasks. The earth floor only needed an occasional going-over with a broom; the beds could be made more or less speedily. The cleanliness of the interior was a function of the time the mistress of the house wished to dedicate to it, if she had no servant to help her: housework came after working in the fields, and caring for the children and animals.

A whole range of activities which were production tasks, though secondary ones, also become part of the women's sphere. The making of cloth by spinning and weaving, for example, was carried out by the woman, if it was for domestic consumption only. Naturally, the importance of this activity depended on how comfortably off the family were, and the degree of urbanisation of the region concerned, where certain kinds of cloth or pieces of clothing could be bought at market. It is true that these activities gradually disappeared with the growth of the textile industries during the second half of the nineteenth century but they nonetheless maintained their importance in peasant thinking, even though they were performed increasingly less often. In the first place, these tasks could be carried out only at certain times of the day, during the evening, which was a time of relaxation and social contact: *Ce que femme file le matin ne vient souvent à bonne fin* (What a woman spins in the morning does not often come to a good end) (Anjou).

Marriage rituals emphasise the symbolic relationship between two, yarn and sexuality; but unlike cooking, which the woman learns to do alone, just as she must encounter her sexual experience alone, spinning is an activity which a young girl can carry out and which can be performed collectively; it is conducted concurrently with her apprenticeship in romantic relations. Often, the young girls would spin during the evenings while the young men came to pay them court: it was, moreover, their trousseau which they were getting ready.

Knitting and sewing were supremely feminine activities, handed on from mother to daughter, and provided a means of socialising the young girl. The boys were sent out into the fields and the girl was kept at home so that her mother could teach her how to handle a needle. Let us observe the mother which Millet painted giving her daughter *The Knitting Lesson*. Everything is quiet in the poor, but well-kept house, with its flagstone floor. The woman and the little girl are seated, and the mother is tenderly guiding her daughter's hand as she leans over her shoulder. There is no better illustration of the feminine transmission of techniques, gestures and attitudes than this painting imbued with tenderness. Knitting was often the occupation of shepherdesses in Millet's work, where, far from the house and looking after the sheep in the fields, they managed to preserve, even in the open air, their feminine bearing. For needlework was also a question of bearing. Even more than a technique, it was a whole controlled attitude of the body which the mother was teaching to her daughter.

The community school would take up this instruction of a quiet and proper bearing, a system which was continued by housekeeping schools which sprang up between the wars, specifically for the daughters of farmers. As an example, here is a text given to the pupils as a dictation exercise, in 1886, in a country school at Vieux-Rouen-sur-Bresle in the Seine-Maritime:

Young girls must be taught needlework at a early age. But, up until the age of twelve and even later, whatever their parents' fortune, they should not be allowed to work any of the imaginative pieces beloved of rich women. The pleasure taken in such work is sufficient to teach a skill in it, whereas it is important that one should learn, at an early age, to perform those tasks which cannot be learned later. Young girls must be taught from their earliest years that calm, self-possessed bearing which is at once a mark of modesty and of grace. They must early be taught those habits which will make them sedentary. I believe thus that, as early as six years of age, sitting next to her mother, the young girl should begin to use her needle for an hour a day, in two sessions, for one must be careful to guard against her becoming put off the most precise and most consolatory of all women's occupations. Hemming, stitches to be worked on coarse canvas, a piece of tapestry-work should be her first undertakings. It is also important to teach knitting when they are very young.

This is an illustration of the belated recovery (at the end of the nineteenth century) of family instruction. It contributes to the reinforcement of the specifically feminine, by imposing a model which, although deriving from bourgeois morality, links with the traditions transmitted within the family. One can see the difference between what is learned unconsciously and that which is taught externally and is enforced.

Over and above all her other functions, the peasant wife is also a mother. She is responsible for bringing up and educating the young child, tasks which she shares with the female world of the household: grandmother, mother-in-law, older daughters, and servant-girls. In this society where infant mortality was still high and in which, even when it was decreasing, one was still constantly aware of it, the mother had to try and keep her child healthy through a variety of practices, more or less related to official medical practice, according to the social class and the particular region.

This heavy responsibility was part of the tasks which fell to rural women, who used a body of magical and empirical recipes which were integrated into a rationale suited to the peasant mentality. It was crucially important for the mother to preserve her children's lives, so that, above and beyond life given and maintained, she could ensure the continuity of her household. In the same way as she appears to be the lynch-pin of the household when her husband goes off to fish or travels to Paris to become a water-carrier during the winter, so too the woman has the fundamental task of keeping healthy and educating the children who will one day succeed the couple. From every point of view, 'the mother ensures the continuity of human life within the life of the family.

Nor is the domain of women entirely confined to the inside of the house. Fetching water at the well or at the spring, or doing the washing at the river took the woman out of the house. Less distantly, within the sphere which constituted her particular domain and which she has symbolically appropriated in the marriage-rites, the mistress of the house had responsibility for the farmyard and the garden. These were domestic activities since they were intended for domestic consumption, but they were also productive since they were often the only activities which could bring a small regular income into the house, since any surplus produce was sold at market.

Though the farmyard was primarily intended to satisfy the needs of the house, the farmer's wife still had the chance of selling at market any surplus eggs or poultry as well as products from the dairy or the garden. Sometimes, as we saw at Lavit, in the Tarn-et-Garonne, the farmyard provided not a secondary but a primary source of production within all the productive activities of the farm. But, whether secondary or primary, the care and the produce of the farmyard are a specifically feminine concern which controls every stage of the operation.

The symbolic relationship between poultry and the woman is perceptible in numerous proverbs linking woman and hen. We have already seen the sexual parallel which was drawn, but that is only one aspect of a wider homology. Hen and woman have the same characteristics, the same qualities, and the same faults.

Just as the hen knowns how to pick up grains, so the woman knows how to be economical.

Le coq a beau éparpiller, si la poule ramass, elle remplit le grenier
The cockerel can scatter grains as much as he likes, if the hen picks it up, she'll fill the barn (Franche-Comté)

The farmyard marks the limits of the territory reserved for women:

Quand la poule reste au poulailler, c'est signe que tout va bien pour le coq
When the hen stays in the hen-house, it is a sign that all is well for the cock (Provence)

Poule et femme qui s'écartent de la maison se perdent
The woman and the hen who stray from the house are lost (Val d'Aosta)

The garden is, as we have seen through a number of rituals, highly feminised. In effect, it is cared for daily by the woman. Day after day, she prepares the soil, sows, waters, hoes, and harvests, and this cultivated area, close to the house, appears as a tiny replica of the fields which the man looks after. In this garden, a vision of future provisions lies before the housewife's eyes: the household soup is growing ready there, waiting to be out in the pot. In proverbial speech the woman is often compared to fruit or vegetables, and the quality of the garden's produce determines to some extent the family reputation: *A la maison et au jardin on connaît ce que femme vaut* (You can tell what a woman is worth from her house and her garden) (Gascony).

For what is emphasised most of all through this gardening are the qualities of patience and hard work, and the ability to carry out the appropriate action each day. Gardening is a productive activity, but also an eminently social one: a housewife who neglects her garden runs the risk of the insult of a charivari.

Activities reserved to men

While feminine activities are more or less identical throughout all French peasant society, even throughout traditional society – everyone has to be clothed, and fed, to bring up and socialise children – and are also identical throughout the year, since they are the fundamental daily activities, activities reserved to men, on the other hand, are dependent both on the economic setting to which they belong and on the period in the productive cycle in which they occur. It is not within our scope here to describe these activities in their technological detail. We seek rather to summarise their principal characteristics in order to compare or contrast them with the tasks carried out by women.

Within the house or with regard to it, the main male activity is to provide the wood. In dead periods of production, during the winter, 'the man chopped the wood and . . . in March he would bring in the faggots and the bundles of wood which finished 'weathering' in the wood-shed ready for the next winter.

In general, the man is only rarely indoors, except to eat and sleep. He is out of the house throughout the summertime, the time of major work in the fields, while in winter, when tasks in the fields are fewer, he devotes his time to repairing his tools and to mending things about the house. It is during the long winter evenings that he does his basket-making with willows and rushes.

The principal labour of preparing the soil, whether for agriculture or viticulture, is performed by the man. For agriculture, if one looks at the tools employed, it is the man who handles the spades, picks, hoes, bill-hooks, pruners and other hand tools which were still widely used during the nineteenth century. As soon as one goes on to equipment drawn by animals, it is no longer a question of an exclusively male domain, but rather of cooperation between the sexes, since, although the plough may be led by a man, a woman may often guide the equipment harnessed to it. The activities linked with planting and sowing are also male tasks: hoeing, and sowing the seed from sacks, or baskets, or bushels. These activities have symbolic connotations: the farmer opens the soil and sows his seed, and the soil, the female womb, brings forth and bears all the hopes of the household.

The preparation of the soil and the work around the plant, in the case of viticulture, are also male tasks: grafting, pruning the vine, putting in props, trimming the shoots, and sulphuring. But, as with cereal harvests, the operations associated with the major tasks of summer, the grape harvest calls for the help of all the members of the household and often also of other men and women who find themselves drawn together in these tasks.

In the animal sphere, one can oppose to the farmyard the care of animals which feature as means of production in the organisation of labour, such as milk-cows or horses. These animals are valued because they are costly, and proverbs emphasise how much the men are attached to them. One should not, of course, take such expressions literally. They show, rather, the relative importance attached to the labour of animals and of people:

Bon Dieu d'en haut, prends ma femme, laisse mes chevaux
Good God on high, take my wife, but leave my horses (Upper Brittany)

Mort de femme et vie de cheval font homme riche
A dead wife and a living horse make a wealthy man (Brittany)

La mort de sa femme n'est pas une ruine, mais la mort de sa vache en est une
The death of a wife is not a disaster, but the death of a cow is (Alsace)

In the South the same kind of statement is made about the beast used for traction and transport: *Homme riche si sa femme meurt, pauvre si sa mule meurt* (A man is rich if his wife dies, poor if his mule dies) (Languedoc).

Draught animals distinguish the farmer from the sharecropper and the day labourer. They are the sign and the means of achieving particular social and economic status, and, just as the hen and the woman, so the horse is the man leading and controlling the equipment of the household.

The state of technology in the nineteenth century meant that male tasks demanded considerable physical energy. The peasants depicted in Millet's paintings, *Men Digging*, *Man with a Hoe*, and *The End of the Day*, are dropping with exhaustion. Yet they are not agricultural labourers, but small landowners of bitterly poor soil which calls for unceasing labour and constant effort. Millet, ethnographer-painter, says of these workers:

I can perceive perfectly well the sun spreading out in the distance, far away over the countryside, its beauty across the clouds. I can see no less well the two steaming horses working on the plain; then there is the rocky spot where an exhausted man, whose laborious gasping has been audible all morning, has tried to straighten up a moment and take breath. All this drama is surrounded by splendour. That is not of my own invention, and the expression the 'cry of the land' is nothing new.

Against the woman's incessant toil one must put the man's physical exhaustion, wearing him out in body and spirit.

The territory reserved for men, therefore, is confined to the work of preparing the fields, whereas the woman's comprehends the kitchen, washing, and the care of small children. But let us not give undue importance to this division of labour. In some regions men perform work which elsewhere is entrusted to women. The greatest proportion of work depends on cooperation between the sexes, whether man and wife together, or wider groups of men and women.

Interchangeability and cooperation

So-called domestic activities are sometimes undertaken by men and reputedly male activities are, in some regions, carried out by women.

If there is one job with feminine domestic connotations, then it must be bread-making. Bread was an essential element in the peasant diet. It was made every week, ten days or fortnight.

Quand une fille sait pétrir et enfourner, elle est bonne à marier
When a girl knows how to knead and bake, she is fit to marry (Bordelais)

Femme qui fait cuire du pain ou qui fait la lessive est à moitié folle
A woman who makes bread or does the washing is half mad [reference to the hard labour involved] (Gascony)

When these operations are broken down – kneading, putting the dough into the bread-tins, lighting the oven, baking – it appears that they may be carried out by either men or women; that one or the other play different parts in the process, even within the same region; and that the men therefore take on a task which is nonetheless reputed to be feminine and domestic. For instance, in Mantois and Vexin, bread-making was entrusted to the housewife. In Brittany, the men were involved in the process of heating up the oven, whether it was a question of the communal oven or of the domestic ovens lit turn-and-turn-about in the little hamlets, within the framework of neighbourly help. In the Mâconnais, there is an even greater confusion of tasks. 'Men and women both made bread,' writes Suzanne Tardieu, who has collected a wide variety of answers from her informants: 'My mother and I made the dough,' said a woman in La-Chapelle-de-Guinchay; 'there were women who mixed the dough, but usually it was the men' (Vergisson); 'the men did the kneading' (Vergisson); 'I did it, and so did my husband' (Laize, Blanzy). Throughout the technical process, which Suzanne Tardieu photographed and analysed in detail, it was a man making the bread.

Here, it is not a regional model but a family tradition which is developing, or, rather, a distribution of jobs which each couple determines for itself. This interchangeability makes one wonder about the stereotypes which nineteenth-century observers assembled, and about a redefinition, perhaps even an elimination, of the term domestic.

Certain activities were carried out by either men or women, depending on the region. Everything to do with livestock was dealt with in this way. While sheep were rather regarded as being the man's province – though how many popular songs speak of the shepherdesses, – cows could be the responsibility of either one or the other. Animals whose products were destined for domestic consumption, such as cows, when there were only a few of them, were cared for and milked by the woman, in this small Breton household or that household in Central France. Even when aimed at the market production of butter, milk and cheese, the dairy could still be entirely within female hands, as in the grazing areas of the Auge region described earlier. In contrast, in Central France, in the Aubrac region which covers the departments of Cantal, Lozère and Aveyron, it was the men who took the cows in the summer to the high pastures, which they call 'mountains'. They would set themselves up in the *burons* – dairies in the high pastures – and make a cheese called *fourme de Laguiole* which would be sold at the end of the summer season. This is rather an extreme example, since the economic system of production is here separate from the household and Aubrac cheese-making is a form of agricultural craft, so to speak, comparable to the workshops of potters or weavers. All that we would demonstrate here is that the cow is not an incontestably feminine animal in the way that the chicken is.

Care for livestock is the point of convergence of male–female complementarity. The cows were cared for by the women, but the byres were looked after by the men, who turned the litter and cleaned out the manure.

The question arises – can such activities still be referred to as domestic? The men took a large share in them; they entered directly into the system of production. In a desire to categorise every task absolutely, have not observers overlooked an essential factor, in the relative interchangeability of tasks from one region to another, and particularly in the advanced cooperation between the sexes, within the same work process? And here, it is very much a question of mutual help between members of the household outside the framework of the mutual help furnished by neighbours and kin when there are major jobs to be done.

Let us look at Millet's painting, *Planting Potatoes*. A man and a woman work together in a luminous atmosphere of tranquillity and tenderness, he works backwards turning the soil, and she follows in the same rhythm throwing in handfuls of the seed-potatoes she carries in her apron. The donkey behind the tree waits in the shade, with a basket on its back where the baby has been put. 'I wanted to show the touching way these two intimately associated people worked together, and to make their actions accord so perfectly that they seemed but a single labour.'

Millet was a somewhat sober observer of peasant life, and the warm atmosphere of work in unison with which the painting is imbued, was doubtless the reflection of some scene he had observed, perhaps in his infancy.

Where is the folklorist who has mentioned that men and women planted potatoes together? They would have spoken of growing potatoes as a male task, without calling attention to the woman's presence in the fields. In all these cultural processes, the woman was eminently present, not only during the major undertakings, but also in the day-to-day activities which had to be carried out.

Why have observers overlooked this participation of women in agricultural work? Though some folklorists might see the woman as constantly working out of doors – particularly those doctors who reproached mothers and nurses with abandoning their babies to go and work in the fields – other observers tended rather to concentrate exclusively on the technology of agricultural operations, and neglected to ask who did what. Moreover, female participation in work in the fields was so much taken for granted in the rural environment that it was hardly mentioned; it was engraved upon the peasant mentality, which ceased to be aware of it: women no more mentioned their occasional help in tilling or sowing than they did the care they devoted to their children. As for the observer, a woman working in the fields seemed so incongruous to him that he just did not see it. Yet the meticulous research carried out in 1945 and 1946 demonstrates this permanent cooperation, a principle of the organisation of rural labour as ancient as the organisation of the peasant family itself, which grew up in the sixteenth and seventeenth centuries, and which had only begun to change under the recent development of new agricultural systems, from the 1950s onwards.

On small family farms, in which activity was governed by the rhythm of the agricultural tasks, and which the researchers visited in 1945 and 1946, cooperation continued throughout the year, and was particularly evident during the great labours of the summer. In order to bring out the nature and extent of this cooperation, however, it would be necessary to examine an hourly timetable of work.

Take a farm of around 17 hectares, in the Tarn-et-Garonne, at

Miramont, farmed by the owners, a couple, with their son, their daughter-in-law and two helpers. It is a mixed farm, and a brief description of the distribution of tasks can be drawn up as follows: the father and son worked in close cooperation, working the land, looking after the grassland, the crops, the upkeep of the vines and the fruit-trees, and were responsible for feeding the larger livestock. The mother and daughter-in-law did the cooking, kept house, fed the poultry, and did the milking. The two servants changed the litter for the cattle and fed them; they maintained the roadways, cut the hedges, and transported the manure. In fact, the division of work seems much less clear if one looks at their timetables in detail: cooperation stands out in a synoptic presentation of tasks. In summer, the women spent little time on domestic activities. They were in the fields with the men in the afternoons, and in the mornings if they had the time. Their particular sphere was that of milking – the animals' litter being prepared by the men – and care of the poultry. The additional time which the men devoted to the fields was spent in preparing meals. Throughout these long days when 20 hours were spent working, at least 14 hours were spent together, sometimes 16 hours if the women spent longer in the fields. This farm was observed in 1945, and had not changed since it was built in 1835, and one can assume that the organisation of labour had hardly changed either.

SUMMER TIMETABLE

Father and son	Mother and daughter-in-law	Servants
	4 o'clock	
Rise	Rise	
	5 o'clock	
Coffee	Preparation of breakfast	Rise
Care of animals	and of snack	Breakfast
Harnessing		Clean pig-sty
	6 o'clock	
Leave for fields		Leave for fields
	7 o'clock	
	Housework	
	Preparation of lunch	
	9 o'clock	
	Care for poultry	
	Milking	

10 o'clock

Snack	Either in the house, or in the fields	Snack

1 o'clock

Quick meal at the farm. It was occasionally taken out into the fields

1.30

Washing up

2.30

Leave for fields

6 o'clock

Return from fields
Care for poultry
Milking
Preparation of dinner

8 o'clock

Return from fields Care for stock		Return from fields Care for stock

9 o'clock

Dinner	Dinner Washing up	Dinner

12 o'clock

Bed	Bed	Bed

At Imbsheim, in the Lower Rhine, a smallholding of 7 hectares spread its interests over cereals, wheat, barley, rye, fodder beet, a few vines, and potatoes: all products consumed by the occupants of the household, whether men or beasts. Only products from the stock-farming entered the commercial circuit. The household was made up of a couple, their daughter and a servant.

WINTER TIMETABLE

Madame K		*Monsieur K*
	7 o'clock	
Rises		Rises
	8 o'clock	
Prepares fire Cares for pig Milking		Cares for cattle

	9 o'clock	
Breakfast		Breakfast
	10 o'clock	
Housework		Fields: transports manure fodder, beet
	11–12 o'clock	
Preparation of food		
	1 o'clock	
Lunch		Lunch
	2–3 o'clock	
Sewing or washing		Repair of materials
	4–5 o'clock	
Milking		
	6 o'clock	
Cares for pigs		Cares for cattle
	7 o'clock	
Preparation of dinner		
	8 o'clock	
Dinner		Dinner
	9–11 o'clock	
Sewing		Accounts, reading

During the summer, there were two great periods of activity: hay-making and harvest.

HAY-MAKING TIMETABLE

Madame K		*Monsieur K*
	4.30	
Rises		Rises
	5 o'clock	
Prepares fire Cares for pigs Milking		Cares for cattle
	6 o'clock	
Breakfast		Breakfast

Housework		Leave for fields
Preparation of snack		Mows
and of lunch		
	8 o'clock	
		Cattle out
	9 o'clock	
Turns hay		Farm
	10 o'clock	
Snack		Snack
	11 o'clock	
Hay-making		Turns hay
	12 o'clock	
	Quick lunch at the farm	
	2 o'clock	
Turning and		Stacking hay
stacking hay		Cattle home
	6 o'clock	
Milking		Cares for cattle
Cares for pigs		
	8 o'clock	
Dinner		Dinner
	9 o'clock	
Sewing		Reading
	11 o'clock	
Bed		Bed

HARVEST TIMETABLE

Madame K		*Monsieur K*
	6 o'clock	
Rises		Rises
	7 o'clock	
Prepares fire		Cares for cattle
Cares for pigs		Breakfast
Milking		
Breakfast		

	8 o'clock	
Prepares packed lunch		Prepares wagon and baskets
	9 o'clock	
Leaves for fields Harvesting		Leaves for fields Harvesting
	12 o'clock	
Lunch in fields		Lunch in fields
	1 o'clock	
Harvesting		Harvesting
	5 o'clock	
Home		Home
	7 o'clock	
Prepares dinner Cares for pigs Milking		Presses grapes Cares for cattle
	8 o'clock	
Dinner		Dinner
	11 o'clock	
Bed		Bed

Men and women follow the same alternation of periods of rest and labour through the annual cycle of the season. During the dead period of the winter they both have a shorter working day, in which the feminine tasks of sewing and washing appear as the equivalent of the masculine task of repairing. The animal domain is separate: the woman looks after the pigs and cows, the man after the cattle.

Bedtime remains the same, summer and winter, and the day is prolonged by rising earlier in the morning; the timetable of the farm at Tarn-et-Garonne shows that the men and women were together from eleven in the morning until six o'clock in the afternoon. During the harvest, their common work-time was even longer, from nine in the morning until six in the afternoon: with the accumulated fatigue of the day, and the foreknowledge of more on the morrow, the evening was cut short, and the restful activities which would usually take place then probably made way to discussions on the quality of the vintage.

Cooperation was a daily affair, lasting for longer or shorter periods depending on the state of work in the fields. These examples go to show that the woman had a normal and continuous place in the fields.

Confining the domain of female work to work around the house, and, inversely, loading all the work in the fields on to the man provides altogether too schematic a view. There was some over-lapping of territories and tasks, despite certain areas of dominance. This cooperation implies a distribution of tasks in working techniques. During ploughing, for example, the woman could help: the man held the plough and opened the furrow, while the women led the team. During hay-making, the big scythe, which was heavy to handle, was a man's tool, as well as everything that went to maintain it, the whetstone in its sheath, the hammer and hand-anvil to straighten the blade. The woman gathered the sheaves with a sickle and bound them; she helped with stacking the ricks. One can find the same sort of division of labour in workshops as well. In the clog-maker's, the man would carve the clogs, while the woman rubbed them down. The division of labour rarely depends on matters of physical strength but, rather, on a model of distribution of roles, authority and responsibility.

Unloading bundles of hay from a cart was done by women, though it was heavy work performed with pitchforks. The farmer stood next to his cattle, without lifting a finger, but keeping a watch out for any errors which could cause an accident.

In an analysis of this cooperation, it is difficult to draw up a general table which would hold true for the majority of rural households; the degree of cooperation, and the amount of feminine contribution to the work on the land depended on the composition of the household and the particular stage of its evolution, on its economic level, on the time of year, and finally perhaps on cultural models which are the most difficult of all to come to grips with.

A large household, employing a number of servants, might relieve a woman of her participation in work in the fields; this is a variable linked to the economic level of the farm. In the same way, the presence of children already able to contribute to the labour force would enable the woman to devote herself exclusively to her household duties. Thus, in a Bigouden village in Brittany, there is a distinction between the women 'who are driven by necessity to the fields and who, side by side with the men, or alone in their furrows, valiantly tackle the job; they are ruddy-skinned, with calloused hands, and go home in the evenings with their shoulders bowed and their step heavy, having manfully accomplished the daily task,' and, on the other hand, the 'mistress of a large farm who never went to the fields. Her husband, her servants, and her sons were sufficient to work the soil. She kept house, that was her job. The floor well sanded, the furniture waxed, the brass shining, the cupboards filled with well-kept clothes, abundant hot meals ready when wanted, her domain was without fault. In the case of servants, the term 'mistress of the house' takes on its full meaning, since there are orders to be given, tasks to be assigned, and decisions to be taken to direct the few servants who relieve the woman from her more taxing duties. But the mistress must observe the crucial rule of conduct: she must rise first in the mornings to organise the day's work, as can be seen by looking at the timetable set out above. From the end of the eighteenth century, this precept was numbered among the pieces of advice given to the good farmer's wife 'who must be the eyes of the house, rising first and going to bed last.'

A folklorist making observations in the Basque country notes the physical strength of the women, who would walk forty or fifty kilometres a day: 'They showed themselves quite as good as the men at working in the fields; they harnessed the oxen, and led them, goad in hand. They drove the cart to the market, or the plough along the furrow. They took the oxen by their horns, mastered them, and made the beasts slow their step or accelerate, according to their wishes.

Female physical strength was not peculiar to the Basque women. The preceding descriptions have shown us the need for it. Whether the tasks are feminine ones, like washing, or whether they are associated with masculine tasks, like hay-making or harvest, the woman must be endowed with solid physical strength, and, if possible, good health, both indispensable to the success of her household. The man relies on the woman to help him, and he relies on a healthy and robust woman. The criteria for choosing a wife based on the externals signs of health – being 'ruddy', being strong – are here explained. Not only do proverbs mistrust feminine beauty:

Fille jolie, miroir de fou
Pretty girl, madman's mirror (Val d'Aosta)

Il vaut mieux dire laide allons souper que belle qu'avons nous à souper
It's better to say hag let's go and eat than beauty what is there for us to eat (Franche-Comté)

and the curiosity associated with idleness:

Fille fenestière rarement ménagère
Gazing out of the window rarely made a good housewife (Champagne)

but they set great store by physical strength and readiness to work:

Le corps vaut plus que le dot
The body's worth more than the dowry (Gascony)

On connaît la femme au pied et à la tête
You can tell a woman by her head and her feet (Languedoc)

Femme vaillante, maison d'or
A valiant woman, a house of gold (Gascony)

La femme courageuse fait la maison bonne
Dauntless woman makes good house (Catalonia)

Une ménagère qui travaille bien vaut sa peau plein d'argent
A hardworking woman is worth her skinful of money (Catalonia)

Brave femme dans une maison vaut plus que ferme et que cheptel
A dauntless woman in the house is worth more than farm and livstock too
(Languedoc)

The high value placed on a body in good health is easily explained in a society in which everything depends on physical strength. The inability to work, caused by sickness, was a calamity. A woman who could carry out physically exhausting tasks as well as having a pregnancy every two years, breast-feeding the youngest child and looking after the toddlers, was certainly a 'treasure'. One can also easily understand the rate of female mortality in the traditional rural environment, before the advent of contraception.

It is known that during the nineteenth century, contraceptive practices had effectively made their way into a number of rural areas of France, and that in the north, in Normandy, rural households were less burdened with children. Nonetheless, in a number of regions fertility was still close to the biological maximum, and the multiple tasks attendant upon looking after young children were added to those of looking after the farm. Mme d'Abbadie d'Arrast gives a very good picture of the harshness of the physiological function of motherhood, particularly in the Pays Basque, where heavy physical work was performed by the women.

For the peasant woman in particular, how burdensome and painful the numerous obligations of motherhood become, with the ties of nursing, and the care of small children; while the father knows only the delight of being fussed over by the children when he returns from the fields. An extra mouth to feed, one of these little brat's mouths, what was that to him, what sort of increase of work did that impose on him? Less than nothing. Whereas the mother, whether in the house or out, busy about her duties, coming and going, had to carry these little ones in her arms, or dragging along at her skirts. When she was pregnant, there could be no letting up; she worked every day, because she had to.

Nevertheless, these tasks 'went without saying'. They were never mentioned by the women interviewed by the researchers, even at Saint-Véran in the Hautes-Alpes, where the families were still very large, even in 1945. Looking after the little children went without saying, it was a duty and a delight, both of which were assumed more or less unconsciously by the women and transmitted in the mother's gestures with her daughter, or the grandmother's with her granddaughter.

This overlapping of the tasks performed by members of the household varied with the seasons. In the winter, the man was more often at home, and more available. During the long evenings where several families gathered together, the jobs were sometimes undifferentiated: men and women together shelled nuts, stripped corn or tobacco;

though most often, it is true, the women worked at their spinning or mending, while the men whittled poles, played cards or dice, or just simply talked together. Finally, the degree of cooperation varied from one region to another, and from one regional culture to another, but that is a delicate question which entails a consideration of roles and territory as well as of tasks, and it would not be possible to venture a hypothesis on the subject without widening the scope of this analysis.

This first level of approach to the organisation of labour has shown the integration of all the members of the household in farming activities and, in particular, the substance of female cooperations: the woman is not relegated to secondary, non-productive tasks as was often previously stated when using ethnocentric classification. On the contrary, her labour was essential to the life and survival of the farm, and thus of the household, in a production context which depended, even in the nineteenth century, even during the early stage of mechanisation, on the necessity for an extensive labour force. In fact, though the winnowing machine represented a technological improvement on the winnowing basket, it still required as much human energy to separate the wheat from the tares as the old-fashioned sieve used to do; the first reapers and threshers were always surrounded by a number of agricultural labourers feeding it material to thresh; and one had to await the invention of the washing-machine before looking after the linen became less of a wearing task than it was when washed in the traditional way.

A woman in the rural environment had no status unless she was married: unmarried she was, more or less, the servant of one of her married brothers or sisters. It was through marriage that she acquired her position as an adult in society, and her right to the responsibilities which she shared with her husband.

Day to day management rarely placed the woman in an eminent position within the household, but she could share the responsibility with her husband. At the level of the household, they were interdependent and complementary, as was noted by Olivier de Serres: 'And just as Tradition conferred on the woman responsibility for the home, and on the man responsibility for the land, so also . . . it was the mother of the family who would care for the disposal of provisions for everyday use, making the consultations necessary for a well-run household: it being occasionally the case, as things fell out, that the man would interest himself in the least concerns of the household, and the woman in the most important.

The future of the household depends on the complementary and interdependent labour of the married couple, and many a rural household could join in the remark made by a café owner in Paris who, a native of Aubrac, ran a small café and tobacconist's with his wife: 'In this job, there have to be two of you, and well united.'

SECTION 2
Work in Modern Societies

I AGRICULTURAL WORK

6 The Work Situation of the Agricultural Worker*
Howard Newby

Editor's Introduction: Probably the most detailed study of farmers and agricultural workers in modern Britain was conducted by Howard Newby in the early 1970s. The focus of the study was Suffolk, and the sample consisted of 71 farms and farmers and 233 farm workers. Though there are clear limitations to the study (for example it does not attempt to deal with hill farms based entirely on livestock), it nevertheless provides an excellent picture of the work conditions on a modern British farm.

Work on the land has customarily been regarded as a qualitatively different experience from work in any other industry. Even today, despite wholesale mechanisation, agriculture remains surrounded by a set of symbolic boundaries which separate it off from other types of employment and create an air of uniqueness with which farmers and farm workers alike identify. The move from agricultural to non-agricultural employment is still regarded as involving a much more severe dislocation than any other kind of occupational mobility. The agricultural worker tends to think of himself as being part of a distinctive breed, divorced by temperament and environment from the urban, industrial majority. The actual work itself is therefore an exceedingly important attribute of the farm worker's personal and social identity – more than many other jobs it defines for the farm worker what he *is*.

This partly explains the importance of the work situation as a structural component of the agricultural worker's overall social situation. However, the nature of the work situation has a number of other important implications owing to the frequent overlap of work and non-work roles. When the rural village was an occupational community such an overlap was virtually complete; and even today the large proportion of workers living 'on the job' (54.1 per cent in the Suffolk

* Extract from *The Deferential Worker: A Study of Farm Workers in East Anglia*, Allen Lane, 1977, pp. 279–89.

sample) ensure that the division between home and work is nothing like as great as in many other industries. It is the purpose of this chapter to describe the nature of the agricultural worker's work and to analyse his workplace relationships, both with the employer and fellow employees. Particular attention will be paid to one theoretical problem; the mode of control operated by the employer, particularly the extent of bureaucratisation, and its implications for the kind of worker commitment and loyalty which ensues. These are the kind of issues usually associated with the so-called 'size-effect' – the effect of plant size on worker identification. In agriculture, because workplace relationships so often spill over into the surrounding community, the way in which employer–employee relationships are handled and legitimated will clearly have implications in the wider social setting, just as the latter will help to define the worker's expectations of his work situation.

By the standards of most other sociological studies of occupational groups it is apparent that the agricultural worker's work situation is a somewhat peculiar one. In 1970 there were over 300,000 agricultural holdings in the United Kingdom, 171,000 of which were full-time with an average size of 154 acres. At the same time there were an average of 1.7 regular whole-time workers for every full-time holding. Therefore one is inevitably dealing with small-scale employers of labour, and, although the trend is towards larger units in terms of production and acreage, so far the rate of diminution of the labour force is sufficiently outpacing the rate of farm amalgamation to reduce the average size of the labour force – in 1965 it was 2.1. In 1970 nearly three-quarters of all agricultural holdings employed no full-time workers at all and a further 13.9 per cent employed only one. So the distribution of the labour force is highly skewed towards the lower size groups: 21.4 per cent of the labour force are employed on their own and 62 per cent are employed on units of four or less men; only 7.8 per cent of the workers are on farms employing twenty or more employees. Comparative data on the distribution of holdings by the number of workers per holding is shown in Table 6.1.

Agricultural work, despite all the technological changes of recent years, remains distinctive in one important respect: the length of the production cycle and the rhythm of working on the land remain largely governed by the seasons of the year. The very length of the production cycle on an arable farm often results in a telescoping of time perception: ten years ago is only ten 'products' ago – almost yesterday to the Suffolk agricultural worker. Technological change, while it has drastically altered the work situation in other respects, has not removed this, for while the pace of work has been affected this rhythm remains. The basis of this apparent paradox is not hard to find. Operations in arable agriculture, unlike those in most areas of manufacturing industry, *must*

Table 6.1   Distribution of holdings by labour size groups, 1972

	Suffolk %	Eastern Region %	England and Wales %
Size groups, regular whole-time workers:			
I	36.4	37.0	49.1
2	20.3	19.9	23.6
3	12.4	12.1	10.6
4	9.0	7.8	5.3
5–9	15.3	15.3	8.2
10–14	3.0	4.1	1.7
15–19	1.5	1.7	0.7
20+	2.0	2.1	0.8
Holdings with regular whole-time workers	47.5	39.8	35.6
No. of regular whole-time workers per holding	1.82	1.58	0.93
No. of regular whole-time workers per full-time holding	2.86	2.73	1.7

Source: MAFF Statistics

take place sequentially rather than concurrently. Thus in replacing hand or horse power by machines the practice of carrying out production in sequential steps is not disturbed, as it is in the changeover from handicraft to mechanised manufacture in industry. As a result the consequences of technological innovation in agriculture have merely been a spectacular change in the implements of production, whereas in industry changes in the organisation of production have been much more thoroughgoing.

This is not to say, of course, that technological change in agriculture has not transformed the nature of the workplace social structure. In particular there has been a dramatic reduction in the division of labour as mechanisation has allowed the production sequences to be carried out more quickly and with less labour than hitherto. On most farms the division of labour among the workers is minimal, with only one major division remaining – between those workers who work primarily with livestock and those involved in crop production which most involves driving machinery. On the smaller farm even this division is bridged. One consequence of mechanisation, then, has been an increased variety in the work of the individual farm worker. Agricultural workers have always had to be extremely versatile, but whereas the nineteenth-century Suffolk horseman's life revolved entirely around his horses, his modern counterpart must not only be a tractor driver and mechanic, but often a stockman and general labourer too. In addition to this increased job rotation, mechanisation has also removed much of the routine drudgery and certainly the physical effort from working on the land. The major drawback has, however, been the isolation of the modern farm worker, increasingly a rather lonely figure in a noisy tractor cab with sometimes only an attenuated and desultory contact with his workmates, of whom there are fewer and fewer around.

To try to reconstruct the work experience of the 'typical' farm worker is a somewhat fruitless exercise, since no farm worker could be regarded as typical in this sense. However, such is the social (and literal) invisibility of much farm work that it seems important to convey some idea of the nature of the farm worker's experience, particularly as it is exactly this aspect of rural life which is usually absent from the conventional English cultural perspective. Most of the farms in the Suffolk sample were arable/pig enterprises, that is to say they were mainly concerned with growing crops, mostly cereals, and incorporated a pig unit which utilised home-produced feed. The end-product of these farms was therefore pigs, although many of the crops, including some cereals, were sold on the open market. Because of its predominance in the sample this type of farm can be taken as an example of the nature of the Suffolk agricultural worker's work, but it must be realised that such a description is intended to be illustrative rather than exhaustive. Certainly there are many Suffolk farming enterprises where the experiences of the workers do not conform with those given below.

A 600-acre Suffolk farm of this type, situated on clay land and away from the river valleys, would in 1972 have employed perhaps five general farm workers/tractor drivers and one pigman, perhaps more, perhaps less depending upon the involvement of the farmer and his family. With the enticing prospect of entry into the EEC and buoyant cereal prices, perhaps two-thirds or more of the farm would be under cereals, barley and wheat, the remainder being taken up with sugar beet, peas for freezing, beans and perhaps a few acres of other vegetables such as potatoes, swedes, cabbages, dwarf beans, brussels sprouts, etc. Small plots of land might be given over to growing bat willows or conifers, which not only have a commercial value but are useful for taxation purposes, while they, together with any residual woodland, provide some cover for that other important source of entertainment and revenue, the pheasant. Although there may be some specialisation over pig production, many farms still see their charges through from farrowing to fattening, using some sort of rota whereby batches of fattened pigs leave the farm perhaps every three weeks or so, destined more often than not for one of the large food-processing firms which often contract out pig production to individual farmers or farmers' co-operatives.

On such a farm the pigman's job is perhaps the most routine, involving a daily round of preparing the feed and distributing it to the pigs, as well as generally keeping an eye on them for any sign of malady. He may also be involved in mucking out at regular intervals, since the muck will be transported by trailer around the farm to make muck heaps, later to be spread on the land prior to ploughing. The pigs will also need to be weighed (which will also involve some help) once a month and appropriate records will be kept. Less predictably the pigman will also look after farrowing, which in many cases will involve the constant supervision and awkward hours to which most stockmen have become inured. The cycle of farrowing, weaning and fattening is quicker than the production cycle on the arable side (it takes between twenty-two and thirty-one weeks from birth to despatch), but the process may also be carried out concurrently so that all the stages are taking place simultaneously. On very intensive livestock units, especially poultry, such tendencies have been followed still further to produce 'factory' farming methods (the term itself is, of course, significant), allowing for an extreme division of labour, associated with routine and repetitive work for those involved. Few Suffolk arable/pig farms could in any way be compared with this, however.

The work of the arable workers tends to be more constrained by seasonal factors, although it is not without its daily or weekly routines. January and February, generally a very slack time devoted to maintaining machinery, tidying up around the yard, oiling and painting, according to the weather, represent the nadir of the farming year. The major outdoors activity is hedging and ditching, a job which most farm workers dislike intensely because of the cold, wet and often filthy working conditions, and because the job is essentially destructive rather than constructive. With more and more fields having been amalgamated and hedges removed, more ditching than hedging is nowadays involved. Increasingly both tasks are mechanised – one sees very few traditionally 'laid' hedges in East Anglia these days – and on some farms the work is carried out by contractors, who possess the necessary equipment, rather than by the farm's own labour force. For the farmer on heavy land hedges and ditches are an irksome nuisance, occupying expensive land which could otherwise be rendered productive, costly to maintain and perpetuating an inefficient field pattern that has been inherited from a pre-mechanised age. Since the job is not a popular one among the workers either, and since there have been cash incentives for field amalgamation, hedges have been removed, and ditches replaced by drains all over south and eastern England. The

result has been a change in the appearance of the countryside – with by
now notorious repercussions among those who wish to preserve the
'traditional' rural English landscape – but for the farm worker a reduction in time spent on a job which he continues to regard with some
distaste.

The end of this slack period depends very much upon weather
conditions and how quickly the land will have sufficiently dried out to
allow men and machinery to venture upon it, but most farmers hope
that around the second or third week in March it will be possible to start
preparing for one of the most frenetic periods of the year – seed-time.
At this time new potatoes are sown and there is some early seed-drilling
if the weather allows, beginning with spring beans. By April the
preparation of seed beds, drilling and rolling are in full swing,
beginning with barley and then wheat, peas and sugar beet. Timing is
of the essence and if weather conditions have been adverse during
March and early April it is not unusual to see drilling taking place at
night by the light of the tractor's headlights. 'Winter' cereals – cereals
sown during the previous autumn which have over-wintered – are
rolled and harrowed and late potatoes are sown. In addition the winter
cereals are top-dressed with artificial fertilizer. All these activities
ensure that the farm labour-force is fully stretched over this period.
Overtime is usually plentiful and welcomed by most farm workers after
the lean winter months and with summer holidays to look forward to.
The necessities of the situation are also fully understood, so that there is
little need for the employer to justify the imposition of long hours and
weekend work upon his workers. Indeed most workers are as anxious to
complete a successful sowing as their employers.

During May there is a further lull, punctuated by some crop-
spraying. In the last week of May the hand-hoeing of sugar beet begins.
Until very recently sugar beet has been sown in a continuous row and a
great deal of hand labour is required for chopping out and singling the
seedling to allow single plants to grow to maturity. The crop also needs
to be kept free of weeds so that later in the year further sessions of
tractor hoeing between the rows may take place. Hand-hoeing is an
important event for a number of reasons. It is almost invariably paid for
by piece-rate, the minimum rate for which is decided upon each year by
Country Wages Committees consisting of NFU (National Farmers
Union) and NUAWW (National Union of Agricultural and Allied
Workers) representatives. Individual farms can, and sometimes do,
vary the rate upwards, so some 'plant-bargaining' is by no means
uncommon. Because of the operation of piece-rates, overtime is virtually unlimited and there is a further opportunity to obtain extra money
for summer holidays. But perhaps the most important aspect from the
sociological point of view is the fact that the operation is so labour-

intensive that casual labour is often taken on, usually in the form of retired workers and workers' wives. Sugar-beet hoeing is therefore something of a social occasion, indeed under modern agricultural conditions it is virtually the last remaining farming activity in which the whole farm labour force (and often their wives) is gathered together with the possibility of easy and continuous communication between them. There is often a quasi-festive air about the proceedings – picnic lunches, etc. – tempered only be the competitive element introduced by piece-rates. Throughout June the usually depopulated fields of East Anglia take on a faintly – and temporarily – bucolic appearance for the one and only time in the agricultural year. However, even this is fast disappearing, since weeds are increasingly being controlled by chemicals and the singling operation has been superseded in many cases by precision drilling and monogerm seeds.

June is also the mouth for haysel or hay harvest. The increased specialisation of most East Anglian farms, and the consequent disappearance of cattle from many of them, means that this is no longer the job it once was. Once haysel began in June and continued until mid-August, when it linked up with harvest; now it is of no concern to most Suffolk farmers and even for those who keep cows it has diminished in importance. A few runs round with a tractor and it is all over in a few weeks. For the arable/pig farm June is a month of watching and waiting once sugar-beet hoeing is completed. It is a time to take holidays or visit agricultural shows. It is also a time for lifting early potatoes, usually with the help of casual female labour, and for irrigating the main crop. Otherwise the tending of crops is limited to spraying – sugar beet for yellow virus, wheat for yellow rust, peas for weevil, etc.

In July the pace of work quickens once more. The early part of the month may be spent on routine maintenance work, the lull before the harvest storm, particularly going over the combine harvester before it is brought into use for its period of brief but intense activity. However, increasingly in Suffolk the main event of this month is pea harvest. Some peas are grown for seed and some for canning, but most of the crop, particularly on farms within easy reach of the factory at Lowestoft, is for freezing. Pea harvest is a fascinating spectacle, as far removed from the traditional smock-and-scythe image of agricultural work as it is possible to go. The keynote of the whole operation, which is carried out with an almost military style of planning and execution, is speed and precision of timing. The production of the crop is closely controlled by the food-processing firms – in Suffolk, mainly Birds Eye – in order to ensure both quality and a continuity of supply. The companies dictate to the individual farmers when to sow, when to spray and when to harvest. The farmers in turn combine into growers' groups in order to bargain with the companies, but also to pool machinery, labour and other resources at harvest time. In the case of one growers' group in the Suffolk fieldwork area this involved in 1972 the purchase of nine 'viners' – the machines which harvest the peas and which look like gigantic combine harvesters – worth £100,000, a water carrier, several tractors and the hire of a fleet of thirty lorries, plus the labour to operate them on a twenty-four-hour basis. This caravan of machinery and men moves around from farm to farm at the instigation of the factory in Lowestoft. The whole operation is radio-controlled from the factory and the peas have to be from field to freezer in ninety minutes, otherwise they are dumped. The harvest is carried out around the clock with a lorry leaving for the factory every twenty minutes (even if it has only a few peas in it).

For the workers, life 'on the peas' represents a qualitatively different experience from life during the other ten months of the year when they are on their own farms. They work shifts, something completely novel in agriculture, but generally receive higher wages. They also have the excitement, and status, of operating bigger, more expensive and more complex machinery than they have been accustomed to. More importantly the work is more disciplined and the mode of control more impersonal and formal than on most farms. However, the greatest significance probably lies in the opportunity which the pea harvest represents for workers from a large number of farms to come together, compare their circumstances and assess conditions on the farms they visit. This allows a degree of comparison over such matters as wages and conditions, not to mention husbandry techniques, which would otherwise not be available to many workers. Some of their verdicts are carried back to their colleagues who have remained on their regular farms and these help to establish and perpetuate evaluations of various farming employers, including their own, in the surrounding area.

Once the pea viners have departed, the opportunity is usually quickly seized to prepare the land for the next crop before corn harvest begins. This involves first muck-spreading and then ploughing in preparation for, later in the year, the drilling of winter wheat or winter barley. By the middle of August pea harvest will have ended, although some of the team is kept together to harvest dwarf beans. By the end of the first week in August, however, most farmers on heavy land will have hoped to have the cereal harvest under way (earlier on light land), beginning with winter barley and finishing around the second week in September with spring wheat. This is traditionally the year's great climacteric, but while it remains a very busy period its importance both as a period of hectic work and as a social ritual has diminished considerably in recent years, though some of the mythology may remain. What was once simply 'harvest' is now often referred to as 'corn harvest' in order to distinguish it from other equally busy, and in some cases busier, periods. As long as it is not too extreme, modern grain driers have even reduced the importance of the weather (although driers can be expensive to operate). As if to perpetuate a version of harvest that is now fading away, farmers who otherwise hardly touch a tractor from one year's end to the next can be seen on board a combine harvester at this time of the year, while they also keep an anxious eye on the sky. The workers also keep a weather eye open, but for rather different motives – for them a difficult harvest means more overtime and higher wages.

Before the 1950s, grain harvesting involved a complex series of inter-connected tasks involving the mobilisation of a large labour force. The crop was first cut and bound into sheaves by a binder and the sheaves were 'stooked' in order to ripen and dry before being carted and stacked. The stacks were thatched to protect them from the weather, and later, over the winter months, it would be threshed to separate the grain from the straw. Today some farmers earn a great deal of money by harvesting the odd field in such a manner and charging the public admission to come and watch them do it. Moreover by growing older strains of wheat without a pith in the straw they can often sell the straw for thatching commuters' cottages for a higher price than the grain. Needless to say, harvest for the most part is no longer carried out in this way. Now all the work is performed by combine harvesters which empty the grain from their tanks directly into trailers or lorries to be taken away in bulk to be cleaned and dressed elsewhere. A combine harvester can complete in a day what would have taken weeks using the old technology. In many fields harvest will take just one day, with possibly one more to bale and cart the straw. Alternatively the straw and stubble may be burned, so that by the end of August it can seem that the whole of the countryside is aflame, much to the consternation of surrounding residents, especially urbanised newcomers.

After harvest there is a brief interlude of muck-carting, ploughing and rolling in preparation for autumn drilling before the busiest time of the year for most East Anglian farms begins around the last week in September. October marks the confluence of a number of farming activities: the beginning of autumn ploughing and muck-spreading, the main drillings of winter barley, wheat and beans and the harvesting of spring beans, sugar beet and main crop potatoes. This month has now replaced August as the really hectic month of the year, when overtime is often unlimited and when work continues over weekends and some-times even into the night. Although this period has none of the aura of corn harvest, in terms of sheer workload it forms the climax of the farming year before the slack winter months arrive. Ploughing and sugar-beet harvesting continue, weather permitting, into November and December and even beyond. The harvesting of sugar beet is now mechanised, thus removing one of the most laborious and detested jobs of the farming year, for pulling sugar beet in often freezing condition was not only uncomfortable and arduous but a cause of sinovitis of the wrist which could result in permanent disability. Ploughing still results in a public statement of the farm worker's skill, but it has become less and less a status-enhancing quality in most rural villages. Some farm workers admit to being bored driving up and down the large East Anglian fields day in and day out for two or three months on end.

Most of the farm workers in the Suffolk sample experienced this kind of work pattern, although clearly it varied from farm to farm according to variations in the husbandry of the holdings and the division of labour among the workforce. Among the factors which emerge as being of importance is the tremendous variety involved in the work tasks, a variety enhanced by changes in the weather, soil and other contextual factors, so that farm workers will readily admit, with only minor exaggeration, that the work is never the same two days running. Most farm workers are also concerned with the production of living and growing things which they see through from beginning to end, so that they feel the sense of achievement familiar to most suburban gardeners when their crops or animals are finally brought to maturity. Compared with most other manual work, agriculture offers far greater non-economic rewards in terms of job interest, judgement, discretion, challenge, responsibility and control, so that intrinsic job satisfaction remains extraordinarily high. This is not to say that agriculture does not contain its boring, repetitive aspects nor its routine drudgery, but few farm workers leave the land because they dislike the work itself; on the contrary many would gladly return were it not for the low wages and poor prospects predominating throughout agriculture.

II INDUSTRIAL WORK

---

7 The Design of Jobs*
Craig R. Littler and Graeme Salaman

This chapter examines some of the major movements and tendencies in industrial work design, which have helped to shape the nature of work experience in modern factories.

Taylorism and the division of labour

The oldest economic principle of production is that of the division of labour. According to Adam Smith, the eighteenth century economist, the advantages of the sub-division of work are threefold: first, labour productivity increases because of enhanced specialised dexterity and 'skill'; second, there is a minimisation of changeover and work preparation time; third, decomposition of tasks stimulates the invention of specialised machinery. An engineer is faced not with a jumble of complex motions but with a limited set of repeated actions that he can reproduce by a machine (Adam Smith, 1776). Charles Babbage, writing in 1832, considered this analysis to be incomplete and added the well-known Babbage Principle. Put simply, this involves stripping a skilled job to an essential core and deskilling all the surrounding tasks. This division is then linked to status and pay differences (Babbage, 1835). The economic dynamic to this continued re-division of labour is labour cheapening, a process which is assisted by the reduction in the learning time for jobs and by weakening the bargaining power of workers.

Productive work involves both mental and manual labour, and what neither Adam Smith nor Babbage conceptualised clearly was that the job specialisation and narrowing which they advocated could be used to divide mental from manual labour. But twentieth century methods of production tend continually to separate mental and manual labour, planning and doing. As factories have increased in size, so planning of productive processes has been taken out of the workshop and placed in auxiliary planning and design departments.

* Extract from *Class at Work: the Design, Allocation and Control of Jobs*, Batsford Academic, 1984, pp. 72–90.

Frederick Taylor's scheme of so-called 'scientific management', put forward in the 1890s, rests upon the principle of the division of mental and manual labour. In addition Taylorism (as it became known) involved:

1 A general principle of the maximum decomposition of work tasks.
2 The divorce of direct and so-called 'indirect' labour, by which was meant all setting up, preparation and maintenance tasks.
3 The minimisation of the skill requirements of any task, leading to minimum job-learning times.

In general, Taylor argued that the full possibilities of scientific management 'will not have been realised until almost all of the machines in the shop are run by men who are of smaller calibre and attainments, and who are therefore cheaper than those required under the old system.' (Taylor, 1903, p. 105.)

If we define Taylorism carefully, it is possible to contrast it with other forms of work organisation – the wave of labour rationalisation between1890 and 1914 based on ideas developed in the British armaments industry; the systematic rationalisation entailed by Fordism in which flow production required the redesign of the whole factory (see below); and the bureaucratisation of the employment relationship, involving institutionalised career systems as in the post office and railways.

This contrast with the other forms of work organisation raises the question of the extent of the influence of Taylorism. Our answer to this question is complex (life is never simple!), so we will baldly state our conclusion and then proceed to qualify it. In general the direct and indirect influence of Taylorism on factory jobs has been extensive, so that in Britain job design and technology design have become imbued with a neo-Taylorism.

However, the line of influence was not straightforward, so that it is necessary to add several qualifications:

1 In Britain there was a time-lag of influence. Indeed, before 1914 the employers rejected American methods of management.
2 Because of this time-lag it was *neo*-Taylorite systems which were eventually introduced, especially the Bedaux system. This combined Taylorism with the First World War fatigue studies and some elements of industrial psychology.
3 The Bedaux system was probably the most important channel for the spread of Taylorite ideas in Britain, but there were other channels, notably the transfer of American mass production industries associated with the emergence of multi-nationals.
4 There continued to be significant worker, supervisor and managerial

resistance to Taylorism resulting in uneven adoption even within the mass production industries.

5 There is the curious paradox that despite the influence of Taylorism on job design, it did not succeed as a managerial *ideology* in Britain, unlike the USA. This paradox arose from the timing and context of implementation.

(For more detailed discussion of the above points see Littler, 1982).

Not all economies accepted Taylorite ideas of job design. A different pattern is exemplified by Japan. In Japan, partly because of the timing and rapidity of industrialisation, no extensive tradition of industrial craftsmanship was ever established. Instead Japanese factories depended on a tradition of work teams incorporating managerial functions and maintenance functions, with few staff specialists. There was a lack of job boundaries and continued job flexibility, unlike the prescriptions of Taylorism.

But in the United States and, more slowly, in Britain Taylorism, with its underlying principles of job fragmentation, tight job boundaries, and the separation of mental and manual labour, became the predominant ideal for job design. However, in practice there are limits to the division of labour implied by Taylorism. As Adam Smith realised, the division of labour depends on the desired volume of output, which, in turn, depends on the extent of the market. If a certain piece of work involved ten operations it would not be economical to employ a specialised, detailed worker for each operation if the total volume of output only required the time of one person. Thus, decomposition of tasks and Taylorite principles depend on mass markets, mass production and the velocity of throughput.

Fordism

This linkage of the division of labour and mass markets was realised clearly by Henry Ford. He largely established, captured and maintained a mass market for automobiles between 1908 and 1929, when the last of over 15 million Model T cars rolled off the assembly line. By that date the USA had about 80% of the cars in the entire world, a ratio of 5.3 people for every car registered, at a time when cars were a comparative luxury in Britain (Flink, 1975, pp. 67 and 70).

The model of production worked out by Ford between 1908 and 1913, to serve this mass market, presupposed the major principles of Taylorism, but went further in the transfer of traditional skills from workers to specialised machines. By 1914 about 15,000 machines had been installed at the vast new Highland Park plant and company policy was to scrap machines as fast as they could be replaced by improved types. In addition, Ford perfected the flow-line principle of assembly work. This means that instead of workers moving between tasks, the flow of parts is achieved as much as possible by machines (conveyors and transporters) so that assembly workers are tied to their work position and have no need to move about the workshop. A crucial consequence is that the pace of work is controlled mechanically and not by the workers or supervisors.

Associated with the new fixed-speed moving assembly line was an accelerated division of labour and short task-cycle times. Ford pushed job fragmentation to an extreme. For example, in 1922, Henry Ford records a survey of jobs in his plants:

The lightest jobs were again classified to discover how many of them required the use of full faculties, and we found that 670 could be filled by legless men, 2637 by one-legged men, two by armless men, 715 by one-armed men, and ten by blind men. Therefore, out of 7,882 kinds of job . . . 4,034 did not require full physical capacity.

(Ford, 1922, p. 108)

Having developed a new industrial technology based on the flow-line principle and extreme job fragmentation, Ford found that control of the production process was not equal to control of the workforce. Worker rejection of the new work processes was expressed in high rates of turnover, absenteeism and insufficient effort. For example, the head of Ford's employment department in 1913 cited a figure of $38 to train up a new worker: a small amount, but with an annual turnover of more than 50,000 workers (i.e. 400%) the total cost was two million dollars (Russell, 1978, p. 40; also Meyer, 1981).

The control techniques developed by Ford in response to these worker problems serve to mark off Fordism from Taylorism. One of Taylor's close associates asserted that he did not 'care a hoot what became of the workman after he left the factory at night; so long as he was able to show up the next morning in a fit condition for a hard day's toil' (Copley, 1915, p. 42). But Ford went outside the factory gates in an attempt to re-mould working-class culture in accordance with industrial discipline and efficiency. The so-called 'Five Dollar Day' offered workers large material incentives for altering their private lives as well as their work behaviour. A worker's bonus, access to company loans and, ultimately, his job depended on satisfactory personal habits (including no consumption of alcohol or tobacco). Home conditions and off-work behaviour were all investigated by the company's 'Sociological Department'! The Five Dollar Day was backed up by the Americanisation programme, directed at immigrants and providing not only language instruction but also moral education into American, middle-class values (see Meyer, 1981.)

At the level of job design the effects of the introduction of the assembly line at Fords on productivity and profits is indicated by the fact that it reduced the time of chassis assembly from 12½ hours to 2 hours 40 minutes (Flink, 1975, p. 77). Fine for the consumer but what does it mean for the producer? An idea of the pressures of mechanical control and of Fordism in practice is vividly conveyed in Linhart's picture of work on the assembly lines at Citroën in the 1970s. (See Chapter 9).

A strikingly similar account to Linhart's is provided by Satoshi Kamata, describing the work experience in a Japanese car factory:

I have really been fooled by the seeming slowness of the conveyor belt. No one can understand how it works without experiencing it. Almost as soon as I begin, I am dripping with sweat. Somehow, I learn the order of the work motions, but I'm totally unable to keep up with the speed of the line. My work gloves make it difficult to grab as many tiny bolts as I need, and how many precious seconds do I waste doing just that? I do my best, but I can barely finish one gear box out of three within the fixed length of time. If a different-model transmission comes along, it's simply beyond my capacity. Some skill is needed, and a new hand like me can't do it alone, I'm thirsty as hell, but workers can neither smoke nor drink water. Going to the toilet is out of the question. Who could have invented a system like this? It's designed to make workers do nothing but work and to prevent any kind of rest.

(Kamata, 1982, p. 22).

The answer of course, is that Ford invented the system, and as these examples from Citroën in France and Toyota in Japan indicate, Ford's competitors imitated his success and installed moving assembly lines with fixed speeds and short task cycles themselves. The factors which fuelled the diffusion of Taylorism and Fordism are considered in the next section.

Diffusion of Taylorism and Fordism
At least for the mass production industries, Taylorism and Fordism became the predominant ideals for organising work in the USA, Britain and many other economies. Two things helped the spread of the ideas and techniques. Firstly, the interwar years were characterised by the internationalisation of technology. In the newer industries, such as electrical engineering, chemicals and vehicles, this was particularly true. For example, one of the largest electrical engineering companies in the USA was Westinghouse Electric. This corporation became a strong advocate of Taylorism, time study and systematic job analysis. In 1924 Westinghouse concluded a technical exchange agreement with Siemens, one of the two largest German electrical firms, which extended the influence of Westinghouse management methods in German factories. Similarly, Mitsubishi Electric of Japan had a similar agreement with Westinghouse in the 1920s. The managing director of

Mitsubishi went to the USA to study Westinghouse techniques and became a strong advocate of Taylorite time and motion studies (Levine and Kawada, 1980, p. 264).

Taylorism and Fordist techniques had of course to be adapted to the labour markets, economic conditions and culture of the receiving society. But one mechanism allowed direct transplants. The diffusion of American management and job design techniques was assisted by the mechanism of the multinational corporation. Ford established subsidiaries in Britain, Germany, Japan and other countries, as did Ford's main competitor – General Motors. Ford first moved to Britain as early as 1911 when the company bought an old car plant in Manchester, and the Dagenham factory, built in 1930–31, was the first major Ford plant outside the USA. Ford's example was followed by General Motors, who took over Vauxhall in 1925. When the General Motors takeover occurred the corporation radically reorganised the existing factory. All machines on the shop-floor were organised on the flow-line principle and assembly was done on moving tracks. Each department and assembly area was co-ordinated to produce one component every twenty minutes (Lewchuk, 1983, p. 96).

The multinational corporation allowed not only the transfer of techniques and machinery but of *people*, who brought with them an extensive knowledge of details and general orientations to mass production. For example General Motors brought over a small pool of American engineers who could train British engineers in the new techniques.

There were still, of course, differences between companies. Citroën of France started an assembly line for its first postwar model as early as 1919 and, lacking qualified engineers, the company later hired American engineers and brought them to Europe. The Austin car company in Britain introduced moving assembly lines between 1922 and 1925 at the Longbridge plant, whilst Morris Motors, perhaps the leading British car firm in the interwar years, delayed the reorganisation of manufacturing methods until 1934 (Fridenson, 1978).

In general, by the mid-1930s Taylorite techniques had spread across Europe whilst Fordism and the moving assembly line had penetrated the largest car firms and spread to other industries such as electrical engineering.

The Limits of Taylorism and Fordism

Even within the principles and practice of Taylorism and Fordism there are limits to job fragmentation and the transfer of skills to specialised machinery. First, there are the economic limits which we have already discussed – the decomposition of tasks depends on the velocity of throughput. Second, there are technical limits. Assume, for example, that in an engineering factor a given piece of work involves several operations such as planing, milling, turning and drilling. These various operations can be economically separated as the volume of throughput increases, each task being assigned to one man, or a group of men, who do nothing else. Thus, a worker may be assigned to drill a specific hole in each piece of metal. If the volume of work increases further, then a drilling fixture or jig may be used and the work of drilling may be further sub-divided by employing one man to put the parts to be drilled into the fixture and take them out again after the operation, and the other man to do the drilling and nothing else. This is an example of the divorce of direct and indirect labour discussed above. But without the further development of machining technology (which has not occurred until recently) it is difficult to sub-divide either of these functions further, no matter how big the market and the volume of output. In other words, the division of labour can be carried down to certain fundamental operations beyond which it must wait upon a transformation of the technology.

Thirdly, Taylorism and Fordism carry co-ordination and control costs. As the division of labour is extended, co-ordination measures must accompany such extension: for example, production planning, supervision and monitoring, and inspection procedures. This is not just a practical, managerial question but also a sociological question related to the development of industry. Early industrialisation in most economies, including Britain, depended on the use of existing forms of group or cultural solidarity and subordination, such as family and kin ties. Later patterns of work organisation, in eliminating such forms, left employers with stark and critical problems of harnessing labour's creative and productive powers. However, formal structures of control cost money and tend to offset gains from an extended division of labour. For example, many employers found that the clerical costs of installing and running Taylorite-type schemes were very high (Littler, 1982).

Fourthly, limits to the direct control methods of Taylor and Ford are set by increasing co-operation costs. If the linkages of workers to the work organisation are largely instrumental and entail very little commitment, then the purchase price of day-to-day worker compliance is inexorably increased during the upturn in the economic cycle when labour markets are tight. More broadly, Taylorite forms of work organisation are acceptable to employers only within certain types of product market. If price ceases to be the predominant factor in exchange, and non-price factors, such as reliability, quality and design, assume a larger significance, then this places a heavier emphasis on worker co-operation and worker commitment. In Taylorite/Fordist organisations workers are neither trained to show, nor are rewarded for, initiative. Here is an account by one American worker:

I am – or was – an American auto worker. I built GM cars for 16 years. Then, in March (1980), I was laid off indefinitely . . . It was not the worker who determines the quality of a car, but the executives in Detroit and the plant supervisors. The worker who performs a certain task 320 times a day, 5 days a week, knows more about the specifics of this particular job than anyone else. Yet, in 16 years, I have never been consulted on how to improve a job qualitatively or quantitatively. There are suggestion programs but their main concern is always 'how to save the company's money'. The auto worker can only build as good a car as he is instructed or permitted to build. We on the line take our cue from those in the head office. If they don't really care about the quality, they can't expect us to either.

(Douglas, 1980)

In this environment workers regard any demand for initiative or commitment as simply a bargaining counter in the struggles with supervisors and employers. Since employment involves willingness to work in exchange for a wage, workers' subjectivity becomes an important element in the production process. These attitudes cannot be made irrelevant by any form of work control or discipline, however oppressive and onerous, so long as the work, however de-skilled or regulated, is done by humans. If they are relevant, then Taylorite forms of work design are likely to have extremely negative consequences for work attitudes. One characteristic response to this phenomenon is to install still tighter forms of work and control regulation (because the workers are so 'bloodyminded'); but as Fox and other writers have noted, this spiral of distrust, regulation, alienation, further distrust, and so on is often identified by management as unsatisfactory even from the point of view of management's practical, commercial priorities.

Job redesign in the 1970s

During the late sixties and early seventies, the apparent problem of technocracy and Taylorite strategies (organisational rigidity and inflexibility, the expansion of organisational complexity to handle fragmented work, the underutilisation of worker initiative, and numerous indicators of worker dissatisfaction) led to the emergence of a job redesign movement, largely based on industrial psychology, and a more broadly based Quality of Working Life (Q.W.L.) movement. The latter is conveniently symbolised by the 'Work in America' report (1973) and the report 'On the Quality of Working Life' (1973) in Britain (Wilson, 1973). These reports, and other writings, propound principles of 'good' job design which are the precise opposite of Taylorian principles. Typically, five have been put forward:

1 Principle of closure: the scope of the job should include all the tasks necessary to complete a product or process. Theoretically, the pre-

dicted result is that work acquires an intrinsic meaning and people can feel a sense of achievement.

2 Incorporation of control and monitoring taks. Jobs should be designed so that an army of inspectors is not required. The individual worker, or the work team, assumes responsibility for quality and reliability.

3 Task variety, i.e. an increase in the range of tasks. This implies a principle of comprehensiveness, which means that workers should understand the general principles of a range of tasks so that job rotation is possible.

4 Self-regulation of the speed of work and some choice over work methods and work sequence.

5 A job structure that permits some social interaction and perhaps co-operation among workers.

(See for example L.E. Davis, 1957 and 1966; Walton, 1974; Hackman and Oldham, 1975).

Through the 1970s these principles were the gospel of a few avant-garde consultants, and though there were isolated examples of new work systems, generally job design remained tied to traditional Taylorian principles. However, through the latter half of the 1970s and the early 1980s the pressure of – mainly Japanese – competition has forced many Western corporations to re-examine their philosophy of job design and control from a solid, down to earth perspective – that of profits.

The recent trends in job design cannot all be grouped together. As several authors have pointed out (Kelly, 1982; Savall, 1981), there have, in general, been three types: reorganisation of Fordist assembly lines, group technology, and job enrichment. We will consider each of these in turn.

Reorganisation of assembly lines

This type of job redesign has been concentrated in consumer industries, especially electrical appliances. Such changes have been associated with increased product variations in more competitive markets. Generally, depending on the type of product and the price structure, a large corporation needs at least two years to get back its investment of setting up a new mass production line. But, partly because of Japanese competition, the pace of change has quickened so that a comfortable cruise along a two year profit path has turned into a bumpy ride. It needs to be remembered that Fordist techniques are product-specific, involving specialised machinery and narrow skills which are not readily transferable. The result has been that mass production facilities have become excessively inflexible and a cost burden, as it becomes harder and harder to consolidate the mass production of a standard product.

Thus the product market pressure has been to create more flexible work forms able to accommodate more rapid product changes without creating an entirely new line (Sabel, 1982, p. 199). For example, in a large British electrical plant the old work system consisted of a fixed-speed straight assembly-line. Work was machine-paced with about 30 people doing one task each – wiring, soldering, assembly, or testing – with task cycles varying between 25 to 45 seconds. Workers could not leave their work stations for as long as one minute and if there was a breakdown or disruption at any point then the entire line stopped. The work re-design carried out in the 1970s consisted of introducing buffer inventories of partly processed goods between work stations and grouping all automatic operations together so that workers were de-coupled from the machine pace by these buffers (see Fig. 7.1). The line itself is not so highly mechanised, the jobs have been slightly enlarged and task cycles are approximately double that of the old line. But the crucial point was that though the initial investment costs of the new line were higher, capacity utilisation increased because of greater flexibility. The new work arrangements could adapt to product changes much faster and thus reduce overall unit costs.

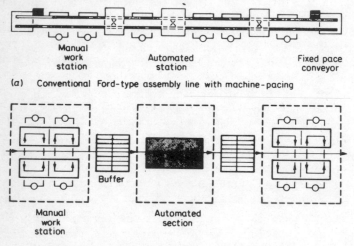

(a)   Conventional Ford-type assembly line with machine-pacing

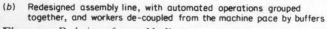

(b)   Redesigned assembly line, with automated operations grouped together, and workers de-coupled from the machine pace by buffers

Fig. 7.1   *Redesign of assembly lines*

Most of the redesign changes in assembly lines have still resulted in production processes with one-man work stations; often more co-operation between workers is possible (see Fig. 7.1), but it is not usually essential to the flow of production. We now turn to a form of redesigned work organisation which explicitly recognises the value of cooperative team work, namely group technology.

Group technology

Group technology represents a realisation by some employers of the value of work groups as a basis for work organisation, because it enables them to move beyond the cash nexus and tap the artesian sources of team-work, group problem-solving and mutual social control. These groups have been tried in mass production industries such as car manufacture in Sweden and Germany; for example, Volkswagen started experimenting with them at its new Salzgitter engine plant in 1975. Normally car engines are built on a conventional fixed speed assembly line with task cycles of about one or two minutes. Instead, Volkswagen began a small scale experiment with four groups of seven workers (two teams on each shift). Within the groups four men worked on assembly, two did testing and one man was in charge of materials. The entire group was de-coupled from the machine-paced line but had to meet a quota of seven engines per team per day. The workers received special training so that they could do all the team jobs and were free to rotate job assignments as they wished. Each group had a team leader (*Gruppensprecher*) who was responsible for liaison with management, and foremen were eliminated (D. Jenkins, 1978).

The results of the Volkswagen experiment highlighted two overlapping problems of such work groups, which have recurred in different situations and economies. First semi-autonomous workgroups run up against the existing power-balance between labour and capital. Employers see such job redesign as an opportunity to undercut the union in the workplace, whilst the unions tend to be opposed to informally elected workgroup leaders as potential usurpers of union influence. This conflict of interests occurred at the Salzgitter plant with the eventual outcome that the team leaders were converted into shop stewards, and foremen were brought back to oversee the groups as Volkswagen wanted to prevent the erosion of management power.

Apart from the issue of autonomous groups as a threat to the existing structures of shopfloor power, there was the question of how the specially trained team workers fitted into the skill and wage hierarchy. The enlarged jobs caused a union/management dispute over wage levels. The unions demanded that the workers should be paid at a skilled rate which Volkswagen resisted. In effect, this re-combination of tasks across Taylorian boundaries disrupted the Babbage Principle of labour cheapening which, as we have said, involves stripping a skilled job to an essential core and paying less for all ancillary and servicing tasks performed by unskilled workers. Volkswagen concluded that they did not want masses of re-skilled workers on the basis that they had no jobs for them – they did not fit into the normal structure.

In 1978 the experiment was ended. Volkswagen management

considered the system too costly and that it was not possible to fill the factory with the 'dreams of another world' (D. Jenkins, 1978, p. 20).

The Volkswagen case is important. It exemplifies the major theme of this chapter: the inherent instability of any particular management strategy as an effort to resolve the basic tension between the need for control and the need for participation as played out against a backdrop of competitive market pressures, technological developments and management/workers (i.e. class) relations. The Volkswagen experiment failed, partly at least, for the sorts of reasons given by General Motors' Director of Employee Research and Training at its Chevrolet division. He remarked that: '. . . the subjects of participation are not necessarily restricted to those few matters that management considers to be of direct, personal interest to employees . . . (A plan cannot) be maintained for long without (a) being recognised by the employees as manipulative or (b) leading to expectations for wider and more significant involvement – "Why do they only ask us about plans for painting the office and not about replacing this old equipment and rearranging the layout?" Once competence is shown (or believed to have been shown) in say, rearranging the work area, and after participation has become a conscious, officially sponsored activity, participators may very well want to go on to topics of job assignment, the allocation of rewards, or even the selection of leadership. In other words, management's present monopoly of control can in itself easily become a source of contention.' (quoted in Edwards, 1979, p. 156).

In general, mass production industries have proved to be a hostile milieu for group technology. In batch production the story has been more complex. It is still the case that the vast majority (up to 80%) of engineering components are produced in batches of less than 1,000. This is significant because traditional batch production costs between ten to thirty times more than mass production of an item. This is because of the need to continually re-set the machines and the considerable delays in the movements of components between machines. Most items spend long periods collecting dust on the factory floor queueing for the next process.

In looking at batch production in the early 1970s, Turner noted that it is complex, because succeeding batches require different machining operations in different sequences. This entails a large amount of variety and great uncertainties (look at the work flow pattern between different machines in Fig. 7.2). Associated with this complex pattern is a lack of complete knowledge of the production system by management, so that instead of a production planning programme there is a monitoring of work-in-progress by an army of progress-chasers and harassed foremen (Turner, 1970).

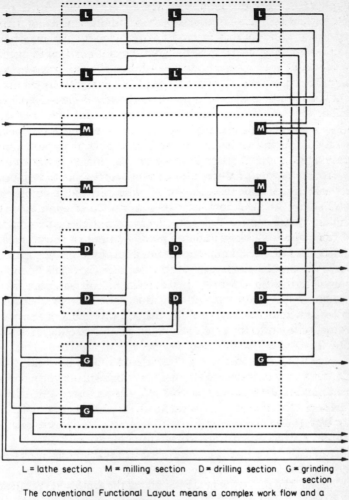

L = lathe section   M = milling section   D = drilling section   G = grinding
section
The conventional Functional Layout means a complex work flow and a
high volume of work in progress

Fig. 7.2   *Work flow in batch production*

In the early 1960s one solution to these problems was the evolution of
so-called 'group technology'. This originally was a technical term
referring to a new lay-out of production based on grouping together all
the machines necessary to complete a particular type of component (see
Fig. 7.3). This in turn was based on classification of all components,
standardisation as far as possible and grouping the components into

'families'. It improved machine utilisation and it speeded up the throughput of work by simplifying work flow.

But in creating a cellular work structure, engineering employers also created new work groups. At first this received no explicit attention, but as skilled machinists' dissatisfaction with their loss of discretion over the sequence of work increased (the machinists could no longer choose the easiest job first, or the safest job when they were tired, or the most lucrative job in terms of bonus) and as employers recognised the potential of job flexibility, the notion of semi-autonomous work groups was given increasing emphasis. This potential was based on machine 'stretch-out', that is, setting up more machines than workers, and re-training so that workers could move from lathe to drilling machine to grinder. But beyond this stretch-out some companies have given the new work groups some discretion over work methods and job assignments, secure in the knowledge that worker discretion is severely restricted by the control built into the system (Green, 1978, p. 18).

Thus, group technology in batch producing industries has created a tendency for the development of flexible work groups based on generalised, skilled machinists with a lack of rigid job boundaries. There is a return, reminiscent of traditional internal contract, of work allocation to the group not the individual (Littler, 1982). Insofar as charge-hands and foremen are eliminated, this reduces control and coordination costs to the employer. Such groups also increase worker adaptability and enable the team to cope with the absences of any of its members. But whatever the managerial advantages of group technology, after a limited spread to about 10% of batch engineering firms in the early and mid-1970s, the process of diffusion came to a halt. This was because the information burden of setting up a reliable group technology production system was too great – there were too many variables and too much unpredictability. Now, with the spread of flexible machining centres and cheaper shop-floor minicomputers the pattern of change will probably accelerate.

In general, the introduction of flexible work groups has occurred in very different industrial sectors and in firms varying in size and technology. The extension of small-scale experiments has often been opposed by both unions and management, and the diffusion of such groups is still very limited (Savall, 1981, pp. 69–71 and 98–101).

In recent years one variant of autonomous shop-floor groups has become popular, namely Quality Control (Q.C.) circles. What are Q.C. circles? Essentially there are small groups of workers (about 5–20), usually led by a foreman or senior worker, who meet regularly to study and solve all types of production problems. In addition such groups are intended to stimulate motivation and involvement on the shop-floor. Unlike earlier human relations ideas, Q.C. circles involve systematic

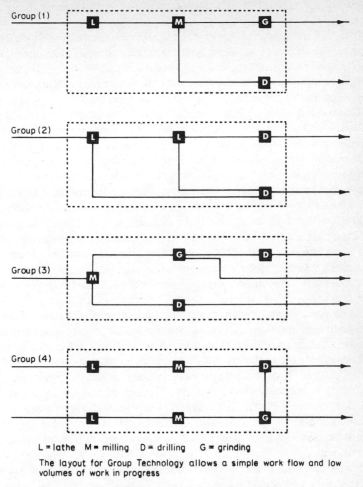

L = lathe   M = milling   D = drilling   G = grinding

The layout for Group Technology allows a simple work flow and low volumes of work in progress

Fig. 7.3 *Typical 'Group Layout' and work flow*

training of shop-floor workers and access to technical assistance to solve problems.

The original idea of Q.C. circles was American: the basis being the notion of improved worker motivation through employee participation in the decision-making process. The concept was transplanted to Japan in the 1950s, where it was adopted and re-worked by several management theorists, particularly Kaoru Ishikawa. The ideas gained popularity in Japan in the 1960s and early 1970s and were re-cycled to the West in the later 1970s, surrounded by the aura of Japanese productivity and economic success. By 1982 about 450 corporations in the

USA and Canada made extensive use of Q.C. circles and about 200 firms in Britain had experimented with them, most notably Rolls Royce. Such ideas have never been totally absent from British shopfloors. The idea of 'briefing groups' designed to bring workers, supervisors and senior managers together to discuss 'common problems' is perhaps more familiar in the British context, but is clearly allied to the Q.C. concept (Hull, 1978, p. 35).

Given that Q.C. circles are *not* the same thing as work groups, what effects have they had, or are likely to have, on job design? The main effect is to bridge the mental/manual divide inherited from Taylorism. Q.C. circles tend to break with the traditional practices and assumptions implicit in most Western managerial control systems. First, there is the assumption of high commitment to the work organisation, so that workers will devote time and effort, even outside work hours, to the analysis of work-related problems. Associated with this, Q.C. circles involve workers (at least in theory) in a genuine study process, requiring company resources and training. Furthermore, study groups are, after management vetting, provided with the means to institute new work practices in order to overcome the problems of productivity and quality.

All of this contrasts sharply with the conventional Taylorite assumption that workers know how to increase productivity or ensure quality but are holding back for no justifiable reason – that worker indifference or even sabotage are the normal problems that management has to face and overcome. Indeed Taylor's starting-point was the pervasiveness of what he called 'soldiering', that, is a deliberate collective slow-down (Taylor, 1903, p. 30). Similarly, conventional factory suggestions schemes maintain the mental/manual divide by assuming that any useful suggestions will be analysed and implemented by management personnel.

One interesting example of the introduction of Q.C. circles in the West is that of Ford. The Ford Corporation, frightened of Japanese competition, decided in 1980 to implement the system in all its 25 manufacturing and assembly plants in Western Europe, involving all 140,000 shop-floor workers. The overall programme in 1980–81 was called 'After Japan'. Ford's stated objectives were to improve the quality of its products, reduce scrap, and encourage worker involvement. The unstated objectives were (probably) to increase labour productivity and change manning levels and traditional work practices (*The Financial Times*, 9 May 1980; *The Guardian*, 11 June 1980).

Ford followed the Japanese patterns of Q.C. circles, with some interesting differences. Each of its Q.C. groups consisted of 8–15 people, including a supervisor plus a representative from the quality control department. The reason for the inclusion of the latter is that the

Taylorian inheritance has meant that production problems and quality control are the responsibility of staff departments divorced from the shop-floor, whereas in Japan the production worker, with his foreman, is much more responsible for checking the quality of his own work before it moves on down the line.

Another difference from the Japanese situation is that in Japan the labour force is all-Japanese, young and relatively well-educated. At Ford the circles often consist of a mixture of West Indians, Asians and Southern Europeans as well as English workers. The first thing that the circles demonstrated as forums of communication was that the traditional managerial methods of communication – posters and job instructions – often meant different things to different ethnic groups!

The attempted rushed adoption of Japanese Q.C. circles by Ford aroused the opposition of the main union – the Transport and General Workers Union. Rank and file union leaders complained that all changes in working practices should be discussed and mutually agreed with the union, and that the proposals cut across existing union structures (*The Financial Times*, 9 March and 25 April 1981). The outcome is that so far Q.C. circles have not been introduced in British Ford plants, but have spread across the rest of the European plants. Other British firms, such as Rolls Royce, have had more success in introducing Q.C. circles but the overall impact of this form of 'Japanisation' has yet to be determined.

Job enrichment

Job enrichment has generally involved a reorganisation of hierarchically-structured tasks, so that lower level jobs expand their areas of discretion. This form of job re-design has been more talked about than acted upon and generally it has been confined to white-collar workers, especially in the financial sector (see Herzberg, 1966 and 1976). In relation to shop-floor workers, 'job-enrichment' has usually meant the amalgamation of direct and indirect labour tasks such as setting up or maintenance, though even this limited step is contrary to strict Taylorite principles. Many shop-floor job enlargement experiments consist of re-combining a set of unskilled tasks in order to solve managerial problems of work-load balance and quality control. The effects are neatly summed up in a well-known statement of one chemical worker:

You move from one boring, dirty monotonous job to another boring, dirty monotonous job. And somehow you're supposed to come out of it all 'enriched'. But I never feel 'enriched' – I just feel knackered.

(Nichols and Beynon, 1977, p. 16.)

Conclusions

The first part of this chapter analyses the significance of Taylorism for job design and argues that its influence, though considerable, did not follow a simple pattern in British industrial history. Taylorism was essentially based on job fragmentation though it was often modified in its implementation and, as we have argued elsewhere, a mixture of labour strategies was possible (see Littler, 1982; Littler & Salaman, 1982).

Fordism was a distinct labour management strategy in that it was systemic, requiring the re-organisation of the entire factory, and involved non-Taylorite control techniques. But it also took over the basic job design dynamics of Taylorism. The internationalisation of technology and the mechanism of the multi-national corporation assisted the spread of both Taylorism and Fordism, especially in the mass production industries.

Taylorism and Fordism as forms of work organisation are constrained by certain economic and technical limits and carry coordination and control costs. In particular Taylorism and Fordism are set within a certain pattern of product markets and inter-capitalist competition. In the late 1960s and early 1970s it began to look as though the accumulation of labour problems plus the shift in product markets, necessitating greater flexibility and with an emphasis on quality and reliability, were creating a crisis for Fordism.

However, reorganised assembly lines and group technology remained limited experiments. In general, these new ideas of job design and work organisation had a very limited influence: they remained the gospel peddled by a few avant-garde consultants. But past history suggests that the succeeding decade (the 1980s in this case) may be the period of the widespread take-up of managerial innovations. Two inter-linked factors reinforce this potentiality – the continuing economic crisis of the 1980s plus the pressures of Japanese competition. The 1980s, like the 1930s, will no doubt spur some employers to cut wages (there have been several cases of this), extend work hours in some form, or impose straightforward labour intensification involving no attempt at work reorganisation. Clearly, mass unemployment has shifted economic power to the employers, so that they can force through previously unacceptable changes amidst a climate of fear and uncertainty about jobs. But there is a limit to what can be achieved by economic coercion. In particular it ignores the changing nature of competition. An emphasis on quality rather than the velocity of throughput means that reluctant acquiescence has to give way to active cooperation. Of course for some employers automation and robots appear to offer a solution – but not enough of one. The crisis of Fordism is neatly exemplified by the present dilemma of Ford Europe. Faced with the large productivity gap between its European plants and Japanese manufacturers, Ford set up its 'After Japan' programme, which as the headlines announced was a contradictory mix of robots, job cuts, a union struggle *and* an attempt to engage the enthusiasm and willingness of the workers (see *The Guardian*, 11 June 1980).

The present Ford (and Fordist) dilemma illustrates the essential tension in the capital/labour relationship – a tension between the need to regulate and dominate the production process versus the need to maximise the creativity and reliability of wage labour. This chapter has revolved around fundamental elements in the history of this contradiction.

References
Babbage, C., (1835), 'On the Economy of Machinery and Manufactures', excerpted in L.E. Davis (ed.), 1972.
Copley, F.B., (1915), 'Frederick V. Taylor: Revolutionist', in *The Outlook*, 111, September.
Davis, L.E. (1957), 'Toward a Theory of Job Design', reprinted in Davis and Taylor, (1972), pp. 215–17.
Davis, L.E., (1966), 'The Design of Jobs' reprinted in Davis and Taylor, (1972), pp. 299–327.
Davis, L.E., and Taylor, J.C., (1972), *Design of Jobs*, Penguin.
Douglas, M., (1980), 'Auto workers can only do as well as Head Office permits', *Albuquerque Journal*, 24 July, 1980, p. A5.
Edwards, Richard, (1979), *Contested Terrain: The Transformation of the Workplace in the Twentieth Century*, Heinemann.
Flink, J.J., (1975), *The Car Culture*, Boston, MIT Press.
Ford, H., (1922), *My Life and Work*, New York, Doubleday Page.
Fridenson, P., (1978), 'The Coming of the Assembly Line to Europe', in Krohn, Layton and Weingart (eds.), *The Dynamics of Science and Technology*, Utrecht, D. Reidel.
Gospel, H. and Littler, C.R., (1983), *Managerial Strategies and Industrial Relations*, Heinemann.
Green, K., (1978), 'Group Technology in Small Batch Engineering'. Paper presented at Nuffield Deskilling Conference, mimeo.
Hackman, J.R., and Oldham, G.R., (1975), 'Development of the Job Diagnostic Survey', *Journal of Applied Psychology*, 60, 2, pp. 159–70.
Herzberg, F., (1966), *Work and the Nature of Man*, Cleveland, World Publishing Co.
Herzberg, F., (1976), *The Managerial Choice: To be Efficient and To Be Human*, Homewood, Illinois, Dow Jones-Irwin.
Hull, D., (1978), *The Shop Steward's Guide to Work Organisation*, Spokesman.
Jenkins, D., (1978), 'The West German Humanisation of Work Programme: A Preliminary Assessment', WRU Occasional Paper No. 8.
Kamata, Satoshi, (1982), *Japan in the Passing Lane*, Pantheon.
Kelly, J.E. (1982), *Scientific Management, Job Redesign and Work Performance*, Academic Press.

Levine, S.B. and Kawada, H., (1980), 'Human Resources in Japanese Industrial Development', Princeton University Press.

Lewchuk, W., (1983), 'Fordism and British Motor Car Employers, 1896–1932', in Gospel & Littler, 1983, pp. 82–110.

Linhart, R., (1981), *The Assembly Line*, John Calder.

Littler, C.R., (1982), *The Development of the Labour Process in Capitalist Societies*, Heinemann.

Littler, C.R. and Salaman, G., (1982), 'Bravermania and Beyond: Recent Theories of the Labour Process', *Sociology*, 16, 2, May.

Meyer, S., (1981), *The Five-Dollar Day: Labor Management and Social Control in the Ford Motor Co., 1908–21*, State University of New York Press.

Nichols, T. and Beynon, H., (1977), *Living with Capitalism*, Routledge.

Russell, J., (1978), 'The Coming of the Line: The Ford Highland Park Plant, 1910–14', in *Radical America*, 12, pp. 29–45.

Sabel, C.F., (1982), *Work and Politics*, Cambridge University Press.

Savall, H., (1981), *Work and People*, Clarendon Press.

Smith, Adam., (1776, 1970 edn.), *The Wealth of Nations*, Penguin.

Taylor, F.W., (1903), *Shop Management*, reprinted in Taylor, 1964.

Taylor, F.W., (1964), *Scientific Management*, Harper & Row.

Turner, B., (1970), 'The Organisation of Production: scheduling in Complex Batch Production situations' in *Approaches to the Study of Organisational Behaviour*, ed. G. Heald, Tavistock, pp. 87–99.

Walton, R.E., (1974), 'Innovative Restructuring of Work' in *The Worker and the Job: Coping with Change*, ed. J. Rosow, New Jersey, Prentice Hall.

Wilson, N.A.B., (1973), 'On the quality of Working Life', Manpower Papers No. 7, HMSO.

Work in America, (1973), Report of a Special Task Force to the Secretary of Health, Education & Welfare, Boston, MIT Press.

8 Women on the Line*
Ruth Cavendish

Editor's Introduction: The following account is based on the experience of the author – Ruth Cavendish – who worked in a motor components factory for seven months during 1977–8. Because of the severe restrictions of the libel laws, Cavendish had to go to considerable lengths to disguise the identity of the company. As a result, the components are called 'UMOs' (unidentified mechanical objects) and some of the technical terms in the chapter are deliberate gobbledegook. Nevertheless, the basic features of working on an assembly line are vividly portrayed.

When I turned up as instructed at the personnel office on the first Monday, the woman in charge gave me a contract as 'assembler', and a clock card number. Then she took me to buy an overall: the firm wasn't responsible for damage caused to our clothes at ʷork, she said. I paid for the overall out of my wages for the next few months at the rate of 20p a week, but never wore it after the first day because the sleeves got in my way. The supervisor collected me and showed me how to clock my card. I must remember to clock three times a day: before we started work at 7.30 a.m., before 12.45 p.m. when we started again after lunch, and at 4.15 p.m. when we went home. Your wages were calculated from the number of hours clocked in, so it's you that suffered if you forgot to clock. Then the supervisor introduced me to Eamonn, the chargehand for the line I was to work on, and they took me to sit with Rosemary, a young Irish woman; I was to sit at her bench and learn the job from her. Rosemary was very friendly – she was pleased to have someone to talk to and share her work, not that I was much help at first. She introduced me to the other women on our line, and to her friends, and showed me where everything was, so I soon felt quite at home, I had no trouble fitting in at all, despite my fears. All the women were friendly and outgoing, which encouraged me to be the same.

From Rosemary's bench you could see everyone in the main assembly, all 200 of them – the women, the chargehands and supervisors.

* Extract from *Women on the Line*, Routledge and Kegan Paul, London, 1982, pp. 15–27 and 40–1.

The shop was light and the women's pink, blue and brown overalls made it quite colourful. You could see which line was stopped, or if there was a breakdown or shortage of components. You could see who the shop steward was talking to. You saw all visitors to the shop, including managers and engineers. You could see who was going to the loo or coffee machine, and how many times a day they went, who was late in the morning, who was clocking out at an unusual time, and who was chatting to whom.

Each line had fifteen 'operators' as we were called, including two 'reject operators' who sat at the end and mended UMOs that were incorrectly assembled or faulty. We sat at benches on each side of the conveyor belt. There was a red light at the head of each assembly line – each time it flashed, every minute-and-a-half or so, the first woman put out a tray containing two UMOs onto the conveyor belt to begin its journey down the line. The conveyor belt itself was only just over a foot wide, and the trays were baskets made of thick dark brown cardboard. A wooden stick was placed across the line at the point where each woman sat, so the tray would come to a halt and she could take out the UMO to do her work. Each time the light flashed, the person in front sent on the tray she had just finished, pushing it over the stick so it would move along the line again, and you sent yours on to the person behind you, so there would be a regular flow of trays.

UMOs were made up from a number of components which we added one by one to the basic mechanism until the UMO was complete. As the trays travelled down the line, each of us added more parts to the UMOs and they became heavier and more cumbersome to handle. By the time the tray reached the end of the line, the UMO was complete: the basic mechanism was covered with modules, sprockets and diactors, and some versions also had three transistors and a filter, each with a cover. Several different versions of UMO were assembled and each version came in a number of models. They were all made from the same basic components but the sprockets, modules and diactors were different for the different 'sets' as we called them. The bulk of the work was for British Leyland and UMOs were assembled for the various Mini, Maxi, Princess, Marina and Allegro models.

My line concentrated on the Maxi and Princess, though we also assembled UMOs for the Marina and Mini Clubman. We did up to 500 or 1,000 at one go which meant doing the same operations over and over 500 or 1,000 times.

To complete that number took between one and two days. The Princess UMO with its three transistors and filter was much more elaborate than the one for the Maxi. It took longer to assemble so the line went slower, or rather they gave us fewer to do and the light flashed less frequently. Two Maxis travelled down the line in a tray every 100 seconds, so we assembled seventy-two an hour, whereas a tray of Princesses came every two minutes and we did sixty an hour. In fact, though, they both belted down the line so fast that we didn't notice the difference in the light flashing – we'd just be finishing the second UMO when the next lot arrived.

The light was controlled by management who laid down the speed for each set. 'Speeds and feeds' weren't negotiable – we could only query whether the light was flashing more quickly than was laid down, and somebody queried it at least once a day. Each operator had to perform several tasks on the UMO as it made its way down the line. Management was in charge of grouping these jobs, and laid down the number of seconds and split seconds allowed for each. To keep the trays moving at a steady pace, all the jobs ought to have taken the same length of time, but some were harder to complete than others, so there were constant pile-ups. The details of all the jobs were specified on the 'layout', a sheet that Eamonn took out of his desk whenever we switched over to a different set. He walked down the line with it, telling each of us what our jobs were on the next set, and making sure that we were sitting in the right order.

Above the benches hung the airguns, power-driven screwdrivers which we had to pull down to operate. On the bench we had a wooden stand to rest the UMO on, or a mechanical jig to fix it in. There were also plastic cartons of nuts and screws of various sizes, and larger boxes of transistors, modules and so on. The men dragged these along the floor to each bench in large black skips, and sometimes the benches were hidden behind walls of skips and boxes so we could hardly see the women on the neighbouring line.

There was little machinery apart from the airguns and jigs. The calibrating machine for making the sprocket register the correct torque was the most complex. There was a separate machine for checking the calibration, another to check the electrical parts of the UMO and a pedal-operated machine for securing it in its case. Some of the jigs were pretty complex to handle, as we had to locate the UMO in them in exactly the right position.

There were eight Irish women on my line, six West Indians and me. Most of them had worked at UMEC for years and knew each other well. It was known as a friendly line, despite some major conflicts – the West Indians said it was friendly because there were so many of them. They addressed each other as 'ladies' and referred to themselves collectively as 'girls'; but the men always talked down to us 'girls'. The Irish women were all under thirty, except for the two who were deaf and dumb – they were in their early forties. The black women were older and most had grown-up children. Many of the women in the shop had a friend, sister or cousin working on another line, and rushed over to sit with her for ten minutes during the breaks. Everyone had known somebody already working at UMEC before they started and they thought I was very brave coming all on my own.

The co-operation between the women on our line also made it more efficient. If someone in front had forgotten to put a small clip or peg on the UMO, we would shout to them to send one along the line and attach it ourselves, or take it up to them to put right. What we were supposed to do, however, was to put out the UMO as a reject, marking down the fault both on it and on a sheet of paper. Then the reject operator would collect it, mend it, and return it to where it had left the line, also marking down the fault twice. Of course, all that took much longer.

For the first few weeks I sat with Rosemary, then I was shunted to wherever someone was missing for the next couple of months, and had to learn about fifteen different jobs. Then Rosemary was promoted to reject operator, and I took over her job permanently. While I was moving around, sometimes to as many as five different jobs a day, I was completely exhausted. I had terrible pains in my neck and back, and found it hard to keep up with the speed of the line – but the trays kept coming so I just had to carry on. All the jobs were fiddly, and I had to concentrate all the time, working with both hands which was very difficult at first, because I wasn't used to using my left hand, or to manipulating tiny nuts and screws at speed. Most days I was worked so hard that I couldn't look up at all, or had to work extra specially fast so that I would have time in between one tray and the next to unwrap a piece of chewing gum, or take a sip of tea.

Even for experienced assemblers it was a terrible strain trying to keep up with the line while learning a new job – although the others came and helped out for a few seconds if they saw you were really stuck and if they could spare the time. It took several weeks to get proficient at any one job, and the first few days were always hell. In no way was it 'unskilled' work; in fact, the firm relied on women staying a long time as they often had to use two replacement workers if one of the old hands was away.

Getting a permanent job meant I had my own bench, and could use its drawer for my tissues, cup and sandwiches; otherwise there was nowhere to put my belongings except on a corner of the bench or on the floor. When I got used to the quirks of my torque-checking machine, jig, airgun and the rest, the work became easier and I could keep up much better. It was very hot in the main assembly, around 75° F most days, even when it was below freezing outside, and very stuffy because the ventilation was so bad. There were only a few fans which made hardly any difference. I was lucky that the one for our line was just in front of me – the two lines next to us didn't have a fan at all; however, ours was pointing up to the ceiling so we couldn't get much breeze anyway. I wore only a thin T-shirt right through the winter months. If you didn't have to work so hard, you could just have fallen asleep from the hot stuffy atmosphere. The noise was constant – the lines rumbled along, the airguns had a high-pitched whirr, and the overhead conveyor system clanked round the corners. You had to raise your voice to talk to the person next to you, like in a crowded pub.

Altogether I must have learnt nearly half the jobs for the Princess and for the Maxi, and three or four for the Marina and Mini Clubman. I wasn't competent at all of these, and there were some jobs I never had a go at, although I watched how they were done. When you were learning a new job, Margaret, the 'training woman', demonstrated it once, then went away and left you to it. She only came back if the chargehand saw that you really didn't know what you were doing or assembled the components the wrong way round. In fact, it was best to learn a job from someone who had been doing it for some time. She would have discovered all the shortcuts and could show you exactly how to hold the components, how to move your fingers and which order to do the different operations, so you could cut out all unnecessary movements. The operators weren't paid for training new workers, of course. In fact, Margaret held the highest position for a woman on the shopfloor; even so she didn't earn much more than us and worked as a barmaid in the evenings and at weekends. She was Irish, in her forties and recently widowed, and she'd been at UMEC for over twenty years.

The first job at the top of the line required very flexible fingers. The basic mechanisms came in cases of twenty, and were placed on a ledge facing the operator. On the bench she had many tiny pieces of metal, of different shapes and colours, a bottle of silicone and a box of tiny wire springs. Her job was known as the 'build up' and involved fixing six or seven of these objects onto the basic mechanism. Some of them were so small and greasy that they jumped all over the place, and the wire springs became intertwined with each other and had to be prised apart. She also had to dip a nut in special grease and magnetise it in a machine before attaching it to the basic mechanism, and she finished by removing a date label from a roll of sticky labels and sticking it on the back of the basic mechanism.

I spent only a few days at this job, while Ann who did it permanently was off sick. It was nearly impossible because my fingers weren't dextrous enough; some of the components were so small they slipped out of my fingers and I couldn't get them on right. It took ages to learn the order they went in and the best way to attach them to the basic mechanism. At speed, I dropped everything or stuck the bits on the wrong way round – but you were supposed to get used to it in the end. Ann had been doing it for two years and was very quick, and she said she had been as useless as me when she started.

The 'build up' was before the light, so your pace of work wasn't regulated directly by the light flashing, and you didn't really know how many basic mechanisms to build up or at what speed. Ann just kept at it the whole time, never giving herself a rest – so she'd always done more than enough to 'feed' the light and keep the line supplied.

Ann was the only quiet person on the line. She didn't chat very much and at break sat with her friend on the next line. She did all the overtime she could, in the evenings and on Saturdays. She was single, about thirty and shared a flat with friends. The others seemed to feel a bit sorry for Ann – as if she was 'on the shelf', even though she often went dancing. She looked pale and drawn, worn out for her age, yet when she came back from Ireland after Christmas her face was shining and rosy, and most of the lines round her eyes had disappeared.

Concentrating on those tiny objects all day gave me eye strain, not helped by the glaring overhead fluorescent strip lighting. The build up was fiddly, but not as demanding physically as some of the other jobs which involved carrying boxes, lifting your arms and turning round. The others thought Ann a bit daft for building up so many basic mechanisms when she could have taken it a bit more easily. She must have been deep in daydreams, because keeping hard at it for eight hours without talking to anyone was mind-bogglingly boring.

The second job was to attach a module to the basic mechanism. On the Princess this was a big job (see Figure 8.1). You had to subassemble the components before screwing them onto the mechanism. First, two 'brakes' had to be screwed onto either side of the basic mechanism in a special jig; it was hard to locate the 'brakes' in the jig so that the screws would go in straight. Then you placed silicone on the basic mechanism, again in a particular position, making sure that the centres of the basic mechanism and the silicone were in alignment, and put a small valve through a hole in the module. Finally, using a different jig, you attached the two components together, screwing the module together with its silicone and valve, onto the basic mechanism with its 'brakes'.

Often the screws had faulty threading, the silicones were scratched or the modules were dusty, all of which had to be rectified before starting the job; otherwise it would be rejected as 'bad work' further down the line, and have to be dismantled and reassembled. When cheaper materials were introduced, sometimes one-third of the silicones in a box of 500 were scratched and had to be thrown away, or a whole batch of screws was faulty. Inspecting them all made the job harder and wasted a lot of time. Frequently the screwing machine decided not to work properly and the chargehand and engineers had an ongoing debate about whether this was due to the screws or the machine – they never listened to the woman doing the job who knew perfectly well which was at fault. Attaching modules to the Princess involved so many different tasks that you couldn't work up any great speed at it even when you

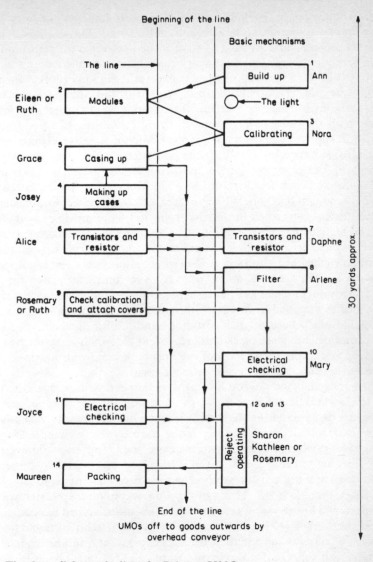

Fig. 8.1 *Jobs on the line: the Princess UMO*

were used to the job; when new women started, the chargehand usually divided it into two separate jobs, the brakes and the modules, for two operators.

Modules were also before the light, across the conveyor from Ann and just under Eamonn's nose. You could hear all his conversations with the supervisors or progress chasers and find out which components we were low on, and how many of this set were to be done. I became quite fast at modules, but hated being at the top of the line. As Ann was so quiet there was no one to talk to, and all the others were behind me so I didn't really feel part of the line. I had to regulate my own speed and could decide to work extra hard and then have a short rest, but I didn't like that either. There was a general rule that there should be quite a large build up of trays with moduled basic mechanisms ready for the next person, the calibrator – in fact, quite a few more than she needed. The women sitting behind thought you were useless if you supplied her with only the UMO she was to send down the line next, although I couldn't see any point in building up too many. In any case, Ann gave you so many basic mechanisms that there was no space on the bench for them unless you attached their module pretty quickly and sent them on. When you had attached modules to two basic mechanisms, you fished out a tray from under the moving conveyor belt and sent them on to the calibrator. Often there were no trays as they were all piled up at the back of the line, so you had to get up and run right down the line to find some. You would always run, never walk, so as to save a few seconds, and avoid getting behind with your work.

Nobody did modules as a permanent job all the time I was there. Any new workers seemed to end up with it and several of them left after a couple of weeks because they couldn't stand it. The nuts, screws and basic mechanisms were black and greasy and the bench was covered in dust, so you had to spend most of the breaks cleaning your hands so as to avoid smearing black grease on your food.

Attaching the modules was also hard on the eyes, with no direct light on the work. The machine for screwing on the 'brakes' was so badly designed that you had to manoeuvre your arms very carefully to pick out the modules from the box in front of the machine. Its handle had a big red knob which was level with my eyes, and I often banged my eye into it trying to get at the modules. Once I banged my hand so hard against it that it bruised and swelled up, and Eamonn sent me to have it bandaged up in first aid. That saved me a few minutes' work so it was worth it, and lots of visitors came over to find out what had happened.

On most other sets, apart from the Princess, attaching the module was a shorter operation and the woman doing it sat at Ann's bench back to back with her. On the Maxi you had to paint two small holes in the basic mechanism with blue silicone, then place a saucer-shaped disc on the basic mechanism, followed by a dial which went on the centre of the disc, aligning pin-head-sized holes in all three. Then you used a magnetised screwhead to pick up pin-sized screws, and screwed them through all three sets of holes to secure the three components together. The silicone was dark and made the holes hard to align because you couldn't see them clearly, and there was a knack to picking up the screws which I never acquired. You could easily misjudge the entrance to the holes, knock the screws off the magnetic head, scratch the dials with the screwdriver, or put the screws in crooked. If you did any one of these you had to unscrew the whole lot with a manual screwdriver and start all over again. If you got flustered there was no time to stop and calm down before having another go – you just had to carry on as fast as you could. By the end of the day you could hardly see straight – everything was swimming around out of focus as your field of vision was concentrated on the tiny holes. I never got the hang of the job at all; Margaret said I was too heavy handed with the screwdriver to pick up the screws straight, but all new women had the same problem as me so you would think they could have used an easier machine.

The other lines in the shop had a separate operator for modules even on small sets. Ann was so fast at her build-up, though, that when we were assembling the Maxi UMO she did modules as well as her own job, working at breakneck speed. She received no sympathy from the others because each was specified as a one-person job on the layout and she was silly to accept the work of two. If there was an extra woman on the line, Eamonn would get her to help out Ann with the modules, but if it was her first attempt at the job she'd make so many rejects that Ann had to take over anyway.

After modules, the UMO was calibrated. Our calibrator was Nora, one of the deaf and dumb women. It was a tricky job and if she did it wrong there was trouble further down the line. I never had a go at calibrating but Nora showed me what she did. First, she 'roached' a box of sprockets – this seemed to mean banging their tips in a special machine. Then the basic mechanism had to be magnetised in an ancient looking box; Nora couldn't wear her watch or that would be magnetised too. Next she attached the sprocket to the basic mechanism, and calibrated it for torque. She had to match up the sprocket with the module, looking at them from left and right as well as straight on. When she'd got it exactly right from all angles, she used a foot pedal to secure the sprocket in position.

The light was by Nora and she 'fed' it, putting out a tray on the line every time it flashed. The tray scraped against a wire in a box fixed against the side of the conveyor and this registered the number of trays that went down the line. For some reason, we weren't supposed to know how many we had done, but we did check now and then to make sure we weren't doing too many.

Nora liked to have a massive build up of trays with calibrated UMOs, sometimes as many as forty, which she piled up all around her. Because of this she could give herself extra rests around the breaks. On other lines, the calibrators missed a light now and then to give the women behind a bit of a let up especially if there was a pile up of trays, but Nora never did. This would have been against the rules – the calibrator was allowed to miss a light only on the instructions of the chargehand, never the women, and as the number of UMOs for the day was laid down, they would have found out if she cheated. Towards the end of the afternoon, Nora read her paper or started taking off her overall, and still fed the next few flashes so the women behind had to carry on working after she'd stopped. This caused a lot of tension. From about 4.07 p.m. we thought every tray she put on the line would be the last one – but there were always another two or three. We wanted her to stop feeding on the dot of 4.10, so that we could also start getting ready to go home. You couldn't leave trays piled up at your position overnight as you'd never be able to keep up in the morning if you had them to do as well as those coming down the line. If the 'swing shift' – the night workers who did a 6–10 p.m. shift – were on they wouldn't do them either and were likely to leave you even more trays in return. Nora became quite anxious that we were talking about her, and kept looking round to see if we were watching her feed the light.

The younger women thought Nora was 'mad for work' because she believed that the more trays we did, the more bonus we'd get. After work and on Saturdays, she did a cleaning job at the shopping centre nearby, and she never got home before 9 p.m. So she was thought to be 'money mad' as well, and the women despised her concern to save; they thought she must be 'loaded' in any case, working all the time and hardly ever splashing out.

Grace did the fourth job, 'casing up', attaching the UMO into its first case. She had to get the cases out of large cardboard boxes, paint over a hole in them with silicone, and clip a blue circuit board for electrical fittings onto the back of the case with five small white pegs. Then she placed the plastic case with a rubber ring through its hole into the jig, slotted in the UMO and secured them all mechanically with a foot pedal, so the back of the basic mechanism stuck through the hole, cushioned by the rubber ring. Then she used another jig to fix diodes through the back of the case, and she painted over any screws that had been scratched by the module operator with black Pentel.

Grace had been casing up for nearly ten years, but often she couldn't keep up as there was much too much to do in the time. Some sets required even more subassembling on the cases, screwing on a small green plastic disc for the diode. Grace managed to have the job retimed and subdivided but only after much fuss. Before, she was always so 'up the wall' – a long pile of trays in front of her waiting to be done and getting longer every time the light flashed – that everyone else complained as well because they weren't being fed trays at regular intervals. Those of us sitting behind shouted to Grace to 'stop chatting and send us a regular feed'. This was a joke but the job was in fact easier if your trays arrived at regular intervals; if not, you'd have none for a couple of minutes, followed by a whole rush of them which would put you 'up the wall' as well.

Grace had to work so fast that she made mistakes, so there were more rejects which made more work for us all in the long run. For a few weeks, any spare worker was sent to help Grace with the circuit board and diode, until she complained so often that they sent the time-study man to retime the whole job. Preparing the case was then made into a separate job with more subassembling, attaching two part-cases together. Whoever did it had to keep Grace supplied with cases but wasn't directly regulated by the light. It was a very boring job and Josephine, one of the young girls, got so fed up with it that she larked around and put Grace 'up the wall' by not making up enough. That cost Josey her job in the end.

★   ★   ★

A tray took about twenty minutes to travel from the beginning of the line to the end. During that time, fifteen of us transformed two small basic mechanisms into complete UMOs ready to be put in a vehicle. The pressure to churn out hundreds of them was constant; it ensured a high level of production for the firm but it certainly took its toll on us. At the end of the day we were all 'jaded', but which limbs ached most depended on the particular job you'd been doing. The 'build up', modules, calibrating and all the checking jobs were hard on the eyes – concentrating so hard all the time and focusing on small holes and objects made your head buzz. Casing up, transistors, covers and packing were heavy work; in the one minute allowed for each UMO you were moving all the time – lifting boxes, changing over trays, throwing away bags and cases as well as doing the actual assembling. Unless you were well organised and knew exactly in which order to do the different movements, the work would get on top of you and you'd be up the wall with no chance of stopping to sort yourself out. But however well you were organised and could keep up with the line, the speed and the amount of work tired you out. The jobs between calibrating and electrical checking were the central ones, controlled by the light; you felt part of a chain and had more contact with the other women. It was like being one large collective worker. Although we were more dominated by the light than the jobs at the front and back of the line we could also enjoy breakdowns more fully. We had nothing 'to be getting on with', like building up more basic mechanisms or assembling diodes, so if the line stopped we had a rest.

Differences between the jobs were minor in comparison with the speed and discipline which the line imposed on us all. We couldn't do the things you would normally not think twice about, like blowing your nose or flicking hair out of your eyes; that cost valuable seconds – it wasn't included in the layout so no time was allowed for it. In any case, your hands were usually full. We all found the repetition hard to take; once you were in command of your job, repeating the same operations over and over thousands of times a day made you even more aware of being controlled by the line. You couldn't take a break or swap with someone else for a change – you just had to carry on; resisting the light or the speed only made the work harder because the trays kept coming and eventually you would have to work your way through the pile-up. If you really couldn't keep up with the line, you were out.

9 The Assembly Line★
Robert Linhart

*Editor's Introduction: Linhart spent nearly a year working on a car
assembly-line at the Citroën works near Paris. As an intellectual he
had no idea of mass production working conditions, until he was
confronted with them in stark reality.*

'Show him, Mouloud.'

The man in the white overalls (he's the foreman, called Gravier, as
they'll tell me later) leaves me standing and goes off busily towards his
glass-walled cage.

I look at the laborer who is working. I look at the shop floor. I look at
the assembly line. No one speaks to me. Mouloud takes no notice of me.
The foreman has gone. So I observe at random: Mouloud, the Citroën
2 CV car bodies passing in front of us, and the other laborers.

The assembly line isn't as I'd imagined it. I'd visualised a series of
clear-cut stops and starts in front of each work position: with each car
moving a few yards, stopping, the worker doing his job, the car starting
again, another one stopping, the same operation being carried out
again, etc. I saw the whole thing taking place rapidly – with those
'diabolical rhythms' mentioned in the leaflets. *The assembly line*: the
words themselves conjured up a jerky, rapid flow of movement.

The first impression, on the contrary, is one of a slow but continuous
movement by all the cars. The operations themselves seem to be carried
out with a kind of resigned monotony, but without the speed I expected.
It's like a long, gray-green, gliding movement, and after a time it gives
off a feeling of somnolence, interrupted by sounds, bumps, flashes of
light, all repeated one after the other, but with regularity. The formless
music of the line, the gliding movement of the unclad gray steel bodies,
the routine movements: I can feel myself being gradually enveloped
and anaesthetised. Time stands still.

Three sensations form the boundaries of this new universe. The
smell: an acrid odor of scorched metal and metallic dust. The sound:

★ Extracts from *The Assembly Line*, John Calder, London, 1981, pp. 13–27 and 111–6.
Translated by Margaret Crosland. Originally published in France in 1978 by Les
Editions de Minuit.

the drills, the roaring of the blow torches, the hammer strokes on metal. And the grayness: everything's gray, the walls of the shop, the metallic bodies of the 2 CVs, the overalls and work clothes that the men wear. Even their faces look gray, as though the pale, greenish light from the cars passing in front of them were imprinted on their features.

The soldering shop, where I've just been allocated ('Put him to watch number 86,' the sector manager had said) is fairly small. Thirty positions or so, arranged around a semi-circular line. The cars arrive as nailed-up sections of coachwork, just pieces of metal joined together: here the steel sections have to be soldered, the joints eliminated and covered up: the object which leaves the workshop is still a gray skeleton, a car body, but a skeleton looking from now on as if it's all in one piece. The body is now ready for the chemical coatings, painting, and the rest of the assembly.

I note each stage of the work.

The position at the entrance to the shop is manned by a worker with special lifting gear. We're on the first floor or rather a kind of mezzanine floor with only one wall. Each car body is attached to a rope, and the man drops it – roughly – onto a platform at the start of the assembly line. He secures the platform to one of the big hooks you can see moving slowly at ground level, a yard or two apart. These hooks make up the visible part of the perpetual motion mechanism: 'the assembly line'. Beside this worker stands a man in blue overalls supervising the start of the line, and he intervenes from time to time to speed things up: 'O.K., that's it, fix it on now!' Several times during the day I'll see him at this spot, urging the man with the lifting gear to get more cars into the circuit. They'll tell me later that he's Antoine, the chargehand. He's a Corsican, small and excitable. 'He makes a lot of noise, but he's not bad. The thing is, he's afraid of Gravier, the foreman.'

The crash of a new car body arriving every three or four minutes marks out the rhythm of the work.

As soon as the car has been fitted into the assembly line it begins its half-circle, passing each successive position for soldering or another complementary operation, such as filing, grinding, hammering. It's a continuous movement and it looks slow: when you first see the line it almost seems to be standing still, and you've got to concentrate on one actual car in order to realise that car is moving, gliding progressively from one position to the next. Since nothing stops, the workers also have to move in order to stay with the car for the time it takes to carry out the work. In this way each man has a well-defined area for the operations he has to make, although the boundaries are invisible: as soon as a car enters a man's territory, he takes down his blowtorch, grabs his soldering iron, takes his hammer or his file, and gets to work.

A few knocks, a few sparks, then the soldering's done and the car's already on its way out of the three or four yards of this position. And the next car's already coming into the work area. And the worker starts again. Sometimes, if he's been working fast, he has a few seconds' respite before a new car arrives: either he takes advantage of it to breathe for a moment, or else he intensifies his effort and 'goes up the line' so that he can gain a little time, in other words, he works further ahead, outside his normal area, together with the worker at the preceding position. And after an hour or two he's amassed the incredible capital of two or three minutes in hand, that he'll use up smoking a cigarette, looking on like some comfortable man of means as his car moves past already soldered, keeping his hands in his pockets while the others are working. Short-live happiness: the next car's already there: he'll have to work on it at his usual position this time, and the race begins again, in the hope of gaining one or two yards, 'moving up' in the hope of another peaceful cigarette. If, on the other hand, the worker's too slow, he 'slips back', that is, he finds himself carried progressively beyond his position, going on with his work when the next laborer has already begun his. Then he has to push on fast, trying to catch up. And the slow gliding of the cars, which seems to me so near to not moving at all, looks as relentless as a rushing torrent which you can't manage to dam up: eighteen inches, three feet, thirty seconds certainly behind time, this awkward join, the car followed too far, and the next one already appearing at the usual starting point of the station, coming forward with its mindless regularity and its inert mass. It's already halfway along before you're able to touch it, you're going to start on it when it's nearly passed through and reached the next station: all this loss of time mounts up. It's what they call 'slipping' and sometimes it's as ghastly as drowning.

I'll learn this assembly line existence later, as the weeks go by. On the first day I must get the hang of it: through the tension on a face, some irritable gesture, the anxiety in a man's glance toward a car body that's appearing when the one before is not yet finished. As I look at the laborers one after another I'm beginning to see differences in what seemed at first glance to be a homogeneous human mechanism: one man is calm and precise, another sweats from overwork; I notice that some are ahead, some are behind; I see the minute, tactical details at each station, the men who put their tools down between cars and those who hold onto them, those who get out of step . . . And the perpetual, slow, implacable gliding of the 2 CVs under construction, minute by minute, movement by movement, operation by operation. The punch. The sparks. The drills. Scorched metal.

Once the car body has finished its circuit at the end of the curving line it's taken off its platform and pushed into a moving tunnel which takes it off to the paint shop. And there's the crash of a new car coming on the line to replace it.

Through the gaps in this gray, gliding line I can glimpse a war of attrition, death versus life and life versus death. Death: being caught up in the line, the imperturbable gliding of the cars, the repetition of identical gestures, the work that's never finished. If one car's done, the next one isn't, and it's already there, unsoldered at the precise spot that's just been done, rough at the precise spot that's just been polished. Has the soldering been done? No, it's waiting. Has it been done once and for all this time? No, it's got to be done again, it's always waiting to be done, it's never done – as though there were no more movement, no result from the movements, no change, only a ridiculous illusion of work which would be undone as soon as it's finished under the influence of some curse. And suppose you said to yourself that nothing matters, that you need only get used to making the same movements in the same way in the same period of time, aspiring to no more than the placid perfection of a machine? A temptation to death. But life kicks against it and resists. The organism resists. The muscles resist. The nerves resist. Something in the body and the head, braces itself against repetition and nothingness. Life shows itself in more rapid movement, an arm lowered at the wrong time, a slower step, a second's irregularity, an awkward gesture, getting ahead, slipping back, tactics at the station; everything, in the wretched square of resistance against the empty eternity of the work station, indicates that there are still human incidents, even if they're minute; there's still time, even if it's dragged out to abnormal lengths. This clumsiness, this unnecessary movement away from routine, this sudden acceleration, this soldering that's gone wrong, this hand that has to do it all over again, the man who makes a face, the man who's out of step, this shows that life is hanging on. It is seen in everything that yells silently within every man on the line, 'I'm not a machine!'

In fact, two stations beyond Mouloud, a worker – another Algerian, but more obviously so, he looks almost Asiatic – is in the process of 'slipping'. He's been gradually moving down toward the next station. He's getting nervous about his four bits of soldering. I can see him becoming more agitated, I can see the rapid movement of the blowtorch. All of a sudden he's had enough. He calls out to the charge hand, 'Hey, not so fast, stop them a minute, it's no good like this!' And he unhooks the platform from the car he's working on, keeping it still as far as the next hook which will carry it forward again a few seconds later. The men working at the preceding stations unhook in their turns, to avoid a pile-up of cars. Everyone breathes for a moment. It makes a gap of a few yards in the line – a space a little bigger than the others – but the Algerian has caught up. This time Antoine, the section manager, says nothing: he's been pushing hard for an hour, and he's three or four cars in advance. But on other occasions he intervenes, gets after the man who's slipping back, won't let him unhook the car, or, if he's already done so, he rushed up to get the platform back to its original place.

This incident had to happen before I realized how tight the time schedule is. Yet the movement of the cars seems slow, and as a rule there's no sign of haste in the movements made by the workers.

So here I am at the factory. 'Settled in.' Being taken on was easier than I imagined.

★　★　★

You feel right down when you come to beg for a little manual job – just enough money for food, please – and you timidly reply 'none' to the questions about diplomas and qualifications, about anything special you can do. All my comrades in the job line were immigrants and I could read in their eyes the humiliations of this 'none'. As for me, I looked sufficiently wretched to seem like a would-be worker who was beyond suspicion. The man in charge of the new intake must have thought, 'Yes, here's a fellow from the country, he's a bit dazed, really, that's good, he won't make any trouble.' And he gave me my pass for the medical examination. Next please. And in any case, why should there be any complication about taking on a worker for the assembly line? That notion's typical of an intellectual who's used to complex appointments, a list of degrees, and 'job analyses'. That's what it's like when you're somebody. But if you're nobody . . . Everything moves very fast here: it's easy to assess two arms! A lightning medical inspection, with the little gang of immigrants. A few movements of the muscles. X-ray. You're weighed. The atmosphere's there already: 'Stand there,' 'Strip to the waist!' 'Hurry up over there!' A doctor makes a few marks on a form. That's all, O.K. to work for Citroën. Next please.

It's a good moment: just now, in early September 1968, Citroën's devouring workers. Production's high and they're filling the gaps left among the immigrants by the month of August: some have not returned from their remote holidays, others will come back late and will learn to their despair that they've been fired ('We don't believe a damn word of it, that story about your old mother being ill, rubbish!') and already replaced. They replace people at once. In any case Citroën works in a state of flux: quickly in, quickly out. Average employment period at Citroën: a year. 'A high turnover,' say the sociologists. In fact, it's quick march. And for me there's no problem: I'm caught up in the flood of new entrants.

I left the recruitment office at Javel on Friday with a document: allocated to the plant at the Porte de Choisy.

'Go to the section manager on Monday morning at seven o'clock.' And now, this Monday morning, the Citroën 2 CVs moving past in the soldering shop.

Mouloud still doesn't say anything. I watch him work. It doesn't look too difficult. On each car shell arriving, the metal parts which form the curve over the windshield have been lined up and nailed into position but there's a gap between them. Mouloud's job is to get rid of this gap. In this left hand he takes the tin, which is shiny; in his right, a blow torch. A flame bursts for a moment. Part of the tin melts in a little heap of soft stuff on the joint between the sheets of metal: Mouloud carefully spreads this stuff out, using a little stick which he picks up as soon as he puts the torch down. The crack disappears: the metal section above the windshield now looks as if it's all one piece. Mouloud has been alongside the car for two yards; when the job's done he leaves it and returns to his station, to wait for the next one. Mouloud works fast enough to have a few seconds free between cars, but he doesn't use the time to 'move up'. He prefers to wait. Here's a new car now. Shiny tin, blow torch, little stick, a few strokes to the left, to the right, up and down . . . Mouloud walks along as he works on the car. A final stroke with the stick and the soldering's smooth. Mouloud comes back toward me. A new car approaches. No, it doesn't look too difficult: why doesn't he let me have a go?

The line stops. The men take out their snacks. 'Break,' Mouloud tells me, 'it's quarter past eight.' Is that all? I felt that hours had gone by in this gray shop, divided between the monotonous gliding of the car bodies and the dim flares from the blow torches. This interminable flow of sheet iron and metal outside time: only an hour and a quarter?

Mouloud offers me a share of the bread that he's carefully unwrapped from a piece of newspaper. 'No, thanks. I'm not hungry.'

'Where are you from?'

'Paris.'

'Is this your first job with Citroën?'

'Yes, and my first time in a factory.'

'I see. I'm from Kabylia. I've got a wife and children out there.'

He takes out his wallet and shows me a faded family photograph. I tell him that I know Algeria. We talk about the winding roads in Greater Kabylia and the sheer cliffs which drop down to the sea near Collo. The ten minutes are up. The line starts again. Mouloud takes his blowtorch and goes toward the first approaching car.

We go on talking, intermittently, between cars.

'For the time being you only have to watch,' Mouloud tells me. 'You see, the soldering's done with tin. The "stick" is made of tin. You have to get into the way of using it: if you put too much tin, it makes a lump on the coachwork and that's no good. If you don't put enough tin it doesn't fill up the hole and that's no good either. Watch what I do; you can try it this afternoon.' And, after a silence: 'You'll start soon enough . . .'

And we talk about Kabylia, Algeria, olive growing, the rich Mitidja plain, tractors and ploughing, variations in the harvest, and the little mountain village where Mouloud's family has remained. He sends three hundred francs a month, and he's careful not to spend too much on himself. This month it's difficult, an Algerian workmate has died, and the others have subscribed to pay for sending the body back home, and a little money for the family, too. It's made a hole in Mouloud's budget, but he's proud of the solidarity among the Algerians and especially among the Kabylians. 'We support each other like brothers.'

Mouloud must be about forty. A small moustache, hair graying at the temples, a slow, calm voice. He speaks as he works, with precision and regularity. No unnecessary gestures. No unnecessary words.

The car bodies go by, Mouloud does his soldering. Torch, tin, piece of wood. Torch, tin, piece of wood.

A quarter past twelve. The canteen. Three-quarters of an hour to eat. When I come back to my place, just before one o'clock, Mouloud's already there. I'm glad to see his face again, already familiar in the midst of this dirty gray workshop, this colorless metal.

It isn't one o'clock yet: they're waiting for work to start again. A little farther on a crowd has formed around the Algerian worker with the Asiatic features whom I saw 'slipping back' this morning. 'Hey, Sadok, let's have a look! Where did you get it?' I go closer. Sadok is cheerfully showing everyone a pornographic magazine, from Denmark or somewhere like that. The cover shows a girl sucking an erect penis. It's a close-up, in aggressive, realistic colors. I find it very ugly but Sadok seems delighted. He bought it from one of the truckdrivers who work for Citroën, transporting sheets of metal, engines, spare parts, containers, and finished cars, and who at the same time bring into the factory small supplies of cigars, cigarettes, and various other things.

Mouloud, who has taken in the cause of all this excitement with one glance, doesn't move. Someone calls out to him: 'Hey, Mouloud, come and see a bit of rump, it'll do you good.' He doesn't move, replies: 'I'm not interested.' And when I come back to join him he tells me in a lower voice: 'It's not good. I've got a wife and kids out there in Kabylia. It's different for Sadok. He's a bachelor, he can amuse himself.'

The porn magazine among the metallic dust and the filthy gray overalls: a painful impression. Prisoners' fantasies. I'm glad Mouloud stays away.

A metallic noise, everyone goes back to his place, the line starts to move again.

'Now it's your turn,' Mouloud tells me. 'You've seen what you've got to do.' And he hands me the blowtorch and the tin.

'No, no! Not like that! And put the gloves on, you'll burn yourself. Whoa! mind the torch! Give it to me!'

This is the tenth car I've fenced with in vain. Mouloud warns me, guides my hand, passes me the tin, holds the torch for me, all in vain; I can't do it.

On one car I flood the metal with tin because I've held the torch too near the tin and for too long: all Mouloud can do is scrape it all off and re-do the operation rapidly while the car has already almost left our area. Then I don't put on enough tin and the first touch with the little piece of wood merely shows up the crack again that had to be covered. And when by some miracle I've put more-or-less the right amount of tin, I spread it so clumsily – damn that little piece of wood that my fingers obstinately refuse to control! – that the soldering's as bumpy as a fairground switchback and there's a horrible lump where Mouloud succeeded in producing a perfectly smooth curve.

I get mixed up about the order of operations: you have to put the gloves on to hold the torch, take them off to use the little piece of wood, not touch the burning tin with your bare hands, hold the 'stick' with your left hand, the torch in your right hand, the little piece of wood in your right hand, the gloves you've just taken off in your left hand, with the tin. It looked obvious when Mouloud did it, with a succession of precise, coordinated movements. I can't manage it, I panic: I nearly burn myself ten times over and Mouloud moves rapidly to push the torch away.

Every one of my joints has to be redone. Mouloud takes the instruments from me and just manages to catch up, three yards farther on. I'm sweating and Mouloud's beginning to get tired: his rhythm has been interrupted. He shows no impatience and continues to do this double work – guiding mine, and then re-doing it – but we're slipping back. We're moving inexorably down toward the next position, we're starting the next car one yard too late, then two yards; we finish it, or rather Mouloud finishes it, rapidly, three or four yards farther on, with the torch cable stretched almost to the limit, in the middle of the instruments belonging to the next position. The faster I try to go, the more I panic: I let the molten tin drip all over, I drop the little piece of wood, as I turn round the flame from my torch nearly gets Mouloud, he just manages to avoid it.

'No, not like that, now look!' There's nothing to be done. My fingers are awkward, I'm incurably clumsy. I'm wearing myself out. My arms are trembling. I press too hard with the wood, I can't control my hands, drops of sweat are beginning to get in my eyes. The car bodies seem to move at a frantic speed, there's no hope of getting ahead, Mouloud's finding it harder and harder to catch up.

'Now listen, getting in a state doesn't help. Stop a minute and watch what I do.'

Mouloud takes the instruments from me and picks up the regular rhythm of his work again, a bit faster than before, in order gradually to make good the time we've lost: a few inches on each car; after ten or so he's almost back in his normal place. As for me, I get my breath back as I watch him work. His movements look so natural! What have his hands got that mine haven't? A car comes: tin, torch, piece of wood, and at the spot where the curving metal was split there's now a perfectly smooth surface. Why can he do the work and I can't?

The 3:15 break. Mouloud sacrifices it to me. The others stretch their legs, form groups, chat, come and go, sit on barrels, or lean against the cars which are standing still. Mouloud begins to explain again. The car in front of our position isn't moving, it's easier. That's the distance at which you hold the torch. And this is how you place your fingers on the stick. There. Press with your thumb to grasp the round part of the metal. In the middle you must press very lightly in order to stop the tin from escaping and you must press more and more firmly as you move away: that's how you get the graded effect. Take the wood to the left first, then to the right. Then a short stroke upward, and another downward. Mouloud repeats the movement slowly: four times, five times. My turn now: he guides my hand, arranges my fingers against the wood. Like that. There. Good, perhaps that'll be all right . . . My brain thinks it understands it all: will my hands obey?

End of the break, back to work. Din of the line. A new car comes forward, slow and menacing: I've got to carry out those movements again with the real thing. Quick, the torch, oh no! I forgot, the gloves first, where's the tin? Good God, how quickly it's coming, it's in the middle of our station already, use the torch, blast! too much tin, get rid of it with the piece of wood, it's gone all over . . . Mouloud removes it for me with his hands. One more try . . . No, it's no good. I'm dismayed, I must have looked at Mouloud in despair, he tells me: 'Don't worry now, it's always a bit hard at first, have a rest, let me do it.' Once more I stand on the edge, watching helplessly: the line has rejected me. And yet it seems to move so slowly . . .

Mouloud decides not to give me the tools again.

'It'll go better tomorrow, go on now, you mustn't worry about it.' We talk about his own beginnings at this station, a long time ago: he got the hang of it fairly quickly, but at first it's not easy . . . By now he's had long experience with soldering and he does it mechanically.

In fact I've heard that soldering is a craft. What qualifications has Mouloud got? I ask him how Citroën classifies him. 'M2,' he replies in laconic fashion. Laborer.

I'm astonished. He's only a laborer? Yet soldering's not as easy as all that. I can't do anything, but I've been taken on as a 'semiskilled worker' (OS2, says the contract): in the hierarchy of the not-very-important, semiskilled is still above laborer . . . Mouloud obviously doesn't want to go places. I don't say anything more. As soon as I can I'll find out on what principles Citroën make their classifications. A few days later another worker told me. There are six categories of non-qualified workers. Starting at the bottom: three categories of laborers (M1, M2, M3); three categories of semiskilled workers (OS1, OS2, OS3). The distinction is made in a perfectly simple way: it's racist. The Blacks are M1, right at the bottom of the ladder. The Arabs are M2 or M3. The Spaniards, Portuguese, and other European immigrants are usually OS1. The French are automatically OS2. And you become OS3 just because of the way you look, depending on how the bosses want it.

— That's why I'm a skilled worker and Mouloud's a laborer, that's why I earn a few centimes an hour more, although I'm incapable of doing his work. And later they will draw up subtle statistics about the 'classification grid', as the specialists say.

That's it. Mouloud has just finished his last car. The hundred and forty-eighth of the day. It's a quarter to six. The line stops. So does the noise. 'So long,' says Mouloud, 'see you tomorrow . . . Don't worry now, it'll go better.' He hurries off to the cloakroom. I remain for a moment in the shop, which is emptying, my head's throbbing, my legs are unsteady. When I get to the stairs, and I'm really the last, there's no one in sight any more. The lights are out and the car bodies are motionless dark masses, waiting for the dawn and a new day's work.

I come home, exhausted and anxious. Why are all my limbs so painful? Why does my shoulder ache, and my thighs? Yet the blow-torch and the stick weren't all that heavy to carry . . . It's no doubt due to the repetition of the same movement over and over again. And the tension needed to control any clumsiness. And it's because I've been standing all that time: ten hours. But the others do it as well. Are they as exhausted as I am?

I think: it's the intellectual's ineptitude for physical effort. That's naïve. It isn't just a question of physical effort. The first day in a factory terrifies everyone, many people will speak to me about it later, often with anguish. What mind, what body can accept this form of slavery, this destructive rhythm of the assembly line, without some show of resistance? It's against nature. The aggressive wear and tear of the assembly line is experienced violently by everyone, city workers and peasants, intellectuals and manual workers, immigrants and Frenchman. And it's not unusual to see a new recruit give up after his first day, driven mad by the noise, the sparks, the inhuman pressure of speed, the harshness of endlessly repetitive work, the authoritarianism of the bosses and the severity of the orders, the dreary prison-like atmosphere which makes the shop so frigid. Months and years in there? How can one imagine such a thing? No: better escape, poverty, the insecurity of little odd jobs, anything!

And what about me, someone from the establishment, am I going to be able to cope? What will happen tomorrow if I still can't do that soldering? Will they throw me out? How ridiculous? A day and a half on the job . . . and then fired for being incapable! And what about the others, those who haven't any diplomas and who are neither strong nor good with their hands, how will they manage to earn their living?

Night. I can't sleep. As soon as I close my eyes I see piles of 2 CVs, a sinister procession of gray car bodies. I see again Sadok's porn magazine among the sandwiches and the oil drums and the metal. Everything's ugly. And those 2 CVs, that interminable string of 2 CVs . . . The alarm clock goes off. Six o'clock already? I ache all over, I'm just as worn out as I was last evening. What have I done with my night?

> *Editor's Note: After Linhart had spent five and a half months in the Citroen works, the management unilaterally announced that the work shift would be extended by 45 minutes to ten hours. This provoked a strike and Linhart was one of the organisers. The following extract recounts the aftermath of the strike and the reimposition of 'Citroën order'.*

It's current practice, in large firms, to relegate troublemakers, restless people, or overtiresome militant trade unionists to isolated places, remote annexes, shops, courses, or stores. Punishment always entails the risk of provoking a row and mobilising people around the victim. Why run this risk if you can obtain the same result without possible appeal? The bosses are the only masters in the organisation of work, aren't they? If the management decides that you're indispensable for the supervision of a lumberroom, a good half mile away from the workshop where you were implanted, you can only comply or give notice.

I knew that. But I hadn't imagined the severe shock that it represents. You feel torn out, like a live limb cut away from the organism, still throbbing. During the first days I missed the familiar universe of the main assembly line and its dependencies. I missed everything. Simon's rapid journeys back and forth as he pushed his carts and carried the leaflets. The little friendly gestures from the Yugoslavs at the roundabout. The women in the upholstery shop. The slow, dignified walk of the Malians. Christian's burst of anger, Sadok's furtive visits, the little meetings on the third step . . . Everything.

For ten hours a day I was shut up in a ridiculous cul-de-sac, reduced to counting the hours and anxiously calculating the effect of our strike. At five o'clock in the evening, one second after clocking out, I would run off without even going through the cloakroom, and arrive a few minutes later, breathless, at the Choisy gates, to get news of the factory, this world which had become suddenly remote, and was forbidden to me.

The news was bad.

First of all the continued erosion of the strike. Then, after a brief apparent respite, the disbanding of the shopfloor committee.

At the end of the second week of the strike, the situation had settled down. Fifty or so workers at the Choisy factory continued to reject recuperation and walked out every evening at five o'clock. Scattered throughout the workshops, on the lines, on piece-work or in laboring jobs, they were now going out individually without hope of stopping production. Their obstinacy, concentrated into this gesture which had now become symbolic, proved every day the existence of a last resistance group to the humiliation of the extra three-quarters of an hour.

In this last group there were workers whom we didn't know, who had never been to the committee meetings, to whom we had never had occasion to speak in the factory.

Conversely, in the end certain members of the committee had given up the daily stoppage.

The majority of the committee members continued to reject recuperation and went home at five o'clock. But an implicit consensus had been established, leaving each man the individual choice of this act. Simon, Sadok, and some of the Malians decided to give up at the end of the second week and submit to the management's work schedules. Although nobody asked them to do so, each explained his reasons, which were due to personal difficulties or to particular means of pressure which the Citroën management could apply to them. Everyone felt their confusion and to what extent this abandonment was painful for them. The others did not blame them for it. We knew that the strike proper, as a collective action, was in fact over, having been progressively limited, planed away, and reduced by the management. We wouldn't cause it to start again. Those who were going on were only keeping to a promise they had entered into with themselves. Primo had sworn he wouldn't give in: no change of tactics would have made him change his mind. The same was true of Georges, Stepan, Pavel, Christian, and a few others.

For a few days it looked as though this situation would continue.

At five o'clock the fifty recalcitrant workers went to the cloakrooms without incident. Their posts had been known for a long time and the adjustors proceeded immediately to replace them on the lines. For the posts on piece-work and the laborers' jobs, absences of three-quarters of an hour had hardly any immediate effect on production.

Order appeared to have returned, production was normally assured during the ten hours of the working day: I imagined that the Citroën system would lose interest in the symbolic demonstration represented by the departure of fifty men at five o'clock. But I didn't know the system well enough. Are the workers devoted to symbols? So are the bosses. To make people produce is not enough. They must be made to submit. Put more exactly, as far as the management is concerned the producers must submit to ensure a certain amount of production: the slightest threat that they will assert themselves again is intolerable, even if there is hardly any immediate material consequence. The system neglects nothing.

Suddenly, at the beginning of March, with no prior announcement, the management began a systematic persecution of the most active workers from the shop floor committee. This selective repression was aimed with such precision at the hard-core elements in our group that I wondered how far the Citroën police spy system had allowed them to get to know our internal functioning.

They fell in succession: Christian, Georges, Stepan, Pavel, Primo.

The method of attack was the same in each case. No firing, but intensive erosion; making life impossible for the man in question. The entire system of supervision, harassment, and blackmail which had come into action from February 18th against all the striking workers in the factory was now concentrated, methodically, on the known 'hard-liners'. The management had chosen a mere ten or so persons to be eliminated. They would know how to make them 'give notice' – and disappear.

Christian.

Dupré spent a week tormenting him. He forbade him to move anywhere in the shop. The Breton, a highly nervous man, had a vital need of action and movement and he only found a certain stability in leaving his rack every two or three hours to take a walk around the shop. This enforced stillness was a severe shock for him. Christian gritted his teeth and held out for two or three days. But he became more irritable, losing composure over details, speaking sharply to neighbors.

Then Dupré began to annoy him about his way of arranging the pieces of rubber. He made him re-do a seat which was supposed to be irregular. Then another. Then he triumphantly informed him one Thursday at five o'clock that the minimum output was increased by five seats and that if he didn't stay to do them a sum would be deducted from his pay. Wild with rage, Christian threw a piece of rubber in the direction of Dupré – without hitting him – and yelled that he was giving in his notice. The other man couldn't have asked for more. He accompanied him to the office without a word, didn't even mention the violent action, and handed him over to the section manager who made him sign his resignation papers. Less than a quarter of an hour later he was outside the door, stunned by his own outbreak and by this sudden departure. Citroën was over for him.

On my arrival from the rue Nationale I found him there, quivering with indignation, desperately upset that they had got him.

'I've been stupid. My nerves gave way . . .'

Georges, Stepan, Pavel.

The three Yugoslavs from the roundabout had organised their work a long time ago, independently of official arrangements. Allocated to the assembly of the locks, they had transformed and regrouped the operations in order to free themselves in rotation from the slavery of the assembly line. Their manual skill and speed had allowed them in this way to take over an area of autonomous functioning in a section where only the decisions of the work-study office were supposed to prevail. The senior staff, who found only advantages in this arrangement – there was never any delay or any defective part – left them alone.

When the decision to get at them was taken, the foreman Huguet had no difficulty in finding the most effective means of reprisal against the three men: he separated them. One fine morning this little corner of Yugoslavia installed over the ten yards of the three roundabout posts was shattered. Three transfers. Pavel found himself in the pressing shop, Stepan in the paint shop, and Georges in the sanding shop (a post that was hated, because it forced you to remain ten hours a day in the midst of iron dust and a whirlwind of minute fragments of metal).

Dispersed and brutally deprived of a rhythm in their working life that they'd built up patiently over the years, allocated to jobs which were especially unpleasant, the three Yugoslavs decided by common agreement that that was enough.

The three of them gave notice the same morning.

They left their posts without a glance at the bosses, who were hanging about them, announced their decision to the office, and allowed their papers to be prepared in silence. But, before going out, they made a complete round of the different workshops to speak for a last time to all the workers they knew, and all those who had taken part in the walk-outs, and all the members of the shop floor committee. They shook hands with everyone. They themselves were already in their outdoor clothes and they shook all the hands covered with dirty grease, oil, metal dust, paint, but they shook them at length, with words of farewell and encouragement. The others stopped working for a few moments, put down their tools, thanked them for all they had done, and wished them luck for the future. That took a long time, but no charge hand, no foreman, no guard dared make the slightest remark or try to accelerate the action. It was only after visiting the entire works in this way, even its most remote corners, that they left through the main door, brushing against the guard without taking any more notice of him than if he'd been a utensil forgotten there by chance.

Finally came Primo's turn.

It was harder with the Sicilian, who was quite determined not to hand in his notice.

It began by the usual method of harassment over work: paintwork to be redone, this coat's too thick, this coat's too thin, etc. No success: Primo complied, impassive.

Then came transfers: he was dragged to the stamping shop, then the sanding. In two weeks he did five or six different jobs, was used as a stopgap and taken away from his work as soon as he began to get used to it.

In the end the management decided to take extreme measures. An *agent provocateur* from the CFT came to insult him while he was working, telling him sharply that the shop floor committee men were only layabouts and that if they refused to work until a quarter to six it was only due to laziness, that in any case immigrant workers were useless and that he, a 'dirty Ita'. Primo's punch cut the man's cheek right open. Two stitches.

And for Primo, immediate dismissal.

Further, Citroën took legal action against the Sicilian: 'grievous bodily harm.'

10 The Nature of Skill: the Case of the Printers*
Cynthia Cockburn

Editor's Introduction: Many occupations are defined in terms of skill, and much of the self-fulfilling nature of work relates to the sense of achieved skill. But what is skill? The following extract analyses the concept of 'skill'. It is drawn from a book that details changes in the labour process of newspaper compositors brought about by the shift to computerised photocomposition in the printing industry. In particular, the book reports the men's feelings about two aspects of the change. The first is the abandoning of the 90-keyboard linotype machine and its replacement by the normal typewriter ('QWERTY-lay') keyboard in photosetting. The second change is the move away from the tough and tangible raw material of lead to the much more widely understood and undemanding materials of paper, card and paste. The differences are also discussed between, on the one hand, those workplaces where the new occupations had been subject to a sharp division of labour (with the men doing keyboarding all year long, others doing paste-up, etc.) and, on the other hand, those workplaces where the union had been strong enough actually to push the division of labour into reverse and win integrated working, entailing all jobs on a rota system.

It is interesting to consider Harry Braverman's account of change in capitalist labour processes more generally, in the light of the experience in the printing industry. He took up and developed Marx's proposition that the more and more effective control of production by the capitalist class must lead to an ever-increasing division of labour and 'degradation' of work.[1] Braverman defined as the first principle of scientific management, 'the dissociation of the labour process from the skills of the workers. The labour process is to be rendered independent of craft, tradition and the workers' knowledge. Henceforth it is to depend not at all upon the abilities of workers but entirely upon the practices of

* Extract from *Brothers: Male Dominance and Technological Change*, Pluto Press, 1983, pp. 112–22.

management.[2] This same prospect was expressed equally starkly by the Brighton Labour Process Group:

Deskilling is inherent in the capitalist labour process because capital must aim at having labour functions that are calculable, standardisable routines; because this labour must be performed at the maximum speed and with minimum of 'porosity'; and because capital wants labour which is cheap and easily replaceable.[3]

The recent experience of compositors points to a greater complexity than these theories allow. If what the men say is true we have, first of all, to distinguish several meanings of the word 'skill'. Then we have to distinguish loss of skill from 'degradation of work'. We should be cautious too, about supposing that deskilling for one group implies an overall deskilling in the enterprise. And finally we need to separate out loss of skill from loss of control. Unless we are prepared to unravel this complexity in the notions of skill and deskilling it will be impossible to understand the individual man's ambivalence or his trade union's current strategy.

To begin this unpacking process: *skill* itself (if we read the men's experience in hot metal aright) consists in at least three things. There is the skill that resides in the man himself, accumulated over time, each new experience adding something to a total ability. There is the skill demanded by the job – which may or may not match the skill in the worker. And there is the political definition of skill: that which a group of workers or a trade union can successfully defend against the challenge of employers and of other groups of workers.

In the nineteenth century (and even perhaps until after the second world war) the three definitions of skill were, for the compositor, more or less co-terminous. In his apprenticeship and working life he acquired abilities that were fully demanded by his job; his unique right to practise the skill was more or less defensible through the union's pre-entry closed shop. For the capitalist employer, existence of a viable skill does not necessarily spell unprofitable production. The stability of craft production can, within certain tolerances, serve accumulation well. As Tony Elger has said in his discussion of Braverman: 'Forms of specialised expertise and craft competence may be embedded within a complex structure of collective labour effectively subordinated to capital accumulation.[4] Nonetheless, craft skill represents a constraint on managerial initiative which may become intolerable in certain economic conditions. The employer then turns to shake off these fetters, increasing the division of labour, intensifying work and introducing new technologies. Increasingly in newspaper production the three definitions of skill came out of synchrony. Computerised photocomposition throws them wildly awry.

The skill the men possessed has been made redundant by the

scrapping of hot-metal plant. The new tasks can be learned all too quickly. (They would of course not be able to take up the new work if that were not the case.) Thus, 'It took me six years, perhaps eight, to learn how to be a good comp and operator. You could take any competent typist from out on the street and I would maintain that within two months she could be doing my job.' Nonetheless, some skill is required by the new work. Some of the men's old knowledge – spelling, for instance, or an aesthetic understanding of how a newspaper page should look – is still useful. Secondly, as the men have found to their cost, typing is quite hard to learn. All of the men found that retraining for the new processes demanded something of them. And if we take 'skill' to designate the accumulated abilities of a person, then learning the new technology has enhanced their skill. It was, as many of them said, 'another string to my bow'. But what is a man's skill if, say, 80 per cent of it cannot be practised? All that is demanded in the new job is perhaps 10 per cent of the old knowledge and the 10 per cent increment recently acquired. In such a situation it is more comfortable to dwell, as many of the men do, on their 'internal', though unsaleable, skill, the acquisition of a lifetime, and continue to claim '*I* am skilled', even if the *job* is not.

Many of the men I talked to were ambitious and keen workers. This applies particularly to linotype operators who, at the end of their apprenticeships, went on ahead of the other comps to learn their 'extra skill' and so to acquire their greater earning power. Many of these climbers were also among the early enthusiasts for photocompositon. 'I thought to myself, I want to be one of the first ones to retrain, to go over. If there is anything going on up there I want to get a look at it.' In a sense they have gone on up a ladder of learning, alluringly set before them, and dropped off the top. For instance, a man said, 'I've gained really. I mean if I can't do anything else I can type. I suppose, now. I could always be a typist in the last resort.' Then, realising where his train of thought had led him, he made a grimace of alarm.

So the men are deskilled in the sense of being deprived of the power to use their original skill. But they have been offered a new knowledge. It is nothing very remarkable but, in the case of the more advanced systems, using VDUs and graphic-display terminals, in an integrated operation in which the men know something of the computer and photosetter, there is a knowledge worth having. (And it seems that this style of working is, if anything, under-represented in the news trade. There are fewer 'idiot' boards, more VDUs, in general printing.) But here the political definition of skill enters, to pay a contradictory role. First as tangible skill is hollowed out, the strength of the political shell becomes critical. If the union cannot lay effective political claim to the whole of this new field of work, to the 'second keystroke', (as the NGA have so far done) the compositor as a *distinct skill group* can kiss goodbye to work altogether. Second, however, political exigencies ironically *prevent* the full development of the new skill, in the man and the job. The full potential of computerised photocomposition is only released when operated as a direct-entry system. It would be a relatively skilled and satisfying job to be one of the few remaining compositors who – as the 'text processor' or 'typographic expert' on the new-style newspaper, assembling complex advertisements or whole newspaper pages on the large video screens of the page-view terminals – works alongside the new-style journalist, editor, accountant, administrator or telephone-advertising clerk to produce a computerised newspaper effortlessly, speedily and cheaply. But that is precisely the situation that the compositors, collectively, must resist. For only a few would get such jobs, the great majority being doomed to redundancy. They are there-fore obliged to stay the torrent of productivity, rather than being permitted to revel in it.

Thus the men had felt during the training period, while being shown the full potential of the new systems, that for the first and last time they were treated as intelligent, interested and competent people – which indeed they are. Reflecting on that time, they now felt it had been a tease, a come-on. Even in 'integrated working' situations the compositor does not personally produce as large a part of the whole product as the remaining compositor would in a direct-entry system. The employer/union bargain has produced a compromise role for comps. From the present perspective, 'Well, it is an idiot system, once you know it. The brainpower aspect goes clean out the window. I feel they are paying me to sit on my backside. All the activity is occurring now inside the computer – and that is pretty quiet!'

As a result of all this, many men were very disillusioned with their work. They would have understood Marx when he wrote, 'The lighten-ing of the labour, even, becomes a sort of torture, since the machine does not free the labourer from work but deprives the work of all interest.'[5] As one compositor put it, 'There was a hell of a lot of pride in the old work. With the new system, it's taken the soul out of the job. I don't buck against it. It's secured [*sic*] my livelihood. But if there is one thing I absolutely dislike about it, that's it, the soullessness of it.' Others said, 'All the skill has gone, basically,' 'It's one big *nothing*.' Many of the men consequently take a more instrumental attitude to the job than they did as craftsmen. 'New technology, great, I'll be mer-cenary shall I? It gives us more money, more time away from the firm. In other words, we've got a job where we get in, do it, go home and forget it.'

The men, then, feel that in one way they *have* been deskilled. And in one way they are right, since in capitalism the means of production are now owned by the employer and in these four newspaper firms the owner had simply scrapped the old plant and scrapped the old skill with it. *Skill in the man* was now out of kilter with *skill in the job*, and the union was only with great difficulty ensuring that *skill as a class political concept* held the line in the turmoil of this employer-inspired revolution.

'Skill' is, however, not only a class political weapon. It is also a sex/gender weapon. Skill as a political concept is more far-reaching than the class relations of capitalism – it plays an important part in the power relations between men and women. The sexual division of labour in society is of great antiquity: men and women tend to do different work. Over very long periods of patriarchal time women's particular abilities and work processes have been arbitrarily valued lower than those of men. It has been a two-way process: women's inferiority has rubbed off on their activities and the imputed mindlessness of the activities has reflected on women. Anne Phillips and Barbara Taylor have pointed out that the skill attributed to a job has much more to do with the sex of the person who does it than the real demands of the work.[6] Other studies have shown how, even in the rare circumstances where men and women do comparable work, the man's work is usually graded higher and rewarded more generously than the woman's. It is of course not difficult to see that men had much to gain, materially and ideologically, from such an overestimate of the skill of men's work and an underestimate of the skill of women's work. In the instance of photocomposition, the sexual character of skill is clear enough. Hot metal was undeniably male. The comps undervalue the typing and paper-handling skills they are now being taught because they see them as female. The men are caught in a contradiction: they must either acknowledge themselves totally deskilled, or acknowledge that many women are as skilled as men. The dilemma accounts for much of the bitterness they feel.

To continue the unpacking of skill: is the loss of skill equivalent to the 'degradation of work'? Degradation can be measured along numerous scales: earnings, hours, conditions, the extent of the division of labour. In all these respects newspaper workers, while being de-skilled, have improved their lot throughout the fifties, sixties and seventies. For most, the change to new technology has brought a marked increase in earnings, a reduction in working hours, and a relaxation of pressure. Besides, it has not further subdivided the work but has in some cases reintegrated detailed tasks. It has produced a more pleasurable working environment. Advances in production are to some extent and in some ways advances for society and some of the gain accrues even to the deskilled worker. If these things are not recognised, it is difficult to understand why, in spite of all their negative feelings, recounted in detail above, very few indeed of the men were prepared to say that they would want to go back to the old processes. Though they like to glorify craft (social historians do, too), there was in reality little that was glorious in the practice of such a craft in the recent phase of capitalist production: it was hard, tiring work. So if, capitalism replaces work that is rewarding but exhausting with work that is boring but easy, you may heave a sign of relief . . . while continuing to mourn the loss.

There is, however, one way in which the men *have* experienced degradation and this accounts in part for their bitterness. Degradation can also be measured *socially*. Does the new work reduce the standing of the old worker relative to others in the working class? Because the work is more generalised and easier, the men feel they are slipping perilously down the worker scale toward the general 'hand' or labourer. 'I think I have gone from skilled to semi-skilled, that's what it is. And I feel a bit let down. It has been a worry in my mind all the time.' 'What should I call myself? What am I now? We haven't even got a job title.' 'It's just a kind of clerical job really. You couldn't call it print.' Compositors, used to holding their head up among other working men, now feel loss of self-respect. 'I daren't think about it, much, but sometimes I do think – perhaps this is a little bit bumptious – I think what if some of my friends outside of print could see me now, what would they think?'

Besides this descent to the common *man*, we have seen how the men feel reduced to the level of women. 'If *girls* can do it, you know, then you are sort of deskilled you know, really.' The men are sensitive to this. 'If some knowing person down the local says, oh that's right, you've all become bloody typists haven't you, he's liable to get his head filled in.' Many compositors talk as though they feel the pull of gravity, levelling them down to what they see (and have always feared) as the undifferentiated mass of the working class: unskilled men, unemployed men, old men . . . and women.

A further consideration is this. It is clear from the instance of photocomposition that the deskilling of one group of workers, and an overall weakening of the position of labour in society as a whole, may be achieved by capital without actually deskilling the overall production process within the enterprise. A newspaper house is a social system of co-operating work groups. Marx called this 'the collective labourer':

The various kinds of collective labour that combine to form an overall collective productive machine participate in quite different ways in the direct process of production of commodities, one mainly with his hands, another mainly with his head, one as a manager or engineer or technician etc., another as a supervisor, yet another as a direct manual worker or perhaps just as an assistant.[7]

The totality of workers, each possessing labour-power of different kinds and different values, comprise a 'living production machine'.

Capital's thrust, in revolutionising newspaper production technology, may be directed mainly to removing the block represented by the composing room, but the owners also hope to make more productive and profitable the activities of journalists, advertising personnel, managers and many others in the firm. If capital gets its way, the composing group as a whole will be destroyed, and unemployment and loss of job opportunities will occur at the societal level. Yet, for those who remain in the slimmed-down newspaper operation, overall skill levels in production may not fall. For example, the massive routine copy-typing or 'input tapping' job, characteristic of phase one of the new technology, will no longer exist as such. 'Typing' on the new keyboards will be a smaller (and more interesting) part of what are essentially other jobs – a part of the work-time of the journalist, editor, graphics person or telephone-answerer. Routine paper paste-up will give way in phase two and subsequent technologies to text manipulation on screen. Small comfort for the majority of compositors discarded from the labour force, but satisfactory enough for those left within the charmed circle. Phase-one technology did indeed bring the expected polarisation of work into routine unskilled occupations and enhanced technological occupations. Phase two, on the contrary, appears to be producing a cluster of semi-skilled, semi-responsible linked occupations.

This effect is not, of course, limited to the newspaper industry. Bryn Jones, in his work on the effect of numerical control on engineering skills, has concluded that degradation of work or overall deskilling does not result from new technology in every kind of enterprise. Contrary to Braverman, he has found that the divisibility of task-skills may be related to such factors as the kind of product being manufactured, the kind of technology on offer and the strength of trade-union organisation.[8] The 'integrated working' we have seen at Times Newspapers and Mirror News Group, curiously flying in the face of 'the capitalist division of labour', may be an indication that such factors will produce, in the newspaper industry of the future, a production process that is characterised by less rather than more division of labour. However, this is not to say that labour will have, in some sense, 'won the battle'. The battle is not only won or lost within one work place, or through the quality of one labour process: it also takes place at a societal level. And skill is not its only trophy.

The question we are led to ask, then, is 'Is deskilling commensurate with loss of control?' A high degree of control over the hot-metal labour process had been built by comps on the possession of a skill. Now that skill is eroded. But the political organisation, the trade union and its chapels, have by no means had their control swept irreparably away. The men have fought back and influenced the way the technology is applied and managed. The worker's closeness to the new technology can be used to rebuild knowledge. Andrew Friedman and other critics of Braverman have pointed out that this possibility is scarcely allowed for in the scenario that predicts the relentless division of labour and degradation of work in capitalism.[9] In that scenario, relentless de-skilling dooms us to ever-diminishing control of work. But compositors have bought time in which some of them at least may build up their competence and know-how on the new equipment in order to re-establish a degree of control based, not merely on political assertion of skill, but on real ability. Of course, there are pressures pushing the other way. Electronic information technology is essentially a gener-alised technology applicable in all industries and throughout society. The comps' protected corner in the labour market is gone. As one told me, pointing up the contrast with the old days, 'I might tell a mate in the pub – we've got this hitch with the line printer. And he'll say to me, yes, we had the same problem at the Express Dairy.' Computerisation of work is happening to every Tom, Dick and Harry. Any one of them therefore might be able to challenge the compositor for his new job. Production processes that can be manned from a large undifferentiated labour market of polyvalent, interchangeable workers is a capitalists's dream. It is in recognition of this that trade unions (the NGA among them) are abandoning the direct equation of 'skill' with 'control', and are reorganising and redefining trade unionism so as to use other (and less divisive) ploys with which to challenge capital's power over pro-duction than the apprentice-based pre-entry closed shop.

A more worrying factor enters here however. Electronic information technology, is precisely *about* control from above. The men are aware of this. 'It's their tool, you know,' said a proof-reader, gesturing towards the new hardware. 'And it tends to have more command over you than your pen did.' Computerised photocomposition is not only used to contest craft control; its very introduction was a gesture of capitalist authority. Though the owners used the persuasive theme of progress, the men for their part made it clear that they felt acted upon: 'We are *victims* of progress,' they said, 'we are *victims* of change.'

Skill, already such a complex concept, has yet another facet. It has a different meaning for the individual from the meaning it has for working-class organisation. The individual producer dates back to a period long before the advent of capitalism. He or she has purely human interests in transformative labour, in production. He or she may very reasonably struggle to retain the pleasurable 'use-value' aspects of skill in the face of changing technologies. The trade union however was born in the same cradle as capitalism; it is a product of capitalist class relations – it has no other *raison d'étre*. Skill for the collective employee of capital, manifest in the trade union, is, sadly, no more than a means to an organisational end. (In the same way, for the capitalist employer, it is no more than a means to the end of producing 'exchange values', the end of capital accumulation.) There may be collective struggle *over* skill, but it is not necessary *about* skill. It is about the value of labour-power and control over production. If the weapon of skill, for the union, becomes blunted, others must be sought. And these, indeed, the NGA is seeking. This is why a union may find itself sometimes required to trample, as capital does, on the individual worker's pleasure in the practice of a skill.

There is always a danger, however, that trade unions, locked in the capital/labour struggle, will adopt the instrumental view of 'skill' in its entirety, forgetting that skill cannot, in the last resort, be evaluated without also evaluating its product. In referring to a 'use-value' aspect of skill I pointed to the pleasure that may be taken in the capability of producing useful things. But it is not only pleasure in the labour process itself that capitalist production destroys by its management disciplines. It perverts the product too. The political pamphleteers of the English Revolution of the seventeenth century, putting printing techniques to work for the first time in a popular movement against overlords and monarchy, could take pleasure in a skill used to produce something useful and purposeful for themselves and their comrades. What pleasure or pride can be taken by the comp in producing the destructive and abusive inanities of the *Daily Star* or *The Sun* – however clever the hot-metal techniques still used to produce those two papers today? Applying skills to bad ends is also a kind of deskilling.

References

1. Marx, K., *Capital*, Vol. 1, Lawrence & Wishart, 1954.
2. Braverman, H. *Labor & Monopoly Capital*, Monthly Review Press, 1974.
3. Brighton Labour Process Group, 'The Capitalist Labour Process' in *Capital & Class*, 1, Spring, 1977.
4. Elger, A. 'Valorisation and Deskilling: a Critique of Braverman' in *Capital & Class*, 7, Spring, 1979.
5. Marx, op. cit. p. 398.
6. Phillips, A. and Taylor, B. 'Sex and Skill: Notes towards a feminist economics', *Feminist Review*, 6, 1980.
7. Marx, K., 'The Results of the immediate process of production', Appendix, *Capital*, Vol. I, Penguin, 1976.
8. Jones, B., 'Destruction or redistribution of engineering skills? The case of numerical control', in Wood, S. *'The Degradation of Work?'* Hutchinson, 1982.
9. Friedman, A. *Industry and Labour*, Macmillan, 1977.

11 Managements' and Workers' Images of a Strike*
Alvin W. Gouldner

Editor's Introduction: Work relations are also power relations, and this crucially affects work experience. A classic study of worker-management authority relations is the work of Gouldner in two books – Patterns of Industrial Bureaucracy *and* Wildcat Strike. *They describe the relationships in a small gypsum mine and factory in Mid-West USA, called the 'General Gypsum Company'. The following extract is taken from 'Wildcat Strike' which focuses on a ten-day spontaneous strike at the plant. It shows that the strike was not in pursuit of wages but centred on issues of authority relations. The 'workers defined their role in relation to the technological system, emphasising their production obligation, and their ties to an impersonal process, but neglected to define with equal clarity their role in the plant's authority system, their place in a hierarchy of human relations.' ('Wildcat Strike', p. 24.) This pattern was disturbed by management changes.*

The various grievances were not all equally stressed by the conflicting parties and, sometimes, the 'same' grievance meant different things to different people. Here we wish to examine these grievances in terms of *who* held them, noting the divergent emphasis and meaning which management and workers gave to the issues involved. If the way in which the conflicting parties saw the strike is known, it may help to explain how they later sought to cope with it. For the solutions they adopted derived in part from the ways in which they looked upon the strike.

Management's Image of the Strike
Our intention is not to outline management's entire definition of the strike but, principally, to focus on its *distinctive* emphasis. In particular, top management's assessment of the situation is vital, for they were the managerial echelon which could make the crucial decisions. While they could not resolve the strike in disregard of lower management's sentiments, they had the final voice.

* Extract from *Wildcat Strike*, Harper & Row, 1954, pp. 53–63.

In larger measure than the workers, top management at the Lakeport office conceived of the strike as the product of a calculated stratagem by the workers. Unlike the workers, they felt that the 'export order' figured importantly in the events that brought the strike about. One of the main office executives began his account of the strike with a detailed statement of the union's and workers' reaction to the export order and emphasised, particularly, the tactical advantages which workers may have thought they possessed in view of the strike at the Big City plant. (Another factory in the group.)

Management also tended to conceive of the strike as a *struggle for control* of the plant. It was not quite a pure struggle for power, not entirely a power conflict, but it is rather close to it and may become even more clearly so in the future, their conception suggested: 'The workers don't look at the strike in the light that "we've got the strength",' mused a main office executive. 'Yet they have a strong desire to run the plants.'

The power conflict view of the strike is important because it implies that workers' grievances are in the nature of an ideology, masking their underlying intentions. Behind each specific complaint, the power politics definition implies, there is a hint of a fundamental challenge to management's status. In this context the problem readily becomes, not the adjudication of each grievance or the modification of the circumstances which elicit it, but rather the need to reaffirm 'who is boss here!' A staff supervisor, one of the engineers in the plant, voices this sentiment:

'The supervisors are kind of kicked around by the union. If there's a grievance they get it too. They [the workers] got a chip on their shoulders. They think they are more important than the Company. All this is going to be changed. They'll know the foreman is the foreman.'

There are at least two important functions served by defining a dispute in terms of its power connotations:

(1) This view allows management to obviate questions concerning the *validity* of the grievances. In bypassing the ethical facet of the conflict, it thus allows management to do whatever is necessary in order to 'handle' or control the situation. In this way, the issue is trimmed to a problem in 'social technology'; the question then becomes one of choosing *efficient* means of control. For if management senses a fundamental challenge, the emergence of a pure power struggle for dominance, it feels justified in choosing *any* solution that will enable it to win.

(2) Moreover, definition of a conflict in power terms is in itself an 'ideological' mechanism, peculiarly useful to those who require some escape from a moral crisis. If a disputant doubts the legitimacy of his

own side's position, his ability to defend himself before a public, or before his own conscience, is undermined. He may sidestep this difficulty, however, by implying that the ethical dimensions of the conflict are really peripheral; that is, he may claim that they are merely window-dressing to conceal the real issue, the pure power conflict.

One section of management, that centering around the labor relations department, had hoped that efforts at a strike settlement would be postponed. They were somewhat sorry that negotiations had begun immediately after the strike started. They had hoped, they said, that the situation would have an opportunity to 'cool off' before talks began. After the negotiations began, they looked upon them as an opportunity for 'catharsis,' providing the worker with a chance to 'blow off steam and clear the air.' Here, too, as in the power struggle definition of the strike, there was a tendency to view the manifest content of the workers' grievances as somewhat secondary; 'getting it off their chests' was held to be the vital thing, rather than resolving the specific grievances about which the affect centered. Emotions and feelings were conceived of as dangerous, and were seen as inhibiting a 'reasonable' settlement.

In effect, a section of top management had tended to conceive of themselves as therapists. In this role, they took account of the workers' unconscious and irrational emotions, which were held to be at the root of the difficulty. To suggest that a section of management tended to use the therapist's role as a model is no mere literary figure. Along these lines, and as partial cause and effect, was the Company's support of a superior 'human relations' program. This employed a series of motion picture strips, which analysed group tensions from a psychoanalytical viewpoint, in terms of the unconscious needs of individuals, and which were discussed with foremen and workers throughout the Company.

The foregoing indicates then, that a section of top management viewed the strike as a combination of impersonal, cold-blooded calculation of the tactical opportunities, and an irrational emotional outburst.[1] This double-barrelled conception of the strike may seem to be contradictory, but this need not be actually so. The production department seemed to be more heavily committed to the 'power struggle' view, while the personnel department was more inclined to the 'emotional outburst' conception. Thus these somewhat mutually exclusive views were not held with equal emphasis by all sections of management.

Nor were they applied with equal emphasis to all groups of workers. There was a tendency for management to speak of the workers' *leaders* as if they were motivated by rational and tactical considerations, while the *rank and file* of the workers were usually held to be motivated by emotional forces.

These two views of the strike do, however, have at least one thing in common. They both by pass the question of the legitimacy of the strike. For questions of 'right' and 'wrong' are as irrelevant in a power conflict for survival as they are in the relations between a therapist and patient.

Management's avoidance of the value aspects of the question clearly suggests that they were uneasy about the moral propriety of their own arguments and behavior. Indeed, main office personnel explicitly indicated this. After discussing the causes of the strike at length with one executive, he finally said that, in his opinion, the 'key' thing was that 'the fellows just didn't have confidence in the company.' 'Why didn't they have confidence in the company?' he was asked. He replied:

'It would be amazing if they had confidence. On January 15th, we changed from Peele to Landman [the second successor to plant manager]. Johnson and Cook were also demoted and *they both had their watches. If a man works twenty years for the Company he gets a gold watch.* From then in he is referred to as "having his watch." Cook became a clerk in his own office [from office manager]. He has his watch too. These changes *justify* the "no confidence".'

In other words, this executive was very disturbed by the demotion of men who had long-standing seniority in the plant. Of course, this executive, like others, believed that impersonal and objective criteria of demotion and promotion, a man's 'efficiency,' should determine his career in the Company. On the other hand, however, most executives also believed that 'seniority' should be given consideration in personnel relations.

Management's adherence to seniority was attested to by their custom of issuing gold watches for twenty years' service. It was also acknowledge in the Company's labor relations manual:

Length of service increases are considered by the Company on the basis of the years of satisfactory service rendered by an employee. . . . For the first two or three years of service in a position such increases are synonymous with merit increases. However, the Company recognizes that an employee continues to become more valuable with years of service, even though increased value is difficult to measure accurately. *Also, the Company feels that an employee with years of service in a position should receive some monetary appreciation for faithfulness.* [Emphasis added]

This affirmation of seniority, in an inter-office memorandum, is indicative of the sentiments of its writers (who were main office executives) and the anticipated sentiments of the managerial corps to whom they were writing. Yet the strategic replacements among foremen had injured precisely those supervisors with the longest seniority.

Notice, too, that the manual indicates that long-standing seniority is taken as an earnest of *'faithfulness'* or loyalty to the Company. In effect, management's drive for efficiency had led them to demote men whom they, themselves, looked upon as unusually loyal to the Company.

Management could not help but feel that, at least in some measure, its own behavior was improper; and for this reason they felt the men justified in withholding 'confidence' from the Company.

This tension between 'seniority' and 'efficiency' reflects a basic managerial dilemma. In order to preserve the security of the enterprise, management wants men who are *both* loyal (and seniority is commonly taken as an index of this) and efficient. Since the loyalty and efficiency of its working force, and especially of its supervisory cadre, are fundamental managerial interests, the choice of one at the expense of the other is bound to place management in a threatening and unsettling quandary.

Since the Production Department was mainly responsible for the costs and level of production, it felt compelled to choose efficiency rather than seniority. The production executives were focussing on the *technological* consequences of their decision since these most directly affected their own department's position. The *social* consequences, the possibilities of conflict that might result from violating the group's seniority expectations, comprised a danger of which they *were aware* but felt they had to risk. The labor relations department, on the other hand, anticipating these conflicts and knowing that it would be *their* responsibility to cope with them, tended to oppose the production department's decision. As one member of labor relations said, 'Under proper leadership, I think that they [the demoted supervisors] could have functioned all right.' Being the more powerful department, the decision of the production executives prevailed.

There was at least one other reason, peculiar to this Company perhaps, why the main office executives paid more than 'lip service' to 'seniority' and were genuinely disturbed at its violation. This involved the Company's distinctive competitive position.

The Company's major competitor is the 'Monotuff' Gypsum Company, whose president is widely reputed to be a bitter 'anti-labor' man. Monotuff is viewed by many of the Lakeport executive staff as the brute antithesis of what they would like the General Gypsum Company to be. Many of General's executive had once worked for Monotuff and were rankled at the latter's methods of treating their employees, managerial or otherwise. As the director of production explained:

'I spent eleven years with Monotuff Gypsum. Believe me our democratic spirit didn't prevail there. A good many of us came from Monotuff. They treat people as machines and tools. They haven't any understanding of human relations. We treat people as human beings.'

General's interest in 'sound human relations' constituted a continuing polemic against Monotuff, and was another arena in which a nation-wide competition could be pursued. For this reason, too, the demotion of the old supervisors upset the members of the executive staff.

The Workers' Image of the Strike

The great majority of workers viewed their strike as a justified and legitimate action. Workers usually defined the strike in ethical terms, holding it to be morally justified. As many of them said, 'We're out to get our rights.' The strike was not interpreted by them, as management was inclined to define it, in the amoral concepts of power. Their hostility toward the 'swearing' supervisor, and against supervisors who overstepped their bounds, expressed *moral* indignation.

Far from presenting their action as a deliberately calculated stratagem, the ordinary worker emphasised its *spontaneity*. They spoke of the plant as a 'powderkeg' which had 'blown up' in the unpredictable manner of a natural eruption, rather than in accordance with the purposive planning of men. Even some of the top union leadership were surprised at the spontaneity and solidarity evinced by the workers. 'This walkout was a spontaneous reaction,' Kayo observed,

'They just walked off the job and went home. They didn't bother to picket or anything. They just stayed home. I've never seen such complete action. The guys came to the union officers and said they were going to walk out, and that's all.'

Each of the grievances that workers actually emphasised as justification for their strike had two facets. In each grievance two different outlooks were operative; one was oriented to established plant practices and was morally indignant at the violation of these custom-grounded expectations. This may be called the 'traditionalist' outlook. The other, or 'marketing outlook,' was oriented to more formal expectations and was hostile at the infringement of the contractual agreement. Different workers gave the 'same' verbalised grievance a somewhat different 'twist' depending on their outlook.

Those oriented to the established practices interpreted the 'swearing supervisor' grievance as an expression of unbecoming 'coldness' and 'unfriendliness'; those having a formal outlook saw the same grievance as a rejection of 'inequality'; to them a swearing supervisor was one who made unjustified claims to superiority. From the perspective of those concerned with established practices, supervisors who 'overstepped their bounds' were violating traditional plant practices which they believed should govern the relations between workers and foremen. In the view of those who were contractually oriented, this same grievance meant that supervisors were wrong in assuming powers that had not been explicitly and *formally* granted to them. This group would not have been so affronted at the violation of established plant practices, if the foremen's behavior had been officially sanctioned.

When those concerned with the defense of established plant practices spoke of 'broken promises,' they seemed to mean that the supervisors had violated a 'trust'. To the contractually oriented group of workers, 'broken promises' meant that supers had broken commitments explicitly acknowledged and contractually binding. When those oriented to the established practices complained that the 'machines went faster,' it largely appeared to be a grievance to the effect that management no longer had any limits to what they wanted. In the formal-contractual outlook, this grievance meant that workers were being forced to work harder without a *quid pro quo*, without more money. Finally, when those concerned with traditional practices complained about 'foremen working' they meant that supervisors no longer left you alone and did not trust you to do your work properly. To those contractually oriented, this grievance meant that working foremen were 'taking another man's job away.'

Each of these two orientations was not only emphasised by different workers, but was occasionally voiced by the same worker. Sodlen, for example, after complaining about the effects of the speed-up at the take-off[2] reveals both viewpoints:

'Other plants with machines like ours make the change in two to four minutes. Can't blame them [management] for wanting to cut down from twenty to two minutes. But the take-off has used the same machinery for twenty years, the bundler and all.'

Thus the union secretary sympathised with both the Company and the workers; he was ambivalent about the Company's speed-up and about the workers' demands; in the end he finds the Company at fault only because it was technologically backward and inefficient.

A similar ambivalence was found among some of the small businessmen in the community, one of whom explained the demotion of the old foremen as follows:

'After all, they're supposed to keep him on because he's been with them for a long time. But a big corporation isn't that way. If they can find someone better to do the job, they put him there. You know, a new broom sweeps clean. Take these old foremen. They were demoted and put to work like the men they used to supervise. The fellows feel stinkin' about this. But after fourteen or fifteen years a guy gets in a rut. So you have to do something about it. After all, they gave them a chance to get on a paying basis. . . . After a guy gets to know you he'll——you every time.'

These comments indicate that the obligatory force of seniority expectations was acknowledged. But so, too, is that of the expectation of efficiency, for as he says, the plant must be kept on a 'paying basis.' And as he adds elsewhere, 'The plant is *right* in making them work more and better if they're losing money.'

In consequence of this split in outlook, two different definitions of the strike were developed by workers. Stated in a purified and extreme form, those who were custom-rooted sought a *restoration* of the past. They wanted a return to previously existent worker-supervisor relationships in which management's expectations would not be constantly changing. They sought no change in the authority *system* as such but instead, tended to focus their aggression on an *individual*, Spiedman. Their strike thus conforms to the classic pattern of a traditionalist rebellion which, in Max Weber's words, 'is directed against the person of the chief or of a member of his staff [i.e., the travelling engineer]. The accusation is that he has failed to observe the traditional limits of this authority [i.e., overstepped the bounds].[3] In brief, they sought the road back.

For these 'traditionalists,' the strike was an expression of resistance against the prolonged and continual violation of their old beliefs. In another respect, it was a demand for increasing the predictability with which their established privileges would be satisfied; that is, for a cessation of 'broken promises.' In greatest measure, their hostility was directed against changes which had affected the *informal* organisation of the plant's social system, for it was in this sphere that their customary rights resided.

On the other hand, the 'market-oriented' definition of the strike, extremely stated again, sought no return to the past but, instead, looked forward to *changes* in the *formal* organisation of the plant as a remedy for their grievances. They dwelled upon the failure of certain formal mechanisms, especially the breakdown of the grievance machinery, in bringing the strike about. In addition, they wanted their trade union to participate in determining the speed of production. 'This is fundamental,' said Bill Kayo, 'Management [in other companies] does this all the time.' They sought, also, a solution to the problem of 'working foremen' by having top management issue more clear-cut directives to foremen ordering stricter conformance to the contract. These 'market men' did not seek to transform the informally established and traditional practices into formal contractual terms. Instead they sought formal recognition of *new* rights and obligations, such as control over speed norms.

For the 'market men,' the strike expressed an effort for formally locate managerial responsibility ('Who is boss here?') and expressed resistence to inadequate contractual conformance. In general, they emphasised the pecuniary implications of the workers' grievances; thus the 'speed-up' was perceived by them as more work for the same money. They also accented the *contractual* roots of the strike. Speaking of the 'radical' group on the union grievance committee, Sodlen commented that they were able to make trouble, ' 'cause of the way the *contract is written.* You can find trouble every day if you want to.' In his view the strike was occasioned by a 'misunderstanding of the contract.'

In many ways, the 'market men' among the union leaders looked upon the strike in a manner very similar to the labor relations executives among top management. For example, these union leaders believed the strike to have come about because some of the men 'lost their heads' and gave vent to irrational feelings. Like top management, too, the 'market men' among the union leaders also viewed their relationship with management as reflecting a power struggle. They felt that sections of management were deliberately acting in a way that threatened the prerogatives and position of the union. Sodlen, for example, said that plant management had once offered the boilermen a larger wage increase than they had been willing to offer the union negotiating committee. In fact, he added, they finally gave the boilermen a larger increase than the one the union committee had recommended. 'They were trying to break us,' declared Sodlen, 'They were trying to show the guys that they could work without the committee.'

If the traditionalists sought a return to a relationship governed by 'trust,' then the 'market men' desired a situation in which trust did not matter; they wanted their prerogatives safeguarded by legal guarantee. If the traditionalists wanted to be able to return to the 'fold,' the 'market men' waned to be 'taken into the business.' If the traditionalists wanted workers and management to be 'friends,' the 'market men' wanted them to be 'partners.' In sum, the traditionalists wanted a return to the old indulgency pattern, while the 'market men' were willing to set aside the informal privileges of the indulgency pattern in exchange for new, formally acknowledged union powers.

Though both of these outlooks were to be found throughout the strike, there seems little doubt that the traditionalists' definition of the strike dominated in the beginning. Suggesting this is the unplanned and 'spontaneous' character of the walkout, the initial focussing of grievances on the behavior of an individual supervisor, the absence of a well formulated set of union demands, the deep feeling against the demotion of the old supervisors.

References

1. The 'power conflict' and 'emotional outburst' views are two widespread conceptions which management groups have of labor-management relations, though not the only ones. Another common view, which is not openly displayed in crisis situations, is a conception of the situation as a 'game.' Thus labor relations directors will often feel and express genuine excitement about their work, and enjoyment in their relations with union representatives. They will emphasise often that their relations with union functionaries are devoid of feelings of hostility. The game viewpoint comes out most clearly when, for example, a labor relations director comments that each side

knows the routine that the other will follow in the negotiations. One labor relations director once remarked to me that the union representative and himself joked about changing sides in a forthcoming negotiations session, and suggested that either one of them could probably do well at the other's job. This seems to reflect the 'objectivity' of the expert so disturbing to his client. Labor relations can take on 'game' characteristics when each party is aware of the structural constraints that the other is laboring under. For example, when the union leader knows that the company labor relations man operations in terms of limits set by higher management and cannot transcend them, and when the labor relations man is aware that the union leader *must* bring home some settlement with which he can pacify his own rank and file. If each tacitly expresses awareness of the other's limitations, and signals his intention not to violate them, then a game is being played in which union leaders and company labor relations directors may develop no little camaraderie. In sum, the game framework is one of stable equilibrium between the two players, not merely because each is satisfying the expectations of the other, but because each is helping the other to satisfy the expectations of some *third* party.

2. The 'take-off' is where the finished building boards are taken off the production line.

3. Weber, Max (1947), *The Theory of Social and Economic Organisation*, edited by Talcott Parsons, Free Press, p. 342.

12 Workers and Bosses*
R.J. Kriegler

*Editor's Introduction: Worker-management authority relations are
affected by the nature of the labour market. Much industrial labour
has been immigrant labour, which is very vulnerable to employer
pressure. Any such pressure can be intensified by employer domina-
tion of local labour markets. Such a situation is depicted in the
following extract, which is a study of an Australian corporation –
BHP – which owns a shipyard and steelworks in South Australia
at Whyalla. Whyalla is virtually a company town. Kriegler
worked at BHP during 1975–6 whilst he conducted his study.*

After the War, Australia experienced a shortage of manual workers and
this ushered in the era of the sponsored immigration programme.
Whyalla, like most other industrial growth centres, shared in this
programme as attempts were made to meet the increasing demands for
skilled and unskilled workmen in shipbuilding and steelmaking. In the
years that followed, Whyalla saw the arrival of thousands of immigrant
families from Great Britain and Europe, and this was reflected in the
town's pattern of growth and in its ethnic composition. In 1947, 95 per
cent of the Whyalla population were Australian-born, but by 1971, 43
per cent of the population in the town were immigrants and another 10
per cent were their Australian-born children. Two-thirds of the immigrants were from the United Kingdom and Ireland and most of these
were skilled workers who were employed, on their arrival, in their
respective trades. Non-English-speaking immigrants, however, were
given the labouring jobs in the BHP works. Even those who were
skilled tradesmen worked as labourers for the first few months, until
their trade certificates had been translated and approved. This took up
to twelve months. Some were never accorded the tradesman status
which they enjoyed in their countries of origin. Today, non-English-
speaking immigrants are still found in disproportionately large
numbers in the heavy labouring jobs. They do the work that many
Australian workmen refuse to accept. An officer of the Commonwealth
Employment Service explained why there was a permanently high
unemployment rate amongst adult males in Whyalla, despite an acute
shortage of labourers at the Steelworks: some the Company will not

* Extract from *Working for the Company*, Oxford University Press, 1982, pp. 121–49.

employ because they are either physically handicapped or in some way unsuitable for BHP's needs, whilst many simply refuse to work for the Company as unskilled labourers. It is this type of work that almost always falls to the most recently arrived European immigrants. Having just landed in a foreign country with their families in tow, they are scarcely in a position to reject any job offered to them, no matter how unpleasant or arduous the work may seem. Consequently, these workmen may be found labouring on top of the coke ovens with wooden clogs strapped to their safety boots to protect their feet from the searing heat. They can be seen stumbling about through the dense clouds of swirling gas, their bodies cloaked in a crust of black coal-dust and tar. Others, less fortunate, find themselves pouring rim steel on the cast-house floor of the steelmaking plant. The temperature on the workman's skin under his clothing has been recorded to be in excess of 65°C. The flesh seems to cringe away from this blistering, incandescent heat. But if steelmaking in its present manner is to continue, then these jobs must be done. In a submission to the Industries Assistance Commission, BHP maintained that it needs a continuing source of immigrant labour to undertake these and similar jobs.

Immigrants are under a great deal of pressure to become assimilated to the Australian way of life, from the moment they arrive here. But getting to know a new country, a new technology and the people takes time, tolerance and tremendous effort. On the job, immigrants are usually supervised by Australian foremen who frequently rely on racial epithets and abuse to get the work done. Inexperienced immigrant workmen who decline to do a job which they consider too dangerous are often threatened with the sack or transfer to riskier or dirtier work. On the other hand, transfers, when requested by the workmen, are very difficult to get. The foreman controls transfers and it is often said that BHP would rather lose a man than transfer him. Workmen rely on overtime to bring their wages up to an acceptable level. Immigrants having to pay off loans for the purchase of furniture or a motor-car say they must work overtime each week. But should a worker refuse overtime once or twice, his foreman is likely to make sure that he does not get an offer of overtime for a long time. Some BHP foremen have to be bribed to hand out overtime. A senior public relations officer of the Company admitted this, adding that 'There have been instances where supervisors got backhanders.' Silenced by the language barrier, and facing economic hardship, many immigrants are forced to put up with appalling conditions and exhausting jobs.

Until about 1970, BHP provided for no tea-breaks during shifts, though workmen were (and still are) given an unpaid thirty-five-minute lunch-break. The trade union leaders in Whyalla, after years of negotiation and threats, were finally able to relate to their members that the Company would provide one ten-minute tea-break per day. The Company made this offer on condition that workmen do not leave their place of work or sit down during this break. This condition no longer applies in the Shipyard and workmen are now permitted to sit down at 'brew-time'; but in the Steelworks workmen are still required to remain on their feet whilst taking their morning tea. (The tea, of course, is not supplied by the Company.) An interviewee who had spent several years working in the Steelworks before coming to the Shipyard, described it thus:

My job over there could have been one of the best jobs in Whyalla, but the bosses managed to turn it into one of the worst. They were the lousiest lot that I've ever worked for in my forty-seven years at my trade. When it came to brew-time (or 'smoko' as we used to call it back in England) we were not allowed to knock off to make our tea until exactly ten minutes to ten. And we were not allowed to sit down. They would stop blokes from sitting down to have the one and only tea break in the day. We weren't even allowed to talk to each other in groups of three or four; they would come up and order us to break it up. It was as near to being in jail as anything I've ever seen anywhere. Of course, it was the supervisors that were causing this; it was, from top to bottom, one scared of the other – scared that they were going to lose their jobs if they did not follow the Company line. But such little Gestapo as you've ever seen.

Another interviewee, who had just been transferred from the Shipyard to the Steelworks, described his work routine:

I know for a fact that there are young girls working as clerks for this Company who earn more money than I do labouring in the Steelworks. I can bring home $150 a week if I work seven days a week plus some extra overtime in the evenings. At the end of each day you are buggered, physically buggered. You're just sort of shattered. And it takes a couple of hours when you get home of sitting down to get over it. There is no hope of being able to play with the children. I go to bed at about nine or ten so that I can get up in time to be back at work by seven in the morning. We are just work machines. They tell you that you are working for BHP for only eight hours a day, but basically you are working for the Company twenty-four hours a day.

*   *   *

We are treated like children at work. For example, when we are supposed to clock off at the end of the day, the foreman comes along at three minutes to four with our cards and instead of giving them to us in an ordinary, rational way, he starts walking towards the clocks which are about 350 yards away and shouts out the person's name. It is usually a nickname which he has made up for each of us. One chap, for reasons only know to the foreman, is called 'shitlegs'. And if you don't dash to his side to accept the card, he shouts 'Too late' and puts it at the bottom of the pack. Once he has handed out the cards, we are to stop walking and if you walk any further, he shouts, 'That's far enough', and you have to stay there. This happens every single evening. The men don't despise him for this because this is just one of the thousands of unpleasant things about the place. It happens so much that the men are not concerned about it any more, they are not even conscious of it any more.

During my first week at the Shipyard, I strolled into a toilet block which was spotlessly clean and I recall how pleased I was that the workmen's toilets were of such a high standard. The next time that I returned to use these amenities, I was in more of a hurry and bumped my forehead against the door because I didn't expect it to be locked. When I raised my head to look at the protruding object that had struck me, I noticed that it was the corner of a sign which read 'staff only'. I was disappointed when I eventually found the workmen's toilets. They were old and in a filthy condition and a large 'U' shape had been cut out of the tops of the toilet doors, presumably to discourage loafing. Staff, I discovered later, were issued with a key to use their own toilets.

In the Shipyard, work commences at 7.30 a.m. There is a ten-minute tea-break and the lunch-break is forty-five minutes (thirty-five minutes in the Steelworks) and then the work proceeds until 4.07 p.m. when workmen pack away their tools. At 4.10 p.m. workers may pick up their clockcards and at 4.15 p.m. the siren sounds and clocking-off may commence. A large sign above the clocks reminds workers that 'Workmen seen running to the clocks will be subject to instant dismissal'. One afternoon, just before the end of the day shift, I noticed that the sky had turned very dark, threatening a thunderstorm. As I walked the long distance to the shipwrights' shop to pick up my clock-card, a spectacular lightning display ensued. By the time I got to the long queues of workmen at the gates, it was 4.12 p.m. and almost immediately a horrendous rainstorm began. There was no shelter whatsoever for the 1300 or so workmen waiting for the siren. The time keeper and security guard stood in their office indifferently watching this pitiful scene as they patiently waited for the clock to move to exactly 4.15 p.m. and only then did they sound the siren. In that three minutes, all the workmen were completely drenched and chilled. It was as if we were being punished, like inmates in a prison, but in this case we were being punished, it seemed, simply for being manual workers, for it would be quite unthinkable that a company would do this sort of thing to its clerical or professional staff.

The offices of BHP's professional and white-collar staff are spacious and well-appointed, centrally-heated in the winter months and air-conditioned during the summer. They take their lunch in the staff cafeteria which is partitioned in order to separate top management (assistant superintendents and above) from other staff employees. The meals are of the highest quality and are subsidised by the Company:

during the time that I was there, a three-course lunch cost a mere sixty cents. In the works, however, the workmen have no cafeteria and they must, therefore, either bring their own lunch and refreshments or buy their lunch from the 'pie cart' which moves slowly through the plant at lunch-time.

At lunch-time, the workmen lie in long rows against the walls of buildings, some on pieces of wood from old packing cases or newspaper, some lying in the dust of the slipway under the ship. If there was one photograph that I wanted to capture whilst I was in the Shipyard, it was this. Somehow, it symbolised the spirit of the place; the degrading atmosphere, the despair, and the lack of communication between the workmen. All but three of the twenty-six interviewees were dissatisfied with the lack of proper canteen facilities for workmen. One of the staff interviewees, though, felt that workmen would not be happy with the type of food served in the staff cafeteria.

Like most other employers, BHP will not pay a workman for a public holiday if he is AWL on the day immediately prior to, or immediately following, that holiday. This rule applies equally to the two-day Christmas break. On Christmas Eve, as on any other day, work does not cease until 4.15 p.m. and, therefore, many workmen go to the pubs or do some last-minute shopping during their lunch-break, often arriving back at work late. Those who returned to work more than thirty minutes late on Christmas Eve, when I was working in the Shipyard, were informed by their foremen that they were to lose their Christmas and Boxing Day pay. In contrast to this, a white-collar friend of mine in the Shipyard was away AWL for the whole of Christmas Eve and returned to find that the Company had given him full pay for the public holidays. Workmen are aware of this type of discrimination and it is a source of bitter resentment for many. Each interviewee was able to relate instances of this kind: here is one of them.

The privileges that are given to these office workers, it's out of all proportion to their worth to the Company. Take a tradesman who has worked for the Company for thirty years and compare him to a 16-year-old office girl who is given full staff privileges. I remember an instance down there where a young office girl was getting married. All her friends from the pay office took half the afternoon off to decorate this motor car in the car park with streamers and so on. That was quite acceptable to the Company. But only about a week after this, an old fitter of thirty years service to the Company was retiring, and a half-dozen apprentice boys, out of respect for the old chap, were in the middle of making a presentation to him when they were ordered back to work. This happened right in front of me, you should have seen the look on the face of old Jimmy. The privileged class win again, because they are in air-conditioned offices and we are building the ships. What they always forget, of course, is that they are completely dependent on us.

A woman who works in the Shipyard administration was not at all surprised to hear these personal accounts. Indeed, she was able to confirm some of them:

The workers must put in a special leave form to their foreman and they've got to give all the details why they need to take it, and they've got to do this a week ahead of time. My boss does all the special leave and I've watched him; quite often he doesn't even bother to read the form, he just says 'No'. It is very difficult for the men to get special leave. I don't know why, because they don't get paid when they are on special leave. Special leave without pay for all workers, but for staff it is almost always leave *with* pay. We get special leave without any trouble and it's on full pay. All that I've got to do is mention to my boss that I need a few days off work to go to Adelaide or something, and I'll get it, no trouble. When I got married, I was given special leave for a week, on full pay. I admit that they were kind to give it to me, but they always try and make the workers feel inferior. They seem to go out of their way to do this.

My interviews with the twenty-six employees overwhelmingly revealed an intense suspicion and hostility towards Company management. Responses varied of course; supervisors and professional staff being more guarded in their comments, whilst most workmen expressed the same frustration, disillusionment and deep-seated bitterness that I witnessed amongst so many of the workmen in the Shipyard. The interviews convey the feeling that years of experience with an inconsiderate and rapacious employer have gradually cemented feelings of collective distrust of the Company. Of the twenty-six interviewees, twenty-four felt that management does not have the interests of the workmen at heart.

*　　*　　*

BHP unofficially encourages and perpetuates the myth that their manual employees earn substantial incomes. Throughout the time that I worked and conducted my research in Whyalla (1975–76) I found middle-class people of the town claiming, with extraordinary authority, that workers earn a minimum of $10 000 a year, most earning more. This claim was also frequently made by senior Company personnel, by professional staff and by white-collar employees of the Company. A clerical worker told me that this information was related to him when he first joined the Company in 1975, whilst a member of the professional staff said that the Company's industrial officer had given him this figure – being a specialist on matters of wages and awards, there was no reason to doubt the word of the officer. Accordingly, the figure of $10 000 is also quoted to curious visitors by the Company tourist guides. What intrigued me was the unanimity and conviction with which this view was held and the ingenious way in which it was used by the middle-class to ward off arguments that seemed, in any way, sympathetic to the plight of manual workers or trade unions. It appeared to form an important part of the ideological arsenal that middle-class people were using to confront complaints, criticisms and accusations from the working-class or perhaps to appease any twinges of conscience that they might from time to time experience.

As a labourer in the Shipyard, it would have been impossible for me to earn $10 000 in one year, even if I worked seven days a week for every week at full overtime rates. Without overtime my annual income could not exceed $5751. At the end of the 1975–76 financial year, I was told the gross incomes of all my interviewees. There was a striking difference between the incomes of the six staff and twenty manual workmen. The mean income of staff was $11 380 (median $11 200) working an average of 5.6 hours of overtime a week, whilst the manual workers earned a mean income of $7825 (median $8000) which included the income from an average of 5.8 hours of overtime a week. All but two of the manual workers represented were skilled tradesmen and the highest income recorded was $9000 by a welder who claimed to have maintained a weekly overtime average of thirteen hours. Furthermore, the incomes also included special rates for working in confined spaces and hot or wet places. The average weekly earnings of these twenty manual workers in the Shipyard was $150.48, which was well below the then national average of $181.00. Moreover, whereas the figure for the Shipyard workmen includes 5.8 hours of overtime, the national figure includes only 2.5 hours of overtime.

Thirteen of the sixteen married *manual* interviewees stated that their incomes were inadequate and that they were having difficulties in coping with the financial demands of family life. The average number of dependent children for these sixteen workmen was 1.7 per family and, therefore, it was not surprising to find that all twenty manual employees were unanimous in their belief that their incomes would not support a family of four children.

As a result of the low wage rates, many Whyalla wives seek part or full-time employment: ten out of the sixteen married manual interviewees had working wives. With only limited employment opportunities for women, Whyalla has a higher proportion of unemployed females than the State of South Australia as a whole. Many female school-leavers find that suitable work is not available in Whyalla and move to Adelaide to find employment. The Whyalla Community Recreation Report states that only 30 per cent of the school-leavers remain in Whyalla, whilst many students return to school because of lack of employment. Most married women do not seek full-time positions and, therefore, they are not represented in the unemployment figures; so that much of the problem is hidden. Female labour is so easy to obtain that employers prefer to engage 17-year-old school-leavers and dismiss them when they reach the age of twenty because they are too expensive on an adult wage. A 17-year-old shop assistant is paid only 42 per cent of the adult wage. Most supermarkets sack a large proportion of their employees over the Christmas and Easter holidays, thereby avoiding public holiday payments. It is no wonder, therefore, that young people in Whyalla consider a shop assistant's job to be a last resort.

A workman wishing to do something about his working conditions and wages, or wishing to complain about being unfairly treated or victimised by his supervisor has, broadly speaking, only two realistic alternatives, that is, if his approaches to higher levels of management have proved unsatisfactory. He may wish to contact his trade union and request some form of action or representation on his behalf, or he may simply decide to resign and seek other employment. Although the former might seem to be by far the most suitable and rational, it is by no means necessarily the most effective. When I started work in the Shipyard, I was informed by my fellow-workers that the union I would be expected to join was the Painters and Dockers Union.

*　　*　　*

After several months had passed I had not been asked to join any union. Finally, I had to seek out the shop steward at lunch-times (it took several). My first reaction to this was one of dismay, for I had fully expected the shop steward to approach me at work, during working hours, and I further expected that the shop steward would be in weekly or fortnightly contact with the men in my squad to see whether we had any complaints or problems on the job. But this, as I quickly discovered, could never occur in the Shipyard or Steelworks because the Company forbids shop stewards to discuss this sort of thing during 'Company time'. Moreover, shop stewards are not allowed to make routine inspections of the working conditions of the men; this is deemed 'union business' by the Company and is, therefore, strictly forbidden during working hours. Breaking this rule usually results in some form of disciplinary action and a report on the employee's disciplinary card. These cards represent a type of dossier on employees and are referred to by supervisors and industrial officers during industrial disputes.

Moreover, the movements of full-time union officials in the BHP works are controlled. BHP only permits union officials to see their members during their lunch-break and then only in the presence of a Company security officer.

Workmen who resign from or have been dismissed by the Company have been known to find it extremely difficult to get work with the smaller contracting firms in Whyalla. Workmen and union leaders claimed that the Company blacklists men who get the sack or resign, insisting that local contractors do not employ them. Contractors comply with this arrangement because they are afraid of losing their contracts with BHP. Several of the smaller firms are BHP subsidiaries. Sometimes, if the contractor refuses, then BHP stipulates that the employee concerned is not to enter any of their plants while engaged in installation or maintenance work for the contractor. According to one of the employee liaison officers, workmen give superficial and usually benign reasons for resigning from the Company. His explanation for this was that workmen feel they cannot criticise the Company as they may have to work for BHP again some time in the future, or they may be hoping to secure work with one of the contractors. A clinical psychologist practising in Whyalla assured me that he did not have any misgivings about discussing the social problems of the town as he was 'one of the few people in this place who isn't threatened or controlled in some way by the Company'. A few minutes later, however, he negated this when he described how many of his patients have psychological problems that originate directly from their work. He explained that, had his practice been located elsewhere in Australia, he would simply suggest to many of them that they change their jobs. 'But this isn't possible here. The frustrating thing about my practice is that I have to help these workmen to adjust to (rather than free themselves from) their inhuman jobs'. Munro suggests that Whyalla is merely a residential appendage to BHP and that 'mental health will not be at its best in Whyalla until a person may say something about the Company, only to have his listener ask "Which company?" '

Those workmen who cannot finds jobs in Whyalla because they have been blacklisted are usually forced to leave the town in search of employment. Workmen seem constantly aware of this ever-present threat and are able to quote case after case where this has happened to friends or workmates. Packing up possessions and resettling elsewhere can be a traumatic experience indeed for many families, especially immigrants who have never seen, let alone lived in, other parts of Australia. They might have to sell their home and furniture, take their children out of school, leave family and friends behind, and pray to find suitable work and accommodation elsewhere. Many families have financial commitments to meet: hire purchase contracts and payments on loans make the prospect of being unemployed quite daunting. Moreover, the flames of financial insecurity are fanned by apocryphal tales of hard times in other parts of Australia. Rumours asserting that there is no work in Adelaide or Melbourne constantly circulate in the Shipyard. Immigrants, and most other workmen for that matter, are not in a position to question the authenticity of these rumours and prefer not to place themselves in a position where they and their families have to find out the truth for themselves. It makes the prospect of being sacked by BHP all the more forbidding and this, inadvertently, acts as a very effective form of social and industrial control over employees. Workmen are fully aware of this form of control.

*   *   *

Close links also exist between the Company and the retail establishments of Whyalla. Several interviewees described how BHP encouraged them to do all their buying on hire purchase. The Company's employee liaison officer, who is required to assist and advise newly-arrived immigrants, took several of the families to large electrical and furniture stores and advised them to buy on credit or hire purchase.

Surrounded by hundreds of colour televisions, air-conditioners, extravagant hi-fi equipment, automatic washing machines and huge freezers, the assistant store manager told me that people were buying these appliances because they were much more affluent than past generations of manual workers. But after I had reminded him what current BHP pay rates were, he admitted that most manual workers cannot afford to pay cash when they are buying appliances; most use the hire purchase scheme. The workmen rely on overtime and shiftwork rates to settle these debts, whilst some have working wives who make the purchase of luxury items such as colour televisions possible. He went on to explain how the retail business in Whyalla is very dependent on, and sensitive to, the rate of steel production. At times, when BHP reduce production, resulting in a sharp drop in overtime and shiftwork, businesses experience 'staggering falls in sales'. According to him, many families are so dependent on overtime, that they have to sell their cars, freezers and televisions when the overtime is cut for prolonged periods. One cannot stress enough the indirect industrial control that an employer can have over a work-force that is deeply entrenched in time payments of one kind or another. Strikes, lay-offs, lock-outs, or simple cutbacks in overtime loom as serious threats to the livelihoods of workmen's families and they are easily encouraged to join the ranks of the other hard-working, obedient and industrially docile instruments of production.

III PROFESSIONAL WORK

13 Engineers and the Work that People Do*
Howard Rosenbrock

1 Introduction

The phenomenon which I wish to discuss in this paper can be illustrated by a plant which was making electric light bulbs in 1979. Production was 800 bulbs an hour, of the type having a metallised reflector and the components of the glass envelope were made elsewhere. They travelled on a chain conveyor around the plant, which occupied an area about 30 feet by 10 feet and was quite new. It was noisy, and the large room which housed it was drab, but conditions otherwise were not unpleasant.

The plant was almost completely automatic. Parts of the glass envelope, for example, were sealed together without any human intervention. Here and there, however, were tasks which the designer had failed to automate, and workers were employed, mostly women and mostly middle-aged. One picked up each glass envelope as it arrived, inspected it for flaws, and replaced it if it was satisfactory: once every 4½ seconds. Another picked out a short length of aluminium wire from a box with tweezers, holding it by one end. Then she inserted it delicately inside a coil which would vaporise it to produce the reflector: repeating this again avery 4½ seconds. Because of the noise, and the isolation of the work places, and the concentration demanded by some of them, conversation was hardly possible.

This picture could be matched by countless other examples, taken from any of the industrialised countries. Beyond the comment that the jobs were obviously bad ones, and that something should have been done about them, we are not likely to be surprised or to feel that the situation was unusual. Yet, as I shall hope to show, what has been described is decidedly odd.

* First published in *IEEE Control Systems Magazine*, Vol. 1, No. 3, September 1981.

2   A Design Exercise

To prepare the way, let us take one of the jobs, say the second one, and suppose that in a first year engineering degree course it was proposed, as a design exercise, to automate it. Picking up bits of wire out of box is obviously too difficult, but we can easily avoid it. Let the wire be taken off a reel by pinch rollers and fed through a narrow tube. At the end of the tube, let it pass through holes in two hardened steel blocks. Then we can accurately feed out the right length, and by displacing one of the steel blocks we can shear it off. If this is all made small enough, it can enter the coil, so that when the wire is cut off it falls in the right place.

So far, so good, but the coil may perhaps not be positioned quite accurately. Then, if we cannot improve the accuracy, we shall have to sense its position and move the wire feeder to suit. Perhaps we could do this by using a conical, spring loaded plunger, which could be pushed forward by a cam and enter the end of the coil. Having found its position in this way, we could lock a floating carriage on which the plunger and wire feeding mechanism were mounted, withdraw the plunger, and advance the wire feeder.

There would be scope here for a good deal of mechanical ingenuity, but of a kind which might not appeal to all of the students. 'Why not,' one of them might ask, 'why not use a small robot with optical sensing. The wire feeder could be mounted on the robot arm, and then sensing the position of the coil and moving the arm appropriately would be a simple matter of programming.'

An experienced engineer would probably not find much merit in this proposal. It would seem extravagant, using a complicated device to meet a simple need. It would offend what Veblen calls the 'instinct of workmanship,' the sense of economy and fitness for purpose. Yet the student might not be discouraged. 'All that is true,' he might say, 'but the robot is still economically sound. Only a small number of these plants will be made, and they will have to bear the development costs of any special device we design. Robots are complicated, but because they are made in large numbers they are cheap, while the development costs will be much less.'

After a little investigation, and some calculation, it might perhaps turn out that the student was right. A plant might even be built using a robot for this purpose. What I would like to suggest, however, is that this would not be a stable solution. It would still offend our instinct of workmanship. The robot has much greater abilities than this application demands. We should feel, like the robot specialist[2], that 'To bring in a universal robot would mean using a machine with many abilities to do a single job that may require only one ability.'

As opportunity served we might pursue one of two possibilities. We might in the first place seek to find some simpler and cheaper device which would replace the robot. Alternatively, having a robot in place with capacities which had been paid for but were not being used, we might attempt to create for it a task which more nearly suited its abilities. It might, for example, be able to take over some other task on a neighbouring part of the line. Or we might be able to rearrange the line to bring some other suitable task within the reach of the robot. At all events, as engineers we should not rest happy with the design while a gross mismatch existed between the means we were employing and the tasks on which they were employed.

3   The Application

The drift of this fable will have become clear. For robot, substitute man or woman, and then compare our attitudes. This I will do shortly, but first let me extend the quotation which was given above[2]: 'However, it is less obvious that robots will be needed to take the place of human beings in most everyday jobs in industry . . . To bring in a universal robot would mean using a machine with many abilities to do a single job that may require only one ability.' There is a curious discrepancy here between the apparent attitudes to robots and to people, and it is this which I wish to explore.

It will be readily granted that the woman whose working life was spent in picking up a piece of aluminium wire every $4\frac{1}{2}$ seconds had many abilities, and was doing a job which required only one ability. By analogy with the robot one would expect to find two kinds of reaction, one seeking to do the job with a 'simpler device,' and the other seeking to make better use of human ability. Both kinds of reaction do exist, though as will be seen, with a curious gap.

First, one cannot read the literature in this field without stumbling continually against one suggestion: that many jobs are more fitted for the mentally handicapped, and can be better done by them. The following are some examples.

'Slight mental retardation . . . often enables a person to do tedious work which would handicap a "normal" worker because of the monotony.[3]'

'The U.S. Rubber Company has even pushed experimentation so far as to employ young girls deficient in intelligence who, in the framework of "scientific management" applied to this business, have given excellent results.[4]'

'The tasks assigned to workers were limited and sterile . . . the worker was made to operate in an adult's body on a job that required the mentality and motivation of a child. Argyris demonstrated this by bringing in mental patients to do an extremely routine job in a factory setting. He was rewarded by the patients' increasing the production by 400 per cent.[5]'

'Mike Bayless, 28 years old with a maximum intelligence level of a 12 year old, has become the company's NC-machining-centre operator because his limitations afford him the level of patience and persistence to carefully watch his machine and the work that it produces.[6]'

Swain[7] remarks that 'The methodological difficulties of using this . . . approach to the dehumanised job problem cannot be glossed over' the meaning of which, one hopes, is that society would utterly reject it. Nevertheless, the quotations should alert our instinct of workmanship to the gross misalignment between human abilities and the demands of some jobs. A much more respectable response to this misalignment is the one which appeals to many technologists and engineers – that is, to carry the process of automation to the point where human labour is eliminated.

This becomes easier in manual work as the robot becomes cheaper and more highly developed. So, for example, in the manufacture of automobile bodies spot-welding is now regularly done by robots, and spray-painting also will soon cease to be a human occupation. Similar possibilities for eliminating human labour in clerical work are opened up by the microprocessor.

When it is applied to jobs which are already far below any reasonable estimate of human ability, there can be no objection on our present grounds to this development. Difficulties begin when we consider jobs that demand skill and the full use of human ability. To automate these out of existence in one step is never possible. They have to go first through a long process of fragmentation and simplification, during which they become unsuitable for human performance.

The mismatch between jobs and human abilities has also been approached from the opposite side by social scientists. Seeing the under-use of human ability, they have developed their techniques[8] of job enlargement, job enrichment, and of autonomous groups. These take existing jobs, and redesign them in a way which makes more use of the human abilities of judgement and adaptability. For example, in an autonomous group the allocation of tasks among its members is not imposed from outside but is left to the group itself to decide. The jobs that result can be better matched to human abilities, within the usually severe constraints of the technology. As Kelly[9] has noted, the opening which is given for the exercise of judgement and adaptability within the group may account for some of the increased productivity that has been observed.

These, then, are the techniques available to us for eliminating the mismatch between jobs and human abilities. There are two which reduce the abilities deployed, one of them inadmissible and the other stemming from engineering. There is a group of techniques which seek to use the abilities of people more fully, and these stem from the social sciences. So far as I know there are no others of significance; and what is remarkable is that engineers and technologists have not produced any methodology for using to the full the abilities and skills of human beings.

The designer of the lamp plant, for example, had made its operation automatic wherever he could do so conveniently. Where he could not, he had used human beings. He might perhaps have used robots, and if so he would have been concerned to use them economically and to make full use of their abilities. He felt, it appears, no similar concern for the full use of human abilities. We may say, paradoxically, that if he had been able to consider people as though they were robots, he would have tried to provide them with less trivial and more human work.

4 A Paradigm

The conclusion we have reached discloses the oddity which was mentioned at the beginning of this paper. It is one that becomes more strange the more one considers it, and we are bound to ask how it arises.

The question has two parts: how do individual engineers come to adopt the view we have described, and how did this originate and become established in the engineering profession? As to the individual, engineers in my experience are never taught a set of rules or attitudes which would lead to this kind of view, nor do they base their actions on a set of explicit principles incorporating it. Instead, we have to imagine something like the 'paradigm' discussed by Thomas Kuhn.[10] This is the name he gives, in the sciences, to matrix of shared attitudes and assumptions and beliefs within a profession.

The paradigm is transmitted from one generation to another, not by explicit teaching but by shared problem-solving. Young engineers take part in design exercises, and later in real design projects as members of the team. In doing so, they learn to see the world in a special way: the way in fact which makes it amenable to the professional techniques which they have available. Paradigms differ from one specialisation to another within engineering, so that a control engineer and a thermodynamicist, for example, will see a gas turbine in slightly different ways. Effective collaboration between them will then demand a process of mutual re-education, as many will have discovered from this or other kinds of collaboration.

Seen in this way, as a paradigm which has been absorbed without ever being made fully explicit, the behaviour of the lamp-plant designer becomes understandable. We still have to ask how this paradign arose. This is a question which deserves a more extended historical study than any I have seen. Tentatively, however, I suggest the following explanation, which has been given elsewhere[11] in somewhat greater detail.

Looking back at the early stages of the industrial revolution we tend to see the early machines as part of one single evolution. Examples of the machines themselves can be found in museums, and in looking at them we see the family resemblance which they all bear, deriving from the materials that were used and the means by which they were fashioned. They were made of leather and wood, and of wrought and cast iron, and in all of them these materials were fashioned in similar ways.

What I wish to suggest is that there were in fact two quite different kinds of machine, similar only in their materials and their construction, but with opposed relationships to human abilities. One of them can be typified by Hargreaves's spinning-jenny, which he invented for his own or his family's use. It is a hand-operated machine, deriving from the spinning wheel, but allowing many threads to be spun at the same time. To use it demands a skill, which is a natural development from the skill needed to use the spinning wheel. This skill in the user is rewarded by a great increase in his productivity. Samuel Crompton's spinning-mule was a similar kind of machine, and even when it was driven mechanically it needed the skilled cooperation of the spinner.

The other type of machine can be typified by the self-acting mule which was invented by Richard Roberts in 1830. What Roberts set out to do was not, like Hargreaves or Crompton, to make skill more productive. Rather he set out to eliminate skill so that the spinner was no longer needed except to supervise a set of machines. Fragments of his job remained, such as mending broken threads, or removing thread which had been spun. These jobs were given largely to children, and they began to resemble the jobs around the lamp-making plant.

For reasons which were valid enough in the early nineteenth century, and which are well documented by Ure[12] and Babbage[13], the second course proved more profitable for the inventor and the manufacturer than the first. When the engineering profession arose later in the century it therefore inherited only one attitude to the relation between machines and human skill, which is essentially the one described above.

Whether this attitude is appropriate at the present time is something which I should question. In a broad economic sense, the under-use of human ability is clearly a loss. Some of the reasons which made it nevertheless profitable for an early manufacturer no longer apply with the same force. Unskilled labour is still cheaper than skilled[13], but much less so than it was at an earlier period. Once only skilled workers could strike effectively[12], but the less-skilled now, by their numbers, may have even greater industrial strength.

Under present conditions, the motivation of workers may be a major preoccupation of managers. By 'quality circles' or other means they may strive to engage the abilities of the workers outside their jobs. By the social scientists' techniques of job-redesign they may seek to make the jobs themselves less repugnant to human ability. For engineers to spend effort and money at the same time on fragmenting jobs and reducing their content seems neither rational nor efficient, if there is any alternative.

5 An Alternative Paradigm

If Hargreaves and Crompton could develop machines which collaborated with the skills of workers in the eighteenth century can we not do the same in the twentieth century, using the incomparable power and flexibility of new technology? A major difficulty is that the problem is not generally posed as a choice between two alternative routes along which technology could develop. The engineering paradigm is not explicit, and it prevails not by a conscious choice, but by suppressing the ability to see an alternative. It is therefore useful to construct an example to show how a valid choice could indeed be made. This is not easy. At least 150 years of engineering effort have been given to one alternative, while the other has been ignored. One path is therefore broad, smooth and easy, the other narrow, difficult and rough. The example, however, need not be taken from engineering. What has been said applies equally to all technology, and will take on a new force as the advance of the microprocessor affects ever newer and wider areas.

What proves easiest is to choose as example an area where high skill exists, and where the encroachment of technology upon skill has hardly yet begun. In this way, both possible routes which technological development could follow are placed upon an equal basis. Following an earlier account[11], the example of medical diagnosis will be used.

Feigenbaum[14] has recently described a computer system called PUFF for the diagnosis of lung diseases. It uses information about patients obtained from an instrument and from their past history. The information is matched against a set of 'rules' which have been developed by computer scientists in collaboration with medical specialists. In the rules is captured the knowledge of the physician, part of which he was explicitly aware of knowing. Another part was knowledge which he used unconsciously and which only became explicit as he compared his own response with that of the computer.

Though still in an early stage of development, the system gave agreement of 90 to 100 per cent with the physician, according to the tests which were used. There is no difficulty in supposing that this and similar systems can be improved until they are at least as good as the unaided physician.

One way in which they might be used is to make the skill in diagnosis of the physician redundant. The computer system could be operated by staff who had not received a full medical training, but only a short and intensive course in the computer system and its area of application.

There might then be no difficulty in showing that the quality of diagnoses was as good as before, and possibly even better. The cost would be reduced, and a better service could be offered to the patient.

Alternatively, diagnosis might still be carried out by the physician, but he could be given a computer system to assist him in his work. Much that he had carried in his mind before would now be in the computer, and he would not need to concern himself with it. The computer would aid him by relieving him of this burden, and would allow him to carry on his work more effectively.

Under this second system, the physician would usually agree with the computer's diagnosis, but he would be at liberty to reject it. He might do so if, for example, some implicit rule which he used had not yet found its way into the computer system; or if he began to suspect a side effect from some new drug. Using the computer in this way, the physician would gradually develop a new skill, based on this previous skill but differing from it. Most of this new skill would reside in the area where he disagreed with the computer, and from time to time more of it might be captured in new rules. Yet there is no reason why the physician's skill in using the computer as a tool should not continually develop.

This is all speculation, but I believe not unreasonable speculation. Which of these two possible routes would be the better? The first leads, step by step, towards the situation typified by the lamp plant. The operators, having no extensive training, can never disagree with the computer, and become its servants. In time, the computer might be given more and more control over their work, requesting information, demanding replies, timing responses and reporting productivity. A mismatch would again arise between the abilities of the operators, and the trivialised tasks they were asked to perform. Social scientists might then be invited to study their jobs, and to suggest some scheme of redesign which would alleviate the monotony or the pressure of the work.

The second path allows human skill to survive and evolve into something new. It cooperates with this new skill and makes it more productive, just as Hargreaves's spinning jenny allowed the spinner's skill to evolve and become more productive. There seems no reason to blieve that this second path would be less economically effective than the first.

The example can be readily transposed into engineering terms. It applies with little change to the future development of computer-aided design. It suggests also that if we re-thought the problem, the operator's job on an MC machine tool need not be fragmented and trivialised, to the point where 'slight mental retardation' becomes an advantage. The task of making a part, from the description produced by a CAD system, could be kept entire, and could become the basis of a developing skill in the operator.

The task of developing a technology which is well matched to human ability, and which fosters skill and makes it more productive, seems to me the most important and stimulating challenge which faces engineers today. If they are held back from this task, it will not be so much by its difficulty, as by the need for a new vision of the relation between engineering and the use of human skill. That I should pose such a problem to engineers will indicate, I hope, the very high position which I give to the role of engineering.

6 Postscript

My paper could end at that point, but some readers may (and I hope will) feel a sense of unease. The argument which is developed above is in essence a broadly economic one. The skills and abilities of people are a precious resource which we are misusing, and a sense of economy and fitness for purpose, upon which we justly pride ourselves as engineers, should drive us to find a better relation between technology and human ability.

Yet economic waste is not the truest or deepest reason which makes the lamp plant repugnant to us. It offends against strong feelings about the value of human life, and the argument surely should be on this basis.

I wish that it could be, but my belief at present is that it cannot, for the following reasons. To develop such an argument we need a set of shared beliefs upon which to build the intellectual structure. Medieval Christianity, with its superstructure of scholastic philosophy, would once have provided the framework within which a rational argument could have been developed. By the time of the Industrial Revolution, this had long decayed, and nineteenth century Christianity did not unequivocally condemn the developments I have described.

Marxism provides an alternative set of beliefs, and a philosophical superstructure, and it utterly condemns the misuse of human ability: but only when it is carried on under a capitalist system. If it is carried on under socialism then Marxism seems not to condemn it unequivocally, and those are the conditions under which Marxism can have the greatest influence. In support, it is only necessary to say that the lamp plant was in a socialist state, and is in no way anomalous there.[15]

Humanism might serve as another possible basis, with its demand[16] 'that man make use of all the potentialities he holds within him, his creative powers and the life of the reason, and labour to make the powers of the physical world the instruments of his freedom.' This indeed underlies much of the thought in the social sciences, yet again it seems that no conclusive argument can be based on it.

The difficulties are twofold. First, no system of beliefs is as widely disseminated as industrial society. Therefore if a conclusive argument could be based on one system of beliefs, it would have only a limited regional force. Secondly, and almost axiomatically, if there is a system of beliefs from which some of the prevalent features of industrial society can be decisively condemned, it will not be found as the dominant set of beliefs in an industrialised country.

My own conclusion is that rejection of trivialised and dehumanised work precedes any possible rationalisation. Tom Bell[17] tells the following story of his mate who, day after day, sharpened needles in Singer's Clydebank works. 'Every morning there were millions of these needles on the table. As fast as he reduced the mountain of needles, a fresh load was dumped. Day in, day out, it never grew less. One morning he came in and found the table empty. He couldn't understand it. He began telling everyone excitedly that there were no needles on the table. It suddenly flashed on him how absurdly stupid it was to be spending his life like this. Without taking his jacket off, he turned on his heel and went out, to go for a ramble over the hills to Balloch.'

No very large part of the population so far has turned on its heel and gone for a ramble over the hills, though a mood akin to that does exist. If industrial society ever comes to be decisively rejected, it seems to me that it will be in this way and for these reasons, rather than as the result of a logically-argued critique. The thought, if valid, takes on a special significance at the present time, when we are engaged in determining the kind of work which men and women will do in the era of the microprocessor.

References

1. Veblen, Thorstein (1898), *The instinct of workmanship and the irksomeness of labour*, American Journal of Sociology, vol. 4, No. 2, pp. 187–201.
2. George, F.H. and Humphries, J.D. (ed. (1974), *The Robots are Coming*, p. 164 (NCC Publications).
3. Swain, A.D. (quoting M.L. Tinkham, 1971), *Design of industrial jobs a worker can and will do*, in S.C. Brown and J.N.T. Martin (ed.) (1977), *Human Aspects of Man-Made Systems*, p. 192 (Open Univ. Press).
4. Friedmann, Georges, (1955), Industrial Society, p. 216 (Free Press of Glencoe).
5. Herzberg, Frederick (1966), *Work and the Nature of Man*, p. 39 (World Publishing Co.).
6. American Machinist (July 1979), vol. 123, No. 7, p. 58.
7. Swain, *loc. cit.*
8. Drake, Richard I. and Smith, Peter J. (1973), *Behavioural Science in Industry* (McGraw-Hill).
9. Kelly, John E. (1978), *A reappraisal of sociotechnical system theory*, Human Relations, Vol. 31, pp. 1069–1099.

10. Kuhn, Thomas S. (1970), *The Structure of Scientific Revolutions*, passim, but especially pp. 181–187 (Univ. Chicago Press).
11. *New Technology: Society, Employment and Skill* (1981), (Council for Science and Society).
12. Ure, Andrew (1835), *The Philosophy of Manufactures* (Charles Knight, London); also *The Cotton Manufacture of Great Britain*, 1836 (Charles Knight, London).
13. Babbage, Charles (1832), *On the Economy of Machinery and Maufactures;* reprinted 1963 (Kelly, N. York).
14. Feigenbaum, Edward A. (1979), *Themes and case studies of knowledge engineering*, in D. Michie (editor), Expert Systems in the Micro-electronic Age, pp. 3–25. (Edinburgh Univ. Press).
15. Haraszti, Miklós (1977), *A Worker in a Worker's State* (Penguin Books).
16. Maritain, Jacques (1939), *True Humanism*, p. xii (Geoffrey Bles, Centenary Press).
17. Meacham, Standish (1977), *A Life Apart*, p. 137, quoting Tom Bell (Thames and Hudson).

14 Thinkwork*
Mike Hales

Editor's Introduction: This chapter is drawn from an 'analytical autobiography'. Hales worked as a chemical engineer and an operations research analyst at ICI. As a professional middle manager he attempts to understand the realities of his work experience as a 'thinkworker'.

And all this science I don't understand
It's just my job, five days a week . . .
(Elton John, 'Rocket Man'.)

What do white-collar workers do, what do they actually *make*? To set alongside the experience of 'middle management' existence in ICI, here I want to lay out the beginnings of a material analysis of that kind of work. By the time that I'm through you'll see, I hope, that what is at stake in the analysis is not only specific kinds of materials, tools, and products (some of which may seem quite trivial in comparison with those of manufacture proper – the chemical factory, the machine shop, the assembly line) but also very general and deeply-rooted structures of power. A proper analysis of the material conditions of work is also a political analysis.

Let's imagine there is such a thing as a typical job that I have been given, as an Operations Research Analyst working for ICI Organics Division. A new plant is to be built producing an intermediate for dyestuffs manufacture, and the design is well advanced. Doubts have arisen in the minds of the project steering groups: will interactions between stages of the process (plant items being occupied when required to receive a batch, and so on) prevent the plant reaching its designed throughput? If so, what modifications can be included before construction is complete: faster cycle times, more complex computer-control procedures, simpler (or better understood) process recipe, quality-control changes, manning changes? As a result of such uncertainties I have been asked, as a member of the Division's central Management Services group, to work with the design team and with technical development workers at the factory where the plant is being built, to construct a computer simulation model of the projected plant

* Extract from *Living Thinkwork*, CSE Books, 1980, pp. 46–58.

and thus to provide some of the data for further decisions of the steering group.

Of all the people I come into contact with on this job I am almost the most junior. A graduate with previous industrial experience and a higher degree, I entered on Grade 11 (there are fifteen grades) of the monthly-staff job-evaluation ladder, the lowest grade in the 'Blue Book'. (The caste system includes Green below and Black above, with other colours rumoured in the higher stratosphere.) The design team is all Blue or Black Book. One member of the team was at university with me as an undergraduate. With unbroken industrial experience as a chemical engineer, he is now on Grade 12 and promotion will soon come, as he moves with the plant from drawing board to factory reality. Average Blue Book salary at this time (1976) is £6,000 pa, I am on about £4,500. However, I'm answerable to neither of the Departments which predominate in the project (Production Department and Division Engineering Department) and this independent, small-p political base for my role is symbolised by the fact that nobody I deal with has technical command over the computer techniques needed to 'model' the problem. As someone whose practice intersects only marginally with the collective practice of 'the team' (I reckon to spend between one and three days a week on the project, mostly in my own office at headquarters) I have quite a lot of autonomy, formal hierarchy not-withstanding. There is too much going on for everything to be closely supervised (except in cost terms) and effects are so diffuse that, after the event, performance is arguable and reinterpretable.

The present centre of activity of the project is in South Manchester, at the office of the firm which has been contracted by ICI to do the detail design work and construction. To work on the model with the team, then, I travel for a full hour across Manchester and meet – by appoint-ment and on non-ICI premises – fellow Blue Book employees of ICI. (As I draft this I recall that one of the most active members of my union Branch back in North Manchester has been put onto the project staff here, thus kicking him into touch as far as day-to-day Branch politics are concerned.) The people I'm meeting have travelled from Yorkshire, Cheshire, and Ayrshire, as well as all parts of Greater Manchester, for this day's work. You might wonder how they make a 'team' on this basis. This is not the only naïve question which is worth answering.

We're in a new open-plan office, wall-to-wall carpet and air-conditioning, in a wing of the engineering contractor's head-office building. Behind the screens over there are the desks, about a dozen, of the design team. The Project Manager has an office on the side, two or three female secretaries occupy another. Very few team members are at their desks – it's murder trying to reach any of them by phone. Some are away at the site, discussing with the factory's engineers, managers, and technicians problems of design, construction, operation, and maintenance. One is at a supplier's factories in Germany, observing trials of equipment she has specified, and bargaining over quantity, quality, time and cost. All graduates, these. A couple of them are down one flight, in the big, open-plan drawing office. No screens here (it is possible to hide behind your drawing board when you want to) just glass-box offices for section heads and administrators. The people here are design and detail draughtsmen (the fashionable euphemism, 'draughtspersons', doesn't hide the reality), non-graduates. One of their number is up on our floor now, in the conference room with the rest of the design team.

In contrast to the desks, the conference room is almost always occupied. Line-diagram meetings, hazard-and-operability meetings, control-recipe meetings, and – when I can squeeze into the schedule – an occasional meeting to design the simulation model, plan its use, and interpret its performance. The process chemist and one of the chemical engineers, with several years experience of the old process at the Yorkshire factory, are in there now with the Project Manager. All three come over each day along the M62 trans-Pennine motorway. They're welcome to it, spaghetti junctions, jams, snow, juggernauts and all. Project Managers are drawn from a small section of the Division's Engineering Department, where the Company's accumulated expertise of process design resides, The department gets smaller all the time, with more and more reliance being placed on non-ICI design labourforces and non-ICI processes, so that engineers in ICI increasingly assume the role of liaison officers and junior project managers, with declining technical skills and increasing responsibilities for organising. Current rumour is that a Regional Engineering group will wipe out several Divisional Departments quite soon.

At the completion of this project some of the team and supporting staff will go on to another. Others will return to their general functions at the factories they came from. And others will be carried as part of the material flow of the project, promoted and uprooted two hundred miles to Scotland, to live with start-up and the early years of the new plant. The underpaid shift workers packing British Airway's in-flight breakfasts have the likes of these to thank for their livelihoods. Those whose lives become closely entwined with the design process have a relationship with their own families which at times is scarcely less remote than this relationship with the breakfast packers. Where does the team start and where does it end? Clearly, there are so many practices intersecting here (there are certainly more than I can mention) that any delimitation of the 'design labour process', or the 'white-collar labour process', or 'the scientific and technical labour process' will be highly contingent. We must have a relatively refined concept of what we're looking for before we can do this in a way which is practically and politically productive. As a first stab at identifying the products of the labour of so-called middle-management mental workers, and the materials on which their labour is expended (the objects of labour), take a look round the design office. What do they work on? The obvious answer – too obvious probably for most of us – is . . . paper. It's everywhere. Manuals, specifications, data sheets, drawings. Memos, telephone message slips. A second naïve answer follows the first: where is the design team – in the conference room; what are they producing – listen . . . sounds! So the design team produces . . . marks on paper and sounds? And its objects of labour are paper and air? Come off it, you're saying, stop playing the mad materialist. Well, I'm not. This is quite serious.

Do you think that it's merely crude materialism to point out that because of the properties of matter these sounds can not reach ears elsewhere; that these papers are, physically, on certain desks and will never be found in other than a limited number of locations? I don't. This is not, of course, the whole story. But there is a level, a whole structure of structures in the practice of white-collar workers, of which these are instances. A practice has a structure in time, space, energy and information (in its mathematical-cybernetic sense): these are dimensions of what I shall be calling, from now on, *objective* structure. Taken together the objective elements and relations of a practice constitute what we can call, for compactness, its *apparatus*. Part of our politically-theoretical attack on labour processes (more generally, on *practices*) must be to discover and delimit their apparatuses, to capture in concept the specific ways and places in which they connect with one another, and to try to say how far the practical whole is locked in a specific shape by the intersections of its objective structures with each other.

But there is also another level of the design team's practice which is perhaps more obvious. At least, the more conventional and stereotyped our notion of scientific practices, the more obvious we find this other aspect: Science, with a capital S, produces Knowledge, with a capital K. A main direction of my argument is that this conventional, idealist, view is dangerously misleading in its abstraction of 'knowledge' from specific connections of historical practice. Hence my flatfooted introduction of paper, air, and so on. To follow what sense there is in the conventional view, however, it is obvious that the *conceptual* production which takes place in scientific and technical practices is more significant than the physical production. For if the process-design practice doesn't produce concepts, what does it produce? Marks on paper? That'll make a lot of chemicals! Nevertheless, no matter how conventionally familiar the terrain we are now on, it's still not easy to find in it the objects that our middle-management specialists work on. More definition is needed.

The conceptual product of the team is 'the design'. It is a complex physical/chemical/logical concept, and the objects that have been worked to produce it (in a quite novel and creative way – the process is genuinely creative) are the knowledges of various sciences: physics, chemistry, engineering science, and other, more empirical, bodies of know-how. Now look again. The design has more sides to it than just 'scientific'; it is a *managerial* and a *business* concept too. The design is a concept of a chemical plant which must:

   i) work, physically, to produce certain transformations in matter, constituting certain physical products from specified feedstocks

  ii) be stable and manageable in operation, within the limits of the Company's manpower resources and policies.

 iii) produce products in such a way that 'adequate' profit can be extracted through their sale in the markets to which the Company has access.

On the way to the final product, then, concepts of a profitable process route and a manageable plant have been produced and worked in together with the 'scientific' concept. In fact many knowledges (more or less formal and explicit, theoretical and ideological) have been taken as objects of mental labour in the design process. They have been worked on, transformed, developed, articulated, to produce a highly concrete composite knowledge, a design. This kind of process of producing and (not all the thinking is creative) reproducing concepts, is the central reality to which we must address ourselves when we look for the political dimensions of the working lives of mental workers. It is not easy to do this in a non-idealist way, but we'll have a go.

The job of ICI workers, as ICI continually tells them (paper-producers most of all), is to make chemicals, and though this is far from an adult truth there is enough in it to make a point. Somehow, through some highly complex and opaque but determining system of relations, the design team is supposed to operate on feedstocks to produce saleable, profitable products. They are supposed to operate on steel and concrete and electronic components to produce an operable chemical plant. This is not just a metaphorical way of speaking. If ICI top managers did not believe that such a connection would in fact operate, there would *be* no project design teams. By extending the intersecting network of practices far enough we could eventually see the connection: the concept ('the design') is given objective form first in calculations and drawings and models, then re-produced in specifications and drawings, once more in equipment and components, and finally in the operational reality of the plant at start-up. Along the way many sorts of labour are associated with reproducing and expanding the material articulation of the concept – literally *re*-producing it. It would take a long time to follow it through thoroughly and in detail, but there is a material connection between the design team and the physical product, chemicals. This highly developed system of connecting practices, linking ideas and artefacts, is what goes under the name of the *forces of production*, in this particular part of this particular industrial sector.

So, it's not just poetic licence to say that the designers produce chemicals. We can follow through the material connections; and if there is no *material* connection, there is no *connection*. That is, if we want to claim that there is a connection between two aspects of reality, we have to be prepared to map out the network of practices which materially constitutes it. It is in this way that we start to put together an *actionable* picture of the politics of knowledge.

How is the remote, real (and as yet non-existent) object of process-design labour brought into the process-design labour process? How is this extensive and complex (if only partial) system of forces of production given its coherence and dynamism? How is it that this particular group of workers, from widely scattered origins and homes, with a wide range of disciplinary backgrounds, comes to spend so much time and sweat (*I* wouldn't want the piles, ulcers, and indigestion of a senior engineering project worker) on producing this very specific object? This is hardly likely to have happened by chance. In this case (which is a relatively simple case within the general range of 'scientific' labour processes) the answer can be given crudely in a sentence. These workers group themselves for this particular, difficult, form of collective labour, and this real object enters so dominantly into their practice as conceptual workers, because they *are* workers – wage-workers, employed by ICI capital. (Why they work so *hard* is another question, and wage-labour doesn't amount to a whole answer.)

The relation between the conceptual object and the real object of the design practice is neither single nor simple, but rather a resultant of various relations of production which order all monopoly-capitalist organisation. There is a hierarchical division of labour between design engineers and detail draughtsmen. Design engineers and their instruments of labour (computers, desks, design manuals, telephones, the Manchester-Glasgow shuttle) are brought together by the grace of ICI-capital, which selectively extends to some of those bound by labour contracts the privilege of materially appropriating, directly in their day-to-day work, these instruments of labour. Plant managers, process workers, and design engineers stand in a wage-labour relation with ICI. And so on. This skeleton of relations of production is what brings the plant into the design office as a product of conceptual labour, and takes the conceptual product back out into the factory. This system of social relations, characteristic of a particular kind of historical society, determines the particular coherence of the design practice and the forces of production as a whole – a coherence which hinges upon contradictoriness.

You and I, if we were chemical engineers, couldn't afford to work this way on our own account. We have to work as employees of somebody who owns the sophisticated tools and can pay for all the running around that is needed. In this way, through wage-labour and private ownership, the new chemical plant is constituted right from the start as an alien thing, confronting first the design team and then, even more massively and materially, the process workers. A *fait accompli*: here you are brother, struggle with THAT. It is the ability to raise a structure in imagination before erecting it in reality that marks off human activity from other kinds. Yet even when this major truth was first put in these terms – by Marx in the nineteenth century – the separation of 'architects' and 'labourers' was deeply entrenched in social practice. Today – in our chemical plant design process – there is one obvious and terrible fact: labourers and architects are not the same people. The process worker is not the design engineer. Nor do they work together. The pre-conceptualising power of the collective architect is vastly greater now than in Marx's day, the forces of conceptual production (state planning bureaucracies, NASA, the R&D establishment) have developed quantitatively and qualitatively. And the collective labourer is relatively more powerless, more *ignorant*, because of the existence of this knowledge-producing estate.

We have here the beginnings of a formulation of a politics of knowledge. How knowledge is parcelled and distributed, aggregated and abstracted, linked and fragmented: these real relations and the practices which carry them are central in defining the forms and the potential of socialist struggle in a world of ICIs.

Let me recap how I've worked my way round to this (as-yet unrigorous) formulation. As an ICI conceptual worker involved in a particular job, my first step was to analyse-out any 'detachedness' that might initially appear to characterise my labour's product. The knowledge which I'm working, with others, to produce is not a disembodied idea, but a product of the labour of a particular group of people, organised in a determinate way (with specific tools and permitted starting-points) to yield a specific end product. This is pretty obvious with industrial knowledge-work in general, but it applies no less to pure science, now or in the past. (This is not to say that organisation is always so consciously or conspicuously imposed on the practice.) Any knowledge implies a definite material system of practices, which produced it and continue to reproduce it as an active element of social thought within a historical social formation. No knowledge exists apart from concrete historical practice, and no knowledge is properly known until its practical connections are known.

The next step was to look beyond the obvious product – a concept – to find a real object associated with the work. Again, this is something you would do in analysing any scientific labour, although the real object of a 'pure' scientific practice won't be anything so vulgarly capitalist as an ICI chemical plant. Some sciences (like old-style pure maths) may not even have a real object at all, being non-experimental and non-observational, as we say. Even if this is so – and it's a tricky question – then it is an exception, to be explained as such, in the same way that we would account for the *presence* of a real object.

The final step is to figure out how the real object came to be there (or absent). How did the particular gang of knowledge-workers come to be beavering away in relation to it (if not actually *on* it, as in a lab – forgetting for a moment the division of labour within the modern laboratory)? What we're looking for is not primarily the motivations of the individual workers, though these are important to the political organiser. We're looking for the material connections which span the distance between knowledge-workers and the larger world, from out of which a certain object (conceptual or physical) has been abstracted to serve as the object of their think work. What practices had to exist in order that this particular abstraction could be made? In the case of the design team, what system of practices is it which makes it socially acceptable for the team to spend time and resources on their particular labour? What system of practices is it which makes it materially possible for the team to piece together the knowledge that they do succeed in piecing together? Where have the objects and tools of the labour process come from, and where have the workers come from, in terms of personal history?

We need answers to questions of this kind, in order to locate historically the forces of production which we encounter in any specific practical context. What we are looking for are those general social relations which appear time and again in giving structure to large-scale practices in society. The search for these relations of production leads to a political analysis of work, for relations of production are relations of social control.

More fundamentally than relations of circulation or distribution, relations of production determine what kinds of power can lie with which groups in society. In this final section I want to rework my description of process design, showing how design workers are implicated in this power game in monopoly capitalist society. Let's look again at the apparatus of the design process and the ways that this links up with the apparatus of chemical production. Although the labour of the design team is by and large conceptual labour, the dead labour is carried into other labour processes massively in objective form: papers, documents. (Equipment specifications, chemical process specifications, flowsheets, detail drawings, construction schedules, component listings and layouts for piperuns, software for the on-line process-control computer, critical-path software for dishing-out job sheets to the construction workers.) Somehow this mass of objectively-ordered dead labour has to act effectively as a link between the design team and many, many others inside and outside the structure of ICI, in such a way that the whole practice is under control. Crucially, at the end of the day, this dead labour must have determined an intensive and extensive ferment of living labour, in such a way that the plant will produce, and produce manageably, and produce profitably. How is this miracle of social control achieved?

In case you're beginning to wonder whether I attribute some kind of esoteric magical power to paper, the first point to note is that the documents don't have to carry all the connections between the many practices involved. There are lots of direct, person-to-person connections; and other less direct connections (through general culture, the Company's and the profession's custom and practice – and also, of course, through the markets for labour and other commodities) which do not rest, in any essential way, on any of the separate individuals whom we would see if we observed the entire project from drawing-office to start-up. But let's see how far we can get with an account of what *can* be carried by the objective products of the design team.

Well, the team will have thought long and hard about the extent to which manual functions can be automated out of the production process, thus securing 'reliability', 'efficiency', 'quality' and suchlike attributes, without increasing costs beyond what the business traffic will allow. These attributes are seen as engineering considerations, but in my terms they represent a set of limited mental approaches within which the relations of capital and living labour can be thought through. The labour to be 'saved' is by no means simply manual; manual' functions are *people* functions, functions requiring living labour. The key skills of a designer lie in thinking through capitalist relations of production in concrete terms. The objective is to give these relations an expanded or new embodiment, in the material form of direct practical connections between living labour (process workers, maintenance workers, production managers) and dead labour (process plant, the on-line computer, the maintenance workshop, the chemical product). In becoming a good engineer it has to be learned that reliability, safety, quality and the rest have no absolute limits. In practice, concrete material limits have to be imposed on them in relation to what can be *afforded*. This negotiation, which precedes the materialising of new forces of production, is political. It is political in a commonplace sense because it is to do with judging how various conflicting and contradictory interests within the Company (unions's, works engineer's, production managers', sales managers', the designers themselves) can be accommodated within the objective limits of a configuration of plant. It is political in a more subtle sense too: it is a process of re-producing the relations of production of a historical social formation. Producing, reproducing, and subverting systems of relations of production is what I mean by politics.

How can the operation of plant be made foolproof? This is a key question for designers. The chemical industry differs from, say, the motor industry in that 'fooling' (meaning sabotage or just arsing about) is not such a noted problem as far as the mythology of the industry goes. Many questions concerning the plant's ultimate manageability come up instead in the form of questions about the chemical stability of the process, and the maintenance of process conditions via (automatic and manual) control procedures. In most cases I think that these issues are resolved in a straightforward 'scientific' or 'economic' manner, with no suggestion that the control of workers' unauthorised *behaviour* is a major but hidden aspect of design (this would not be true in many cases of transfer-line design in the motor industry). Although they are less emotive and explicitly political, however, the questions of managerial control over the workers which are considered in the design of chemical plants are no less basic. ICI managers are constantly grappling with the problem of how intensity of labour and active commitment to the Company's business interests can be simultaneously improved. Such questions are inevitably raised in the design process, because the plant manager-designate and his leading shift managers are members of the design team.

Among other things, they want to know how the plant will work in terms of labour allocation and supervisability, and how the cultural reality of the Weekly Staff Agreement (WSA) will interact with the new plant's task requirements. It may not often be the case that the best design, in a techno-commercial sense, has to be compromised in order to meet the practical needs of plant management at this level. (It might happen, for example, that a particular outlying work station would be brought closer to the main paths of activity within the plant by using more expensive automated equipment, in order that a more senior process worker – who would distort the pyramidal structure of WSA job-grades within the plant or Area – will not be required to occupy that place in the labour process.) Whether the technical content of the design is affected or not, however, the point to be made is that this kind of pre-negotiation of reality is an intrinsic part of the design activity. In concept, the forces of production – as they will be materialised in steel and concrete and flesh, in the real labour process – have to be brought into as harmonious a relation as possible with the exigencies of managerial control as well as with market relations. The design codifies the outcome of this navigation of a contradictory reality, as carried out within the ranks of management and technical aides.

The concept of the labour process of chemicals production, as carried out into the world by the design documents, is substantially complete in most technical essentials and many other details. The conditions (of health and safety, of isolation, of ignorance and awareness, of interdependence) in which work will take place are already closely determined. There certainly will be things that the design team have overlooked, or have decided to leave to be resolved by trial and error, or could not have foreseen. There will be loopholes and shortcuts and changing conditions (of manning or culture or mechanical functioning or profitability) that the process workers will discover and exploit, to reclaim some ICI time for non-ICI objectives personal objectives such as relieving boredom or gaining satisfaction, collective objectives such as reducing health risk and increasing income and minimising insecurity. But to go further than this – to challenge the general determinants of how they spend this large part of their lives, working – they will have to surmount or destroy a vast obstacle. This is it: although many of the most fundamental conditions of the society they live and work in have been consciously worked in to the technical apparatus of their working day – put there by the plant's designers – these designed relations are far from obvious. Because they have been thought at such a concrete level and then materialised in the apparatus of production, the generality of these relations has been made effectively invisible.

The concept of what work may and may not produce, the open- or closed-ness of the forces of production in relation to collective social effort, is not written on the face of reality as the workers confront it. The social process lies behind the plant and the daily routine, and although its social and political content can be read back into it, the fact has to be stressed that all the living labour embodied in the plant took place at some other time, in some other place, involved some other workers: effectively a different world. The dead conceptual labour of the designers confronts living labour in the designed labour process with a flat challenge: Either do the obvious (which we have actually made obvious so that you will not have to think about it) or unravel the social and historical conditions that are woven into the situation – and do it in your spare time, because *you* are not paid to think.

This is the reality of what I call *preconceptualisation*. It is a political reality because preconceptualisation is an extremely general and well entrenched relation of production in monopoly-capitalist societies. In exploring how we are constrained in what we do 'at work' – not necessarily, in any iron-clad logical sense, but historically – the notion of preconceptualisation is crucial. In its place in labour-process theory, this concept offers some novel ways of thinking about a socialist politics of production.

15   The Housewife
S. Gail

I married as soon as I graduated, explicitly anti-domestic, and bent on proving to myself that it was possible to combine marriage (an intense personal relationship mainly, but also a family much later) with unprejudiced exploration of literary values often remote from healthy-mindedness, hygiene and a stable society focused on the family . . .

We had a flat which accumulated fluffy dust balls ankle-deep till a parental invasion was expected. Then we spent a few hours together making it respectable in order to avoid intrusive criticisms.

Carl was conceived unexpectedly that year, and the summer before he was born we moved to another flat. This was a great, rambling old place which we shared with an eccentric poetical colleague. He used to empty his pipe into my buckets of soaking nappies, and leave his part of the flat open to mating couples when he was away. I was shaken out of my cavalier attitude to housework. The baby immediately caught enteritis, and I was shattered by guilt when the doctor attributed this to the dirty flat. The housework proved enormously difficult in itself, partly because I was still tired, partly because the place was so large and dilapidated. I was humbled by the discovery that what I had considered work fit only for fools was beyond my capacity. Worst of all, Joe, who had regarded my non-domestication with complete tolerance, suddenly found the dirt and untidiness depressing, and begat status yearnings. As a man with a wife, a son and a salary for the uncongenial job foisted on him by Carl's appearance, he wanted a clean shirt every day, not just as something practical, but as his *right*. We were jolted out of our self-sufficiency, and reverted desperately for a while to Mummy's and Daddy's standards. If Joe was indignant when the dinner was burnt, I felt he had every right to regard me as a failure. And I sterilised everything that came remotely into contact with Carl, becoming deeply involved in germs. This provoked some passably hysterical scenes with

* Abridged from R. Fraser, *Work*, Vol. I, Penguin Books, Harmondsworth, 1968.

our unfortunate poet, who held a generous communistic view of flannels and tooth-brushes.

The following autumn Joe got a university post, and we moved to the flat we are in now. . . .

I have long since passed the point where control of the housework seemed unattainable, and Carl as he grows older requires fewer and fewer elementary attentions. But I realised recently that I have developed an absurd cyclical pattern which stretches over a period of one or two months. I work up to a point where every room is in so organised a state that it requires only a few touches every morning to keep it perfectly clean and tidy (by my standards). Even the occasional job like dusting books or cleaning the cooker are done, and I move briskly from room to room in quite the efficient manner. The hearth is not only brushed after I've laid the fire – it is wiped and polished. As I work evangelical hymn-jingles from my carefully obliterated past well up in my mind. But I cannot achieve that degree of irony. It would be hubris, and the walls might fall in if I started chanting,

I'm H–A–P–P–Y.

Perhaps this stage lasts a week or two. Joe has his clean shirt every day *and* clean underwear; Carl is bathed several times. Then suddenly I flop. Every gesture requires an effort of will. The flat quickly sinks into chaos, dishes are washed under the tap as they are needed, and the airing cupboard stinks of urine because I have dried Carl's pants out instead of washing them. On Sunday evening I pick over the litter on the bedroom floor to find Joe's clothes to wash for Monday. The dinner comes out of tins, and far from presenting a clean hearth, the fire doesn't even get lit. Worst of all, that oasis in the afternoon when Carl is asleep and I can at last get down to my books, I waste destructively by going to bed. I have usually reached that point of tiredness where it takes some moments of fumbling to fix a plug in its socket, and there is an area of buzzing and shimmering between me and what I am trying to do, so I sleep. But my dreams are of the things I am trying to forget; static dreams, like a nauseating plateful of steaming sprouts.

What seems most undermining is that housework is anathema to concentration and intensity. Joe tells me I am freer than he is – I can do things in my own time without pressure from anybody. But that seems to me poor compensation for the sameness of jobs that require perhaps less than a quarter of one's mental awareness, while leaving the rest incapable of being occupied elsewhere. When something happens to stimulate me to my former awareness – an enjoyable social occasion, or the tutorials which I still give once a fortnight in the university – I feel I have come back to life; I am ashamed to admit that quite frequently I come home afterwards in a mood of savage rejection. I intended of course to carry on with my thesis quite as if nothing had happened after having Carl. I wanted him very much once I was pregnant, but expected him to play a limited role whose boundaries I was going to set. Alas! Long after I had pulled myself out of the morass of the first few months, come to look on Carl as something other than a cataclysm, and worked myself into a fever pitch of busyness to get everything necessary done first (I used to run to the shops), I was still not getting my thesis written. Two substantial chapters were already done, I was amassing ample material for a third – it was a genuinely interesting subject – and there, except for one joyous week last summer when they were both away, it still stands. I began to feel guilty about this failure too, because I had been so overweeningly confident in my ability to look after a baby, do the housework, and write a thesis, that I was still drawing a research scholarship. When it became obvious that I really was not capable of getting the thesis written in the circumstances, I had out of honesty to resign the money. My self-respect began to rot away. Step by step I dropped all the small rituals of vanity, and for a while it was a great effort even to bath. . . .

I let the flat get dirty when I am depressed, and the dirt depresses me further, even though I do not consider myself immoral for slipping into that state. Yet even this is not simply true; my happiest moods may coincide with the worst disorder. Then I am absorbed in thoughts of something else, and no longer notice my surroundings. Even when the flat is at its best it seems slightly sordid; we can't afford the spatial escape a car would give us, and mental 'escape' has to do instead.

My hair-style is also an indication of the mood I am in. I grew it long one period when I was feeling resigned to this female role. Shortly after I had Carl I cropped my hair down to about an inch all over. It was a rejection of femininity because the dependency feeling pleasantly aroused by pregnancy, far from disappearing after giving birth as I had expected, intensified beyond all bearable limits. Feeling motherly seemed to be the last thing I would ever find time for, and an enormous chasm opened between me pregnant, and me with a deflated belly, my hands immersed in filthy nappies. I would not be so crudely symbolical with my hair now. I have achieved a measure of true independence within myself in the teeth of the last two years, and feel no need to flaunt it in the face of men. It is there, and does not need their recognition to exist. It was never a burden to me to be a woman before I had Carl. Feminists had seemed to me to be tilting at windmills; women who allowed men to rule them did so from their own free choice. I felt that I had proved myself the intellectual equal of men, and maintained my femininity as well. But afterwards I quite lost my sense of identity; for weeks it was an effort to speak. And when I again became conscious of myself as other than a thing, it was in a state of rebellion which I had to clamp down firmly because of Carl. I also grew very thin, and I still do not menstruate. This self-imposed penance, or this disgust at my subservience, had repercussions on all of us, some of which have still to be worked out. In a sense it is a triumph and a release not to menstruate. I have my sexual self intact with almost no danger of being called to account for it by pregnancy. But it seems that now I can achieve nothing unequivocally. I should hate Carl to be an only child; I know too well what it means to inflict that on him. But treatment of amenorrhoea is lengthy, and success uncertain. Meanwhile the time when I shall no longer be housebound recedes into the distant future.

My most obvious way back to feeling creative is to write the thesis, and I think I shall soon be able to tackle it again. The practical problem of libraries is minor compared with the fear I have felt of not being able to concentrate in the same way as before. It is not only mental concentration that is sapped by baby care and housework, it is personality concentration as well. A baby demands the whole of you. Before I had him I could turn away from everybody, into myself or my books, if I needed to; it was on this basis that I had resources and kept myself balanced. But I remain turned towards Carl even when he is asleep. At first this was a terrible burden. Now I bear it lightly, but not so lightly that I have felt safe so far in resuming the thesis in the odd periods of free time I have. . . .

Perhaps this seems to be an aside from 'work', but Carl and housework are so closely interwoven that I cannot mention one without the other. This is especially true since I could never consider the possibility of staying at home as a housewife, even part-time, if I had no child to humanise the work for me. Office or factory work seems more annihilating because even less of me would be involved, but if I were given the choice between that or housework I would rather be out working in any conditions. My feelings of satisfaction or happiness are never connected with the housework, and are often in strict opposition to it, because Carl's vivacity and lawlessness oppose the reign of order and hygiene. I have of course received such a specialised education, voluntarily, that I would have to undergo a radical character change in order to fit the new mould adequately. That is a possibility, but one I have rejected. The other possibility, which I sought urgently for a long while, is to have other babies; I would then be so engrossed in the work entailed that I would not have time for thoughts of freedom till I emerged on the other side, maybe. But I have explained how this has not come about. I am not a bad mother most of the time, and might be a much better one in social conditions which did not try to integrate two hostile activities, but I am an incurably bad houseworker because I cannot pretend it is an essential, personalised task. Joe's work is much more necessary – we all live on it. Housework is housework, whoever does it. . . .

The mornings are always my worst time – the day stretches ahead in dreary sameness, with no possibility of anything unexpected; I would rather listen to anything or nothing than Housewives' Choice. The thought of all those millions of women performing exactly the same gestures as me, enclosed in their little circular activities, and perhaps with no desire or possibility of ever escaping, depresses me more than I can say. By the evening I am battered down to size, and Roundabout and Playtime, which are much younger programmes anyway, afford a very welcome relief.

When the housework was still new, I used to take a little pleasure in finding ways of doing the jobs quicker and better. But it is an exhaustible subject of interest, as you can tell by the way I keep veering off it. Now I am simply bent on eliminating as many tasks as possible. This is sensible to a certain extent. Joe did not notice the sheets were unironed last week, so it seems pointless to iron them any more – but it does cut the ground from under my feet. Another factor that undermines my interest is having to keep my mind on two things at once. I used to get very tense carrying on with a task while making sure Carl was not getting into trouble. I have overcome that by freeing the surface of my mind from thoughts altogether, leaving it swimming aimlessly so that it can be called into action by an alarming sound. This is a further loosening of concentration, and one that has to be practised for a distressingly large part of the day, often leaving me too empty for real concentration when the chance comes. And, as I said, any inclination I might have to take my work seriously is comically scotched by Carl himself, in his constructive moments as much as his destructive ones. Anything I do attracts his attention, so if I tidy a room he picks up the object as I put it down. Or if I clean windows on his level he comes after me, imitating my movements with his hands, and smearing what I have just done. Even if I give him a duster his fingers slip off; it is the movement he is intent on, not the sense of the gesture. I begin to feel hilariously unreal.

It is constantly niggling not only to be doing jobs that require so little valuable effort, but also jobs which are mainly concerned with simply keeping level with natural processes – cleaning jobs, whether of objects or for people, which once done are not done for good, and will have to be done all over again, just as if I have not already made the effort, the next day, or even within a few hours. There is something so negative about this role that society heaps entirely on to the shoulders of women, that of making sure things do not get dirty, and people do not get unhealthy. I want to believe in health as something basic, neutral, to assume that all the essentials are cared for, or at least will not magnify themselves into a full-time occupation. In my research I always felt at the end of a day's reading, writing or teaching that I had somehow added to life, enriched my experience, moved forward in a quite tangible sense . . .

Life that does not move forward seems to me to stagnate, and in this sense I cannot help seeing Carl as a parasite. He can move forward to the time when he will no longer need me only on the understanding that I am prepared to stand still and grow older quietly, without too much fuss. My life slips away uncharted precisely when I am most eager to find out what I am capable of. I sit crouched in a chair, feeling all that useless and unwanted power suppressed inside me. I neither feel I have married the wrong man, nor that I don't want Carl, but I often wish that I had not had such confidence in my ability to ignore the established meaning of marriage, and had waited a few years longer before marrying. Sometimes I want to stretch out my arms to bring the whole imprisoning structure of home and family crashing around me, annihilating me with the rest. This is the only possibility, unreal as it is, that presents itself vividly to me. To walk out is never a real, live image, although I am curious to know how much of me would be left if I did. This, all round me, is my only creation so far, however incomplete and shoddily achieved; my split function goes too deep to be resolved by such a gesture.

Can you imagine what would happen to a man who was suddenly uprooted from a job in which he placed the meaning of his life, and delegated to a mindless task, in performing which he was also cut off fairly completely from the people who shared his interests? I think most of the men I know would disintegrate completely. (The maternal 'instinct' is a comfortable male myth; a woman can only give freely if she is in a position where she does not feel deprived herself.) This is only a small example, but after two years of the sights and smells of a baby, Joe still refuses to change a nappy, except once a fortnight when I am literally not there to do it. He plays with Carl better than I, because the responsibility is not in terms of his own personal success. But chores are a different matter . . .

The way the family is structured leads inevitably to tyranny, against all one's clearsightedness and efforts to avoid it. Financial and patriarchal tyranny in Joe, however discreet its expression, is a reality, and it drives me to tyrannise over Carl. Then Joe will often reassert justice – by siding quite rightly with Carl against me. I would not believe a girl who claimed this had not happened to some extent in her family, because I know how hard we have struggled to avoid it.

Housework in these circumstances also constitutes an outright attack on femininity. It suddenly becomes a problem to keep slim, an impossibility to look attractive all the time. . . .

As in everything else, men's viewpoints prevail, so there are no new nursery schools being built. And there are so few state places that, in this town at least, you have to put the baby's name down by the time he is six months old. I have managed to get Carl into a private nursery school in a few months' time, afternoons only; some of those afternoons I shall spend teaching to pay for it, and I hope there will be some left for writing my thesis. He was sociable enough to spend half days at school months ago. . . .

I know many of his frustrations could be sorted out by a good nursery class, where he was given something constructive to do, and more company of his own age than I can arrange at the moment.

It would obviously be beneficial to Carl not to have to live with me so much. Perhaps it is unfair of me to blacken other more adaptable women with my dirt, but I feel it should be more widely recognised that it is in the very nature of a mother's position, in our society, to avenge her own frustrations on a small, helpless child; whether this takes the form of tyranny, or of smothering affection that asks the child to be a substitute for all she has missed. . . .

There are odd moments exquisitely satisfying in themselves, moments when I identify myself with Carl's discoveries. I suddenly see into his mind as if it were my own. One day he bent down to scratch a pale spot on the pavement with his fingernail, to find out if it was raised or level. Maybe without my book knowledge I would not have noticed, or not realised what he wanted to know. Or I can anticipate his discoveries; he looks at a toy vehicle sideways, and I ask him how many wheels it has. He answers two, so I turn it upside down for him to see all four.

In postscript, it is obvious that Carl is quite the best thing that has ever happened to me. And Joe isn't a tyrant.

---

16   Being Out of Work⋆
A. Sinfield

The Experience of Unemployment
Of all the reactions to being out of work for the first time, surprise is the most common. This point has emerged in every study of unemployment, certainly since the war, that I have ever read. It indicates the lack of awareness about the problems of being out of work among the rest of the population and may help to account for the generally unsympathetic and often very suspicious attitude towards the unemployed. As one apprenticed tradesman in his early twenties commented in 1979: 'It's changed my attitudes to the unemployed. I used to think they were just skivers and was quite a lot against them, but now that I've experienced it, it's no joke, man' (Newcastle, 1980, p. 35). Another in North Tyneside said, 'once you've been on the dole yourself, you begin to think differently about the other people there. You can't help it, and you realise that perhaps they can't either'. It was the actual experience of unemployment that led these workers to alter their own opinions of what it was like to be out of work and so to start breaking down their own stereotypes of the unemployed.

Some men spoke with considerable contempt of the others they met at the dole but this distancing did not seem to appear among those who had been out of work for a couple of months or more. It is perhaps more common among those who seem to feel the acutest shame and stigma at being out of work themselves. 'This feeling that people are looking down on you was sometimes accompanied by the ironic comment that the respondent himself had probably done the same when he was working' (Newcastle, 1980, p. 32). Keen awareness of the status of being unemployed comes through in interview after interview. Men who have lost their jobs, and are officially registered as unemployed while looking for work, have gone out of their way to emphasise that they are not unemployed but redundant.

Each time unemployment tends to rise, there are suggestions that the

---

⋆ Extract from *What Unemployment Means*, Martin Robertson, Oxford, 1981, pp. 35–57.

stigma of unemployment has been substantially reduced, which not only eases the strain and tension for the unemployed but reduces the social pressure on them to get back to work at the first possible opportunity. To some observers, increased unemployment itself is seen as acting to reduce the speed with which the total declines.

It is therefore important to emphasise the continuing feelings of stigma and shame expressed by many of the unemployed. These feelings may be reduced at a major redundancy but the quotations above show that it may return very quickly. Joe Kenyon has been giving welfare rights advice for many years and is continuing to get letters or phone calls that begin 'I have never been out of work' or 'my husband has never been out of work'. A harmless thing to say, you might think. But think about it some more. 'Never been out of work' – does it mean that this should carry some kind of privilege, as against the one who has been out of work before? If one can claim, with an injured pride, that this is the first experience of unemployment, then one is establishing more deserving status. The implication is that those with repeated experiences of unemployment have a more questionable claim for sympathy and special help.

Obviously, the impact of unemployment on those out of work and their families varies enormously. There is a great difference between two weeks and two years on the dole. It will be all the greater if the short-term unemployed has already found work before his last job ended while the long-term unemployed has become disabled or finds his skill is no longer needed, and may despair of ever working again. There will also be differences between individuals because of their different personalities. But one general thesis has begun to appear more and more frequently in discussions of the unemployed and is now in danger of becoming part of the conventional but unproven wisdom about the impact of unemployment on the individual. In the late 1930s a hypothesis on the 'psychology of unemployment' emerged from a detailed review of literature by Eisenberg and Lazarsfeld:

First there is shock, which is followed by an active hunt for a job, during which the individual is still optimistic and unresigned; he still maintains an unbroken attitude. Second, when all efforts fail, the individual becomes pessimistic, anxious and suffers active distress; this is the most crucial state of all. And, third, the individual becomes fatalistic and adapts himself to his new state with a narrower scope. He now has a broken attitude. [1938, p. 378]

Despite their cautious qualifications to this hypothesis, stressing the very poor quality and imprecision of much of the research, and despite the fact that others, such as E. Wight Bakke, produced other patterns of unemployment, the pattern of 'shock – optimism – pessimism – fatalism' has tended to receive increasing support. In general though, the hypothesis has been illustrated and supported rather than tested and validated. Writers have, I think, tended to look for these patterns among the unemployed they have interviewed and failed to give enough attention to the exceptions or differences that they may encounter.

In some extreme forms the accounts suggest such an inevitability in the successive stages that there can be no escaping them. Once the unemployed has reached the final stage of fatalism, it has become a permanent adjustment to continuing unemployment. Silent toleration appears to be easy acquiescence and acceptance. Some of these studies provide no evidence on the standard of living or the level of income. Given the persistent belief by the public in the adequacy of the many different benefits available today, it is not surprising that the impression is fostered of someone who has settled down to a not too intolerable life on the dole. One final twist in this argument is that increasing unemployment may actually encourage this belief.

As Richard Harrison pointed out in his detailed review of research into the impact of unemployment for the Department of Employment in 1976, 'the idea of a series of stages may well apply to people in their prime years with a history of steady employment. But the great majority of these workers are amongst the first to find work again. If their unemployment is prolonged, though, it is clear that it brings many people face to face with acute personal dilemmas and fundamental questions about their identity and value to society' (Harrison, 1976, p. 340).

For very many unemployed, however, the idea of a fixed pattern of stages does not seem appropriate. In interviews, the two main and contrasting reactions can be summed up by 'I never thought it would happen to me' and 'That's your fate'. It is the very rawness and sharpness of the shock that makes the first pattern much more evident, particularly in the single interview. A man who has never been out of work and has only just been made redundant will often be very eager to talk about the injustice and outrage. The vividness and even bitterness may be all the sharper if he has spent most of his working life with one company and doubts whether he will ever find another job. In some interviews with a man like this, I have had to ask very few questions: he is more than prepared to tell me the full story with very little prompting. Whether shock is followed by optimism or pessimism is likely to depend upon age, health and the level of resources, including past pay and any final settlement. Knowledge of the local labour market and of the demand for any skills he has or the extent of his informal contacts may also be crucial.

By contrast, the unskilled man in his forties, now in his second or third spell out of work this year, may be laconic to the extent of disconcerting the most experienced interviewers. He realises that he is becoming more vulnerable to unemployment, especially if he is disabled or his health is deteriorating, and he knows that the market is becoming much slacker at the same time. There is little new or different about this time out of work: if he is fortunate in getting back to work, he is aware that it will probably not be long before he becomes unemployed again. The most inept question, such as 'What is it like to be out of work?', which will set the first man vividly talking, may simply elicit a blank or puzzled stare from the second. For him, being out of work is part and parcel of being in that sort of job. He doesn't expect it to change – in the end, the older are always being pushed out by the younger and fitter. But this does not represent a fatalism that accepts continuing unemployment. It is often very much more a reaction to a repetition of unemployment and the uncertainty of the job search.

These are obviously extreme examples, but I have frequently met both types. Now that unemployment has been rising for many months, more of the redundant, especially the older ones, may lose their volubility and simply be numbed by what looks even more like the premature end to their working careers. But this change is by no means evident. Interviewers continue to remark on the almost unbelievable optimism with which men who coped with unemployment a decade ago opt for the attraction of the lump-sum redundancy payment expecting to find work again in a couple of months at the latest.

In between the two extremes there is a wide range of experiences. Very little appears to be known about the impact of unemployment on the married woman. The pressures and tensions she encounters, losing her paid job and 'only' being left her housework, may depend on the extent of her family responsibilities and the need to find employment again quickly – whether to maintain her own independence and career or to restore the family's reduced resources. Tensions and frustration may be all the greater when two members of the same household are out of work. The impact on the school leaver may change dramatically as the weeks stretch into months and many of those who left at the same time find work. His or her fatalism may be much more a matter of accepting the abandonment of previous ambitions and settling for a series of uninteresting but physically demanding dead-end jobs.

For all unemployed people, the level of demand seems particularly important. A skilled man with sound experience and good health may be able to accept the delay until work returns after a seasonal decline because he expects to be taken on again. This is very different from the man made redundant whose skill is no longer needed. Movement between jobs may be a useful way of gaining experience for teenagers without any skills and be a sensible way of coping with the monotony and boredom of many of the jobs available for younger school leavers. But, as Phillips (1973) has said, 'such gains become deadly' when unemployment is high. Employers may prefer to take those straight from school who have not built up what is now seen in a declining labour market as an unstable work record.

The other main factor that I believe affects the reaction to unemployment and influences its impact is the range of resources the unemployed person can command, whether they are economic or social, in terms of family support or help and guidance through colleagues and neighbours. In my view, some of the more psychological analyses have completely overlooked the impact of reduced income on the unemployed and their families. The lack of resources may increase the burden of unemployment and at the same time make it more difficult to escape back to work.

Very often the impact of unemployment is revealed most clearly in interviews with men now back in work. It is perhaps hardly to be expected that families hard-pushed to cope with the burden of unemployment will tell a complete stranger what loss of work is doing to them, their families, their marriage and their lives. The family tensions and arguments often come out much more vividly in recollection. Men I have often regarded as quite hardened or accustomed to unemployment in my first interview with them when they were out of work, have spoken angrily and with great relief of the hardships, pressures and often unremitting monotony of that time once they are back in work. This is brought out in two interviews with workers made redundant in Newcastle in 1978. Both were in their fifties and had been back at work six months before the interview.

It affected me a lot when I was unemployed. I didn't think I was going to get another job. It was very depressing and got worse the longer I was unemployed. It wasn't so much the money or the way I felt. It was degrading – in the dole office or when people asked me what I was doing. People would say – 'are you still unemployed?' 'Are you not looking for work?' I was looking. It was very degrading. I have worked all my life and got angry. People who have never been unemployed don't know what it is like; they have never experienced it . . . When you are unemployed you are bored, frustrated, and worried, worried sick: at least I was. Of course it is worse for the man who has got a family: he has got responsibilities. So you worry for the wife and the bairns.

The second man had taken a poorer job as a labourer, which he had got through a friend after four months out of work.

When I was unemployed I was very worried: I thought that was it, I didn't expect to get another job. I slept in late until about 11 a.m. I got very bored. Hours in the early afternoon were the worst – hours when I thought that I used to be working. I wasn't ready for retiring yet: I can still work, I wanted to work. I got very jealous of those who were working. My wife is right when she said it affects me as *a man*: it isn't the money so much as the feeling men have. [Newcastle, 1980, p. 34]

My impression is that there are more references to humiliation and anger and depression in the comments from those back at work, but fewer references to the importance of income. In the interviews with those out of work, the opposite pattern often emerges. Change of location can also make a difference. I have noticed that interviews in the home, often in front of the family with members joining in, may pick up many of the deprivations that are being experienced at the present time. Interviews with groups of unemployed outside the benefit office or in a pub are often much more focused on work and the loss of it. They also talk more of the job search discussed in the next section.

The Search for Work

You meet people and they ask you what you are doing and you say you are unemployed and you know what they are thinking. You can tell yourself that you don't care what they think but deep down it gets you. It always gets you. Sometimes people will say you are still not working? You are not trying man. I have got a job. There's plenty of jobs for those who want to work'. But I am trying. [Craftsman redundant for 12 months – Newcastle, 1980, p. 36]

One of the greatest ironies in the creation of the mythology of the voluntary unemployed is the success of some in finding work. In a work-oriented society that condemns idleness there is strong encouragement for the successful job-searcher to congratulate himself and play down any element of good fortune. This seems all the more likely to happen when the search has been long and difficult because of the shortage of jobs. Besides, many people do not have to register very long before they are successful in finding a new job. More than 1 in 4 spells of male unemployment lasted less than four days according to a detailed analysis of all spells between June 1971 and 1972 (Stern, 1979, p. 69). However, this was a time when unemployment rose quickly but fell equally rapidly; unemployment is now more than twice as high and still rising. Even so, during the high level of unemployment in 1975, the number of unemployed registering for less than four weeks never fell below 180,000.

Many people looking for work find it harder to get a job than they expected. This includes skilled men made redundant in their thirties or forties who generally have much less difficulty in finding work unless their particular skill had become obsolete. When Tress Engineering closed on Tyneside in June 1978, only a third of the redundant workers believed their chances of getting any jobs were poor, although many more had less confidence in being able to get a similar job. But one year later more than one-half had found that looking for work was worse or a lot worse than they had expected, and this included men who had succeeded in getting a new job. Many of the skilled who had been more optimistic initially had been much more shocked by their experience. In total, over a quarter had to change their minds about the type of work they were looking for. Most of the men took the first job they were offered and less than 1 in 5 said they had actually turned down the offer of a job. Most of these were skilled men, half of whom had turned down a job in favour of another that they preferred or because it would have involved moving home. Those without any skill had been much more pessimistic about their chances in the labour market and hardly any had turned down a job offer (Newcastle, 1980).

It is often argued that many unemployed could find work quicker if they did not set their sights too high and were not cushioned by generous or at least high benefits. The evidence for this appears to be largely anecdotal and is not supported by the findings of many surveys over the last fifteen years. One study in 1979 showed that a majority of unemployed men had tended to come from low-paying jobs, but only 3 per cent would be receiving more in benefits than they had previously earned (the average gap was £34 per week). Those who managed to find a new job generally suffered a reduction in earnings but their new take-home pay was still on average £28 more than their benefit income. Those with relatively higher benefits because they had many dependants were generally looking for higher earnings and tended to take longer to find a new job. There was no evidence, however, that they were not looking for work as hard as the others. They put fewer restrictions on the type of job that they would take and had made more job applications than those with low benefit incomes. They were also most likely to be suffering financial hardship (Smith, 1980). The natinal DHSS Cohort Study (Moylan and Davies, 1980) of men becoming unemployed in the autumn of 1978 also found that there was little if any evidence of the earnings target being set too high.

I have been struck by the sheepishness or defensiveness with which men explain why they have taken a job for a low wage, including one beneath their benefit income. Many see it as a defeat: unlike others, they have neither succeeded in getting back to work quickly on their own terms nor had the guts to hold out for the type of job they used to have. Taking lower pay often means accepting a poorer job with less status and requiring less of their skill – it means a lowering of standards that may be never regained.

In examining the job-search and its intensity, one has to take account of the differences among those out of work. Most importantly of all, the demand for workers in some occupations is very much lower than in others. Opportunities for unskilled workers are particularly limited. In September 1980, when unemployment had been rising and vacancies dropping so steadily, there were 162 people registered as general labourers for every job known to the employment service. The average number registered unemployed for all other occupations was ten. The chances also varied very greatly by region, and an analysis within these would probably have shown even greater variation in job opportunity. Workers also differ in their previous experience at finding work and the resources they can bring to bear. In some occupations there are traditional patterns of finding employment – for example through the Seaman's Pool or the local Sheet-metal Workers Union. Some companies only take on people through the job shop while others prefer people to 'exercise their own initiative' and call at the factory gates.

The atmosphere is very different when there is only a temporary lull in employment. Tradesmen in the shipyards may expect a recall when work returns. There are certain known places to look for notification of jobs besides the job shop and an efficient work-seeker who intends to stay within a certain range of jobs may save himself the tedious and depressing trudge from factory to factory that generally still has to be made by those without a skill. This can change very quickly when there is a more general slump. Even in good times the older unemployed man whose health is deteriorating or skill becoming obsolete may have to turn to other ways of looking for work.

Amongst the great majority of those I have interviewed it has become very evident that there is no single 'right way' to look for work and what is seen as luck has often tended to dominate the job-search, especially for the unskilled. This helps to account for the fatalistic attitude expressed by many men without skills.

I am a great fatalist – whatever comes along, that is your fate. Oh, but you have got to go and look for work, you have got to push yourself. Perhaps you will be going to one place and there won't be work – at another there will be. That's your fate.

This has been brought home to me in interviews time and time again.

I got my last job myself – not that I can say I got it by looking for it. I had been down to the yards looking and had no luck. On the way back I stopped to talk to some men working on the corner just over there [he nodded across the road from his house] and I got taken on.

For these men there was no spur of efficiency, no premium on effort, and the pub or the betting shop could be as good a place to find work as the factory gate or the job shop. One hot tip for a job may be dud; the place was filled weeks ago. Another time this may lead to a job. 'I don't know what to say to him when he comes back in', said one wife of a semi-skilled worker who had been three months out of work, 'I don't know why he does it.' Good fortune in finding work is acknowledged, but this type of success only confirms one's own inability to dominate and overcome the situation. One apprentice plumber eventually found work.

It wasn't easy, not easy at all. I wanted a trade, something I could learn that would be useful not just any old job. My father has a trade and I wanted to have a trade too. I looked around; went to all the building sites, in town. I even went to one building site 7 weeks in a row. Even then I never got a start. It was through a neighbour I got the job I'm in now. He told me they were looking for apprentices, so I went down next day and was told to start the next week. [Gow and McPherson, 1980]

The role of the family and friends in helping the unemployed to find work is very important and is obscured by much research that simply asks those out of work what methods they are using to find a job. Without prompting, few will think to mention their family or friends. But this of course does not mean that a relative or friend who hears of a suitable job may not follow it up or speak for the unemployed to the employer. Parents, for example, have often asked their employers about possible jobs for their children and vice versa. Informal contacts are still so important in finding and keeping work that the unemployed often say 'it's who you know, not what you know' that determines the chances of re-employment. Over half of the men who found work after the Tress redundancy in Newcastle did so through informal contacts. This was much more common amongst men who were likely to have greater difficulty in finding work. Older workers or those without skills found particularly severe problems in an area where unemployment among men had been at least 10 per cent for many years. Yet four men, all over 50 and without a skill, found jobs within three months – all, significantly, through relatives working for their new employers (Newcastle, 1980, p. 12). Similarly in North Shields, an unskilled man of 63, the oldest I met who found another job after being made redundant, was taken on by his son's employer: 'he told my lad when he knew the timberworks had closed 'If he's as good a worker as you are . . .'' '.

The informal method has advantages to both employer and jobseeker. The employee-contact has virtually approved the job for his unemployed friend and told him its attractions and faults and at the same time effectively given a reference on his friend to both the employer and his work colleagues. The fact that a relative or friend spoke for him may well lead a man to put up with much more than he might otherwise do in the initial, often difficult, settling-in period. The employer also knows this and so may be more willing to take him on. Contacts and the chance to vet informally on both sides therefore play a valuable role in bringing job and job-seeker together quickly and efficiently. Their importance is all the greater in unskilled and less skilled jobs, although in taking on apprentices employers also often give preference to the families of their own workers or those they have spoken for.

But any practice that discriminates in favour of some will leave others more disadvantaged. Those who do not have good contacts and are not established or accepted in the local community become more dependent on their own unassisted efforts or the help of the job shop. In North Tyneside we found that this worked against men in their forties and fifties living by themselves and with no regular family contacts. Their poverty reinforced their isolation, cutting them off from the main source of jobs (North Tyneside CDP, 1978). This may well help to account for the higher rate of unemployment among those who are single or no longer married. Immigrant and ethnic minority groups are also likely to find these patterns of recruitment working against their attempts to find work until they have become established and accepted in the local community. Many careers officers or job centre staff do not appreciate that this places an additional premium on their own efforts to help 'outsiders' find work. By continuing to use this established and accepted practice, employers and others have the effect of discriminating against, for example, black school leavers. The higher unemployment rate among West Indian as opposed to Asian teenagers may be partly an effect of this pattern of recruitment combined with the differing occupational and industrial structure of the two groups. There are more Asians than West Indians in employing positions, such as small businessmen and shopkeepers, so that there is likely to be a larger pool of jobs known among the Asian community in the same informal way. And, as the number of vacancies falls further short of the numbers looking for work, one might expect that a greater proportion of jobs will be filled through informal contacts.

Higher unemployment brings a marked reduction in opportunities for those who lack both skills and contacts, and enormously increases their frustration and tension. In the last resort the nature of the jobsearch is decided by whether the employer or the unemployed is looking harder for the other. When employers are more concerned with finding the essential worker to complete the work team, their attitude and behaviour are very different from those who dismiss the idea of putting up notices outside factory gates with jobs for labourers because 'we would be deluged if we did. We only advertise skilled jobs and tell the job shop about unskilled vacancies'.

The Organisation of the Unemployed

Given the isolation, boredom, monotony and general emptiness of life described by those who remain out of work for a long time, some means of promoting closer and easier contact among the unemployed would seem valuable. Of course, the places where they are brought together most of all are the job centre and the benefit office – many new registrants, have commented on the general silence of the slow shuffle forward with the majority appearing to be very withdrawn. The exceptions, chatting or calling out to others in the queue as they come in, generally seem to be neighbours or workers from the same company.

But the atmosphere generally discourages contact amongst the unemployed. The way in which the very need to compete for the work available and the isolating experience of being out of work tend to set one person apart from another has worked against organisation of the unemployed. But from time to time, as unemployment has hit particularly hard at one community or one company, there has been some effort at organisation. With the rise of unemployment in the early 1960s, which was particularly severe in the more depressed areas, clubs and associations sprang up in a number of areas only to disappear when the initiators themselves returned to work. And this is a key problem for any organisation of the unemployed – that the most active and competent organisers are also likely to be people most skilful at obtaining work. The exception will be the organiser who is so militant that he becomes blacklisted or unacceptable to employers.

★　　★　　★

The absence of any lobby or pressure-group for the unemployed has been a major obstacle to presenting their case and a more sustained and widespread critique of the scrounger mythology. This is all the more important because many union members who are hard pressed by high rates and the standard rate of tax on below-average earnings are all the more prone to accept stories of affluence and comfort on the dole without the daily stress of having to earn a living.

Poverty out of Work
'One of the enduring myths about unemployment is that its link with poverty has been broken' (Walker, 1981). This is not only a very persistent myth but a very powerful one, which allows or even encourages the rest of society to accept higher levels of unemployment more easily. Benefits are so generous and numerous in the welfare state, it is argued, that being out for work for a few weeks or months does not bring the hardships that it did in the 1930s. Besides, wages are much higher and many families have two adult wage-earners so they are much better prepared to cope with unemployment. Even people who discount stories of scroungers, dole-dodgers and unemployables may find reassurance from these beliefs as unemployment continues upward. There is a world recession, and inflation is severe for those in work. If unemployment is part of the cost of getting the economy back on its feet, this can be endured if the benefits available can take the sting out of worklessness. After all, that is exactly what they were intended to do. The ideal of 'the welfare state' encompassed the belief that benefits should be sufficient to keep those dependent on them out of poverty and give enough support to save them from having to take the first job

that came along, however bad its pay and conditions.

When the sharply rising numbers of unemployed mean more people suffering more and longer spells out of work, it is particularly important to examine the financial impact. Despite the increasing number of benefits, the many changes and what have now become annual upratings of benefits, the main finding has remained depressingly the same in every study of unemployment since the war that I have examined. One detailed survey in Coventry, Hammersmith and Newcastle in 1971 concluded that 'the majority of the unemployed were living . . . on what can be described as no more than subsistence incomes' (Hill *et al.*, 1973). This picture was supported by a national survey in 1973 that found that the costs remained 'substantial for all groups' and the unemployed 'were by no means compensated by the level of social benefits received' (Daniel, 1974). Official analyses show the much greater risk of poverty among those out of work for three months or more compared with households where the main wage-earner was in work. During the high unemployment of 1976 the unemployed were twenty-one times more likely to be in poverty.

The combination of low pay with previous periods of unemployment and sickness leaves few of those out of work with any resources apart from state benefits after a month. In the national Cohort Study 7 out of 10 men still unemployed after a month reported that they had 'no unearned income *and* no income from a wife's earnings *and* savings of less than £500' (SBC, 1980, p. 34). Those who report little or no financial hardship have not only received the highest state benefits but have generally also been supported by private and state redundancy payments in a lump sum, severance pay and payments in lieu of notice. In the Cohort Study, the total receiving any of these payments came to less than 10 per cent. The majority therefore have to manage on incomes around supplementary benefit level. In particular, the inadequacy of the rates to support those with children has been emphasised time and again by the Supplementary Benefits Commission and has even been acknowledged by the present government. 'I accept', said the Minister for Social Security to a House of Commons Standing Committee in February 1980, 'that the provision for children under the Supplementary Benefits scheme is not good enough, has never been good enough, and will not be good enough following the [review] changes' (SBC, 1980, p. 84).

The inadequacy of the standard of living possible on supplementary benefits is documented very clearly in official research carried out in October 1974 (at that time the value of benefits in relation to average net earnings for a married couple appears slightly higher than it is today). Only 1 in 20 of the unemployed on supplementary benefit said that they were 'managing quite well' and most were single men. The majority of families with two or more children said that they were 'getting into difficulties'. On measure after measure of deprivation and disadvantage, families with children were found to be worse off, particularly if unemployment had been prolonged. Most people had to cut back on their expenses, but there were far more economies amongst families. The larger families were much more likely to be living in overcrowded accommodation and to have used up any savings. The greater poverty of families was also shown by their 'unmet needs' in terms, for example, of the clothing, bedding and household equipment that the Supplementary Benefits Commission set out in their guidelines. 'Three-quarters of the men with children did not have one complete change of clothing, a warm coat and two pairs of shoes' and families as a whole tended to be very poorly clothed (Clark, 1978).

Subsequent research has produced more evidence of acute financial hardship, particularly as unemployment becomes prolonged. Enough for 'existence rather than living' was the conclusion of the Manpower Services Commission's own detailed study of people out of work for over a year in the middle of 1979 (Colledge and Bartholomew, 1980). Another survey in the same year reported that the most frequent answer by the unemployed to what was the worst things about being out of work emphasised the financial problems. Half the men had fallen behind on regular payments, such as rent, rates, mortgages and fuel bills (Smith, 1980).

The wretched position of families deserves emphasis because of the particularly vicious circle in which they are caught. Many of their needs cannot be deferred, and extra heating for very young babies and winter shoes and coats for growing children all bite into the weekly budget. One family where the father had had very little work after contracting tuberculosis fifteen years ago ate particularly poorly. The parents never had any breakfast, and had just a sandwich at lunch and some form of hot meal in the evening – with no supper, they added. They found Thursday and Friday before benefit arrived the most difficult days on which to manage. As I got to know them, I discovered how very frugally they lived. Over the years they had clearly put a lot of thought into budgeting, buying savings stamps for heatings costs and so on. Most of their clothing was obtained from the Nearly New shops and charity sales. These more deprived groups are all the more likely to get caught in the trap of having to pay more to purchase clothing and other essentials through clubs and local stores with high interest rates. 'This put further pressure on a weekly income already tightly stretched to cover basic necessities' and this state of chronic poverty became even more acute as unemployment lengthened. Not surprisingly, therefore, one-third of the families who had three or more children had debts of £50 or more (Clark, 1978). Yet families, especially large ones, are the group that most people in work believe to be best protected, if not cushioned, by the bounty of the welfare state. Many unemployed families are acutely aware of this, mentioning, for example, fights that children have got into at school: 'his dad said they were supporting people like us'.

The combination of a reduced budget and more contact between husband and wife enforced by the lack of daily work routine has been shown to cause increasing tension within families, especially when relations may not have been too strong in the first place. Many men report that the most frequent rows are over money and children, and studies report disturbing evidence of violence and family break-ups linked to unemployment (Colledge and Bartholomew, 1980).

Observing the pressures and strains that poverty and prolonged unemployment place on many families, my own research has made me much more conscious of the many ways the double impact wears them down and turns them in on themselves. The silent endurance of deprivation and rejection does not make headlines, and is astonishingly often dismissed as apathy or lack of will. Going without what most of society has come to expect is a daily burden. It may be particularly upsetting for unemployed parents at a child's birthday or Christmas, but it is a constant and very undramatic struggle. Often the extended family will take some of the strain, feeding children some evenings or weekends, keeping up their pocket money and paying for winter shoes and clothing. The poverty of many families out of work would be very much sharper if retired grandparents did not help and so reduce their own limited resources.

In many ways, however, poverty is an isolating experience. Joe Kenyon has noticed in his work with claimants how people become 'locked into poverty' so that their home becomes a prison. When they had a job, it was somewhere that most were glad to return to; but poor and out of work they find their home is 'a mouth that eats up' their money before they start to buy food for themselves. In their attempts to cope, they cut themselves off from others. The Supplementary Benefits Commission has defined poverty today as 'a standard of living so low that it excludes and isolates people from the rest of the community'. Poverty-caused isolation deprives people of the social contacts that not only help them to survive the crisis but may also be their main way of finding work and so their only chances of escaping poverty.

Given the persistent evidence of poverty in the surveys of the unemployed, even official ones, it is tempting to imagine some malevolent conspiracy of silence. While much of the hostility encouraged by stories about scroungers and the work-shy may play an important part in distracting public attention, there are many other factors that serve to disguise or divert attention from the financial problems of the unemployed. Ironically, one of these factors is the experience of many short-term unemployed who may receive substantial income tax rebates on top of their earnings-related supplement, insurance benefit and any lump-sum payments from their employer for redundancy, severance or in lieu of notice. They may dislike the experience and be glad to be back in work, but clearly they have not endured any poverty.

So far, I have been concerned to show that the link between poverty and unemployment has not been broken. But concentration on this aspect alone may reinforce long-held assumptions about what is a matter for concern during unemployment. Unemployment may not mean poverty to many of those out of work but it nonetheless represents a significant loss and deprivation. High unemployment makes it unwise to risk time 'looking around' for a better offer; many more people experience only a short time out of work but go back to lower-paying jobs. Older workers who are fortunate enough to get another job at all are particularly likely to go back to a job with less status and reward, and this seems true in any occupation or profession. Even if they return to the same level, they have often missed the next step up the ladder and from then on find they are competing with younger, better trained colleagues.

The combination of material and career loss may be much more significant than people care to admit or maybe realise during their unemployment. In detailed interviews with husbands and wives in a sub-sample of her survey of redundant managers, Jean Hartley found only one family that said they had a much reduced standard of living and, in general, there was not much evidence of 'cutting back' in a major way (Hartley, 1978). What became evident on closer examination was that managers often used their savings or obtained credit rather than change their life-style while they were out of work, hoping that they would soon find a job. 'Several were already seriously in debt and one manager cashed in his pension . . . the majority of managers expressed anxiety about their savings: when to use them, how much to use before changing their job plans, what to do when savings ran out.' In his interviews with professional and managerial men. Robert Slater found (1975) that families also drew on 'potential savings'. These are savings families would have made had the man not been unemployed and for the first few months they used up these before touching any capital – one example would be wives' earnings normally saved for special expenditure on the home or towards a move to a better one. It is also very common for the unemployed to cash in insurance policies with the treble loss of continuing protection, a poor surrender value and a much higher premium if a new policy is taken out later.

Maintaining your current standard of living and risking future financial problems may be a small price to pay when it maintains your self-respect and confidence and makes it more likely that you will get the job you want. 'Do not take the first job you are offered' is the advice given by those counselling redundant executives. 'Think positively and aim high' (*Sunday Times*, 13 December 1980). Most people approve these strategies and recognise the importance and difficulty of keeping up one's confidence in the face of continuing unemployment. Yet many of the same people are often very critical of the refusal of any job offer and of what they see as the inappropriate spending or mis-spending of the poorer unemployed with whom they are less able to identify. In one survey I asked unemployed families if there were any things they spent money on which they felt they should not. The wife of one particularly good family of four, living in two very dilapidated rooms, replied: 'What, to cheer us up, do you mean? Oh yes, sometimes Jack would get his dole on a Friday afternoon and on his way home get pasties, bacon and eggs. We couldn't really afford it, but we were so sick of it all.' I have mentioned this in discussions and it has been used to support the view that the poor obviously need more advice on how to budget and manage.

This is a particularly good example of the ways in which social familiarity or distance helps to influence how we perceive the problems and strategies of others. Social distance reduces our ability, quite simply, to see the needs and difficulties of those furthest removed from our own daily lives. When the problem is concentrated disproportionately, as is unemployment, among the poorer and less powerful members of our society the danger of the failure to recognise the need for action is all the greater. It is one of the less evident of the 'hidden injuries of class'.

References

Bakke, E. Wight (1933), *The Unemployed Man*, Nisbet.

Clark, M. (1978), 'The unemployed on supplementary benefit' in *Journal of Social Policy*, 7, 4, October, pp. 385–410.

Colledge, M. & Bartholomew, R. (1980), *Study of the Long-Term Unemployed*, Manpower Services Commission.

Daniel, W.E. (1974), *National Survey of the Unemployed*, Political and Economic Planning.

Eisenberg, P. & Lazarsfeld, P.F. (1938), 'The psychological effects of unemployment' in *Psychological Bulletin*, pp. 358–90.

Harrison, R. (1976), 'The demoralising experience of prolonged unemployment in D.E. Gazette 84, April, pp. 330–49.

Hartly, J.F. (1978), 'An investigation of psychological aspects of managerial unemployment'. University of Manchester Ph.D thesis.

Hill, M.J., Harrison, R.M., Sargeant, A.V. & Talbot, V. (1973), *Men Out of Work*, Cambridge University Press.

Moylan, S. & Davies, B. (1980), 'The disadvantages of the unemployed', Employment Gazette, August, pp. 830–1.

Newcastle-Upon-Tyne City Council, (1980), *Redundancy in Newcastle-upon-Tyne: a Case Study*, Newcastle: Policy Studies Department.
North Tynside Community Development Project (1978), *In and Out of Work*, Home Office.
Phillips, D. (1973), 'Young and Unemployed in a northern city' in Weir, D. *Men and Work in Modern Britain*, Fontana.
SBC (1980), *Annual Report 1979*, HMSO, Cmnd. 8033.
Slater, R. (1975), 'Coping on the dole', in *New Society*, 14 August, pp. 367–9.
Smith, D.J. (1980), 'How unemployment makes the poor poorer' in *Policy Studies*, 1, 1, July, pp. 20–6.
Stern, J. (1979), 'Who bears the burden of unemployment?' in Beckerman, W. (ed), *Slow Growth in Britain*, Oxford University Press.
Walker, A. (1981), 'The economic and social impact of unemployment: A case study of South Yorkshire' in *Political Quarterly*, January.

SECTION 3
Work in Non-Capitalist Societies

17 A Worker in a Worker's State[*]
M. Haraszti

Editor's Introduction: Haraszti is a Hungarian writer who worked as a factory worker at the Red Star Tractor Factory. He wrote up his experiences in a manuscript entitled 'Piece-Rates', and his attempts to publish this were met with arrest, a delayed trial in 1974 followed by a suspended sentence and heavy fine. The book focuses on the importance of piece-work in shaping the experience of being a machinist operating milling machines.

I discover a change in myself. My interest in materials, techniques and ways of economising my strength is first coloured and then dominated by an obsession about making money. I surrender to an oppressive, unspoken but all-powerful taboo: never approach work to make it more exact, easy, enjoyable or safe.

One day, it struck me that I had almost come to hate the innocent, friendly and talkative woman whose job it was to give out the work allocations. Before my eyes, she split a batch of 150 pieces – all of which could have come my way – into two lots of 75. Actually, she did this only to ensure that the fitters received a steady flow of finished pieces from us millers. Two months earlier, I would have been pleased to have been landed with only 75 jobs of this sort because the work involved was particularly nerve-wracking. Every piece has to be hammered into position, and after every operation the wharf has to be cleaned from the surfaces of the clamps completely, or the next piece would not be true to measure. But since then, I had found a way of doing them three times as fast as the official speed, and the quality inspector still accepted them. That's why I was so furious when I learned that I might not get the other half of the run, and that, even if I did get it, I would have to reset my machine and have it checked all over again. This job has not become any less demanding, only now it is 'good' work and it is impossible for me not to like it.

When I have work of this type – and it is always more trying because looting inevitably means speeding things up.[1] I can't help wishing, however monotonous it is, that it will go on for ever, that my cuts will be slight enough not to need treatment, that the worker who should take over from me will be sick so that I can carry on and do overtime, that no

[*] Extract from *A Worker in a Worker's State*, Penguin, 1977, pp. 53–65.

one talks to me, that nothing will come into my mind which might distract my attention or interrupt my will, that I will have neither hunger nor thirst, and that everything will be exactly the same tomorrow. My basic ideas have not changed (perhaps only because I haven't always been here, and I won't have to go on doing this job for ever?), but somehow I am split. In the showers, I feel guilt as I recall the rage in which I repeated the same movements, minute after minute. I say 'guilt' because I have discovered that this rage comes from the tension of looting, and nothing else.

Of course, I have to do 'bad' jobs too, when I try to lose as little time as I can; this sort of work allows you to get jobs in which looting is possible, which in turn lets your wage reach a half-way acceptable level. When I do a job which doesn't allow for looting, all that I feel about myself is hate and bitterness; my brain won't admit that even with such work I should be pushing myself to the limit. I am easily distracted because I only have to look at my work-sheet to know that, at best, I am working for thirteen fillérs a minute.

In the end, the only way out is to become a machine myself. The best workers are very good at this. It is as if an immovable mask was glued to their faces, whatever the type of work they are doing. Their eyes seem veiled, yet they never miss a thing. Their movements don't seem to require any effort. They follow predetermined trajectories, like inert objects under magnetic control. Throughout the whole day, they keep to a fast even pace. Just like the machines, they don't rush into things when they are feeling fresh, nor do they slow up when they're tired. They give way to 'nerves' only when the proportion of 'good' work to 'bad' is really grim. Otherwise, their behaviour reflects reality: 'good' and 'bad' jobs, 'paid' and 'unpaid' work, run together in the course of a day. The benefits they squeeze out of them and the wages which come from them are equally indifferent to such distinctions.

In itself, the difference between 'good' and 'bad' work is born of illusion, there are no clear criteria for determining it.

After I had worked out the pay for eight hours work with 100 per cent performance, I told my shift-mate the figures I had arrived at. He was surprised and incredulous. 'I knew that you had to get a move on, and that the prescribed time was only there so that they could show something on the paper, but I never realised that if I worked honestly throughout my shift, at a 100 per cent performance, I still wouldn't reach the nominal hourly pay rate. Well, you never can trust a piece of printed paper!'

Particularly when jobs are of a new or unusual kind, whether or not they are 'good' or 'bad' does not emerge until you do your accounting afterwards. This is especially true if you are a beginner. Even with experience, you can never tell in advance just how 'good' or 'bad' a job is. There is only one thing that's absolutely certain: 'Don't stick to the technical instructions!' This is the only way to make sure that we don't miss a 'good' job. But experience does not enable us to work out our gains with certainty – just to make, at best, a rough guess.

Insecurity is the main driving force in all payment by results – both piece-rate and contract work. It chases us remorselessly every minute of the day. That's why payment by results is held to be the best incentive of all.

The manifest coercion and dependence which characterise payment by the hour change into a semblance of independence with piece-rates. Workers on assembly lines, or on automatic or semi-automatic equipment, serve machines which they do not control, which run at a constant pace, and whose output is fixed in advance. In return, they get a predetermined wage – usually at an hourly rate. Such workers can only increase their earnings by stepping up the number of hours they work, by doing overtime. Within the official limits, their precise hourly pay is fixed individually: you get so much, and you, so much. The boss fixes your pay and he can arbitrarily increase it entirely as he sees fit.

The time-rate worker knows, therefore, what is expected of him and what he can expect in return. He does not have to make an economic analysis for the essence of time-rates to stare him in the face. His eight hours have been bought from him. The machine holds to its inescapable rhythm. It cannot be deceived. He has as little influence over the price of his working day as he has over how, when, where and in whose interests the value which he produces (and of which he receives a part) is used. There is little chance of his getting bogged down in details, and coming to see part of his work as 'paid' and part as 'unpaid', or to rate some of his jobs as 'good' and others as 'bad'. He does not envisage that astute tricks or individual effort might turn the system to his advantage. If he regards something as unjust – for example, his rate of pay – then, as he broods over ways and means of bringing about a change, he must either come to see the whole system as unjust, or accept it in its totality as a fate which says: 'That's the way it is.' Whatever position he arrives at, coercion, dependence, and obedience – the very essence of paid labour – are quite clear to him, however well paid he happens to be. Whenever he possibly can, he reduces his suffering. When he works faster, or infringes the technical regulations, he doesn't do so, like a piece-rate worker, to produce more. On the contrary, when he feels that his output is more than is being asked of him, he slows down. In a word, time-rates are straightforward: an 'incentive wage form'.

A worker paid by the hour knows that he can't demand anything; he has to accept that something will be handed out to him in the end. The piece-rate worker also knows about what he can't expect. But he is bound to believe that he can do one thing through his own efforts: make money. When he earns his pay, he thinks he is getting the reward for a private struggle. Every day, he starts at zero. Every day the mirage of limitless possibilities shimmers on his horizon. The florints that he earns are the spoils of a battle, involving something which appears to depend upon himself. Beside those external factors about which he cannot do a thing – materials, regulations, pay rates, controls – stands his own will. He himself works his machine.

It is not enough that the conditions are skilfully set up for the compulsion of work to take over. A totally alien flow of time fragments his life. His working day is disguised minute by minute by the renewed effort of will he incessantly squeezes from himself. His belief that in all circumstances it is possible to extract more money than he has been allocated is subtly reinforced. He does not notice that his will has been taken into account in a cold calculation, in which, whether he breaks through the set limits or stays within them, it comes to the same thing. His efforts only generate further profits and new demands upon himself.

Uncertainty is the great magician of piece-work. It puts life back into those details which the time-rate worker does not even think about when he installs himself in front of his machine: the speed of the spindle; the technology of the process; the pay. If a man on hourly pay feels cheated, then he feels that he has been cheated totally, absolutely, and in every way. The piece-rate worker, however, just would not start work at all if he began the day with a resigned, passive feeling that he was going to be cheated. For him the chance of something extra is essential. Of course, he knows perfectly well that he is being cheated. But his active participation in this trick against himself makes it impossible for him to see the deception; or to identify it with his conditions of life, as can the worker on hourly wages.

Instead, he has a sharp eye for petty discrimination, injustice or manipulation, and fights against such things in the belief that such victories can be set against the defeats. He tends to judge everything in terms of pay, and when he has a good month, he believes, from the bottom of his heart, that he is not the dupe but the victor.

If the time-rate worker notices that his rate of production is faster than it was two months ago he says to himself, 'They have speeded up the conveyor, modified the machine, replaced the tools, or altered the raw materials. It is up to them. I can't do anything about it.' But when a piece-rate worker discovers that the norm for a particular job has been tightened, he remembers that he recently increased his output in the hope of the temporary advantage of a better pay-slip. How could he admit to himself that his will was part of something that had been willed outside of him, and that what has happened has, in one way or another, been planned? He must look for another explanation and think about the instance as a temporary setback, an exception rather than the rule.

How much work do we do? My neighbour the turner, who returned from military service two years ago, claims that he has to produce a lot more now to earn the same wage as he got before he went into the army (and today with such a wage he can hardly make ends meet) even though he is still on the same machine doing the same work. Everyone else agrees, even those turners who are paid by the hour and work on semi-automatic machines. The millers are not short of things to say about this, M, for example, likes to talk about the Golden Age when he worked on one machine only. Or take his shift replacement, who once watched a weight-lifting champion on the television. When he heard the commentator enthuse that there were no real limits to man's prowess, he reacted: 'All these blokes have to do is to lift up one milligramme more than the others, and they are covered with gold.' Warming to his punchline, he went on, 'They certainly don't have to eat shit. But I am forced to push through twice as much, and no one thinks of putting me on the T.V.'

The real meaning of piece-rates lies in the incessant increase in production. The bosses do not have to impose it. It is enough for them to register that it has happened and then to incorporate it officially by changing the norms. Of course, there are sometimes abuses and injustices: occasionally management pushes matters and goes a bit too far in setting the new norm, even though the compulsion to loot would get the same result anyway. But clever management simply acknowledges the results which have been achieved, and bases further increases upon them.

*   *   *

We learn a new lesson about the logic of wage labour, a lesson which can be put like this: a man who creates wealth is compelled to work in a way which destroys the quality of that which he produces, and his own health as well; simultaneously, he is forbidden to work in this way, as if he would ever choose to do so of his own free will.

The idlest and most far-fetched artist could never have imagined that he who creates all existing goods could work without complaint under a system of 'incentive' pay which means that he has to surpass 100 per cent production in order to obtain, for himself and his family, just enough to live, so that he can start the next day all over again. His beliefs too take on a form which corresponds to such production and are put to a use of which he is not informed. Because they, too, are given 'incentives' by appropriate moral rules, and he is forced to compete with his workmates. But as soon as his productivity has reached a level which assures him acceptable living standards, his output is condemned as too high, and he is sanctioned, in the following way: the production level which he has just achieved, although condemned, is nonetheless recorded. Henceforth, he must reach that same output for less pay, which proves in turn to be insufficient for his daily needs. To cap it all – Sisyphus could have learned a thing or two from them – the door of 'incentive' wages is again thrown wide open, revealing its infinite horizons, and on again goes the record of moral incentives, everything begins and nothing finishes.

There is no way out of this. To make our living, we are forced to provide the rate-fixers with irrefutable arguments for the revision of the norms, and so for the reduction to an ever more unreal level of the time per piece and consequently the pay per piece. This incites us to speed up the rate still more to try and reach a greater level of production. Therefore we prepare the ground, slowly but surely, for yet another increase of the norms.

The cunning threat of the production graph contains this inescapable trap. There is only one thing to do: forget it. But for how long? Doesn't the very first production meeting of the year anticipate the exact extent to which it will be possible for us to forget the chains that we have wound around our own bodies?

After an interminable litany of production data, the foreman pauses a second and then says, in a solemn voice, 'During the first quarter of this year, the level of production in this section exceeded 130 per cent, just as it did in the final quarter of last year. You will therefore understand, comrades, that the current norms are out of date. Believe me, the officials who fix the norms are very patient. Management believes that a general revision is long overdue. The section held its own very well during the rat-race at the end of the year, and it was only because of this that I was able to use my weight to prevent any revision until today.'

Most of us are smoking cigarettes with heads lowered, or staring through the window at the factory yard, which never seems to alter. Everyone remembers that at the last production conference, the chief foreman said: 'Management counts on all turners, and more especially on this section, to do everything possible to end the year on a successful note. The government's economic Commission has set us the task of ironing out this factory's main difficulties during the course of the coming year. It is in the interests of everyone that, by pulling our weight, we get on top of the situation into which the factory has fallen through no one's fault. I need scarcely add that we are in duty bound by the trust which the superior authorities have placed in us.'

We knew what he meant all too well. Our factory's products proved unsellable. In the fifties, they had benefited from the prestige attached to the mechanisation of agriculture and were therefore subsidised. It had now become essential to turn round the factory's whole production programme in the shortest possible time. This transformation began during the sixties, but the introduction of the economic reforms made it a matter of urgency: the government gave us an ultimatum.

Many left. Many new workers came, mostly from the country – to them the wages were all that mattered. But quite a few of the older workers, precisely those who should have foreseen that a massive revision of the norms would be the climax of this change-over, and who should have put the others on their guard, for example by slowing the rate of work or threatening mass resignations, were the very ones who gave in to this sentimental appeal. They reckoned that they could loot unpunished: after all, they were no longer doing this only for themselves, but because they had been asked to play their part in the great transformation.

It would be an exaggeration to maintain – although the factory journal naturally did so – that these workers, who already knew from past experience what kind of thanks to expect, speeded up their work out of 'love for the factory' or through 'pride in labour'. It would be more accurate to speak of a blind and desperate faith in justice, of the belief that perhaps, after all, this exceptional situation would lead to a truly exceptional transformation. If the management asserted that, in the final analysis, only the workers could save them from the sufferings of a pitiless reorganisation, surely this time management would grant the workers some recognition for their efforts?

I watch the workers' reactions. When it becomes clear in the production meeting that all their hopes have been in vain, they do not give way to anger but begin to console themselves: the money we made in the rush at the end of the year is ours, and they can't claim that back from us. Anyway, the justice we had longed for would not have meant more than this: the revision of the norms would not have taken place at once, but would have been postponed for, say, a year. Clearly, in their heart of hearts the workers never believed in their hopes for a second. This was why their hope could change so fast into the hopeless but bearable certainty that tomorrow is another day, and that they will manage somehow.

Reference

1. 'Looting' consists of speeding up the machines, cutting corners, ignoring safety factors in order to produce a reasonable daily wage under the piece-work system.

18 Manager Qiao Assumes Office*
Jiang Zilong

Editor's Introduction: It is impossible to obtain autobiographical accounts of life inside a modern Chinese factory. However, the following short story provides an excellent insight into some of the tensions and conflicts in Chinese work organisations. The author works at the Tianjin Heavy Machinery Plant in China, where he has been a forger, manager's secretary and a deputy secretary of the Party branch committee in a workshop. The story was written in 1979 and should be seen in context as part of the reaction against the political radicalism, political factionalism and near civil war of the Cultural Revolution years (1966–76). In its place, and clearly expressed in this story, is a more single-minded commitment to economic modernisation.

Comeback
There was an awkward and rather unusual silence at the enlarged Party committee meeting of the Electrical Equipment Bureau, especially since Huo Dadao, the director, was presiding over it. It was like the lull before a storm. Although the 'Gang of Four' had been out of power for two and a half years, the Heavy Electrical Machinery Plant had yet to fulfill its quota. The situation was intolerable. Unless the whole bureau was to be let down, a capable man had to be sent there to put things right. The problem was who to send. Quite a number of cadres in the bureau hadn't much to do. A few were qualified but fewer still were willing to be appointed. People were anxious to be promoted but who wanted to take over such a mess?

Having notified the committee members beforehand about what would be discussed at the meeting, Huo remained calm, his eyes closed as if in meditation and then sweeping across all the faces in front of him.

Then his gaze fell on a dark tanned face, tough and fleshy, with bushy eyebrows, deep eyes, and high cheek bones. An image of strength! He was Qiao Guangpu, the director of the Electrical Appliance Company under the bureau. Qiao was fidgeting with a cigarette he had taken out of Deputy Director Xu Jinting's packet. Though he had given up smoking ten years before during a period of illegal detention, he often fidgeted with other people's cigarettes or sniffed them when-

* First published in *Peoples Literature*, July 1979. Translated by Wang Mingjie.

ever he was agitated or concentrating on something. Staring at the cigarette, his lips firmly shut, Qiao clenched his teeth in anger, while the muscle of his left cheek twitched. Huo smiled imperceptibly, certain who would break the ice and what would be the solution.

The expensive 'Tulip' cigarette in Qiao's hand was crushed and he reached out for another. This time Xu stopped his hand and said, 'Listen, Qiao, if you don't smoke, don't waste them like this. No wonder the smokers all steer clear of you at meetings.'

Everyone roared with laughter.

Without raising his eyes, Qiao began to speak in a steady voice, 'I'd like to work in the Heavy Electrical Machinery Plant. I hope the bureau Party committee will consider my request.'

His words dropped like a bombshell. Surprised, Xu offered him a cigarette and asked, 'Are you kidding, Qiao?'

It was indeed the surprise to end all surprises that Qiao should volunteer to work in a factory. He was already a company director, an important yet easy job. He had the help of the head of the bureau plus the factory managers to do all the donkey work. If things went well he'd be promoted. If the reverse, he could shift the blame on to the higher-ups or his subordinates. All he had to do was pass on instructions and issue orders. A director had a lot of freedom and power – an easy job for good pay, an ideal one in the eyes of many old cadres. Yet Qiao wanted to leave such a post to be a plant manager. What had got into his head?

Qiao's eyes scanned the meeting room and finally met Huo's. For an instant they exchanged significant glances.

'I'm fifty-six and pretty fit,' said Qiao. 'My blood pressure's a bit high, but that doesn't matter. If I fail and the plant doesn't fulfil the quota set by the state, I'll pack up and go back to cadre school to raise chickens and ducks.'

His determination left him no room for second thoughts. Huo raised his eyes and looked at Qiao with deep appreciation. Here was a man of action, on whom one could depend.

'Is there anything else?' Huo asked.

'Yes. I'd like to have Shi Gan with me to be the Party secretary. I'll be the manager. We were old partners,' replied Qiao.

This caused another stir. Everybody knew that Shi Gan was no longer the man he used to be. A modest man, what he needed was a peaceful life. Would he be willing to take the job?

For a moment Qiao was silent; his cheek began to twitch again.

'That's what you think,' someone said. 'But how can you be sure Shi will want to be your partner this time?'

'I've sent a car to the cadre school to fetch him. He'll have to accept whether or not he wants to. Besides. . . .' Qiao turned to Huo and continued, 'if the Party committee agrees, I'm certain he'll go with me.

By the way, I'd like to say a few words about job transfer. A Party member must obey the Party's decision. Of course, one's opinion must be considered beforehand, but it is the Party which has the final say and which assigns posts to its members regardless of rank.'

As he glanced at his watch, Shi entered, looking like an old peasant. But the way he entered and his composure showed that he was an experienced cadre who had frequented the room. He was small and slow-moving but his shabby appearance concealed his shrewdness. Though he was just turning sixty, his lined face made him look older. He nodded like a stranger in response to their warm greetings, keeping his mouth shut as if afraid to utter a sound. Refusing the seat Huo offered him, he remained standing as if not knowing why he had been summoned.

Qiao rose to his feet and said, 'Shall I first talk it over with Shi, Huo?'

Then, he took Shi's arm and walked him out of the room. After they had settled themselves down in armchairs in Huo's office, Qiao looked at Shi, distressed to see that he seemed a different man.

In 1958, after completing his studies in the Soviet Union, Qiao had been appointed the manager of the Heavy Electrical Machinery Plant and Shi Gan was made the Party secretary. As a result of their efforts, the plant soon became a model. Shi was a witty, humorous fellow, and a good talker. During the Cultural Revolution, however, much of what he had said was criticised. During his illegal detention, Shi often remarked to Qiao, 'All my troubles were caused by my tongue. It spills out whatever's in my mind.' He got particularly irritated when interrogated by the so-called rebels at criticism meetings. If he kept silent, they accused him of being uncooperative; if he answered them, it only added more fuel to the flames. Qiao, who was also often criticised at the same time, had a way of dealing with his interrogators. He called it switching off. At first, like Shi, he listened attentively to those criticisms, but the more he listened the angrier he became. Very often he perspired profusely and afterwards he was completely exhausted. Then gradually he got used to it. Qiao was fond of Beijing opera, so when a meeting was held he'd switch off and silently sing an aria to himself. Quite pleased with himself, he told Shi about his method. Unfortunately Beijing opera was not Shi's forte and it didn't work for him. Once, in the autumn of 1967, Shi was ordered to stand on a makeshift platform on two trucks. As he got down at the end of the meeting, he slipped and fell to the ground, unfortunately biting off the tip of his tongue. Saying nothing, he swallowed the blood in pain. Ever since then the two friends had been separated. Shi never spoke again in public. When his injury had healed, he was sent to do physical labour in the bureau's cadre school. Later, if he was offered work in the city he would refuse, saying he couldn't talk. When the news of the arrest of the 'Gang of Four' was announced, Shi went to the city and drank some wine in celebration. But he returned to the cadre school that night, for he could not leave his 'three armies'. As he was responsible for hundreds of chickens, dozens of ducks and a flock of sheep, he was nicknamed the 'commander of three armies'. He had resolved to live in the countryside for the rest of his life. But early that morning, Qiao had sent a close friend to fetch him under the pretext that there would be an important meeting.

Having told Shi what was on his mind, Qiao waited hopefully for his support.

Under Shi's strange, inquiring gaze, Qiao became rather uneasy. It seemed to convey a disturbing remoteness and distrust between old friends. At last, Shi spoke in a low, indistinct voice, 'Why on earth pick on me? I won't take the job!'

'Listen, Shi!' Qiao's voice was anxious. 'Do you really want to hide away like a hermit in the country? Are you as scared of struggles as others say?'

Shi nodded. But Qiao jumped to his feet, denying it. 'No! You're not like that! You can fool others but not me!'

'I've only got half a tongue. . . . I'd bite off the rest if I could!'

'Nonsense! You've got two tongues. One to help me and one to convince people. You often encouraged me in a crisis. No one can replace you. You're the best Party secretary I've ever met. You must come and work with me now.'

Shi signed, his eyes had an agonised expression for an instant. 'I'm a disabled man,' he said. 'I can't give you any help. I may even disappoint you.'

'Pull yourself together, Shi! You're more than a gifted speaker, you've got a good head on your shoulders. You've lots of experience and guts. On top of that, we've worked well together for years. All I'm asking is that you give me advice at crucial moments.'

Still shaking his head, Shi replied, 'I'm way out of date and I've no energy left.'

'What crap!' Qiao was about to lose his temper. 'You're as fit as a fiddle. How can you talk like that? OK, you lost part of your tongue, but that doesn't mean you lost your whole head!'

'I mean I just don't give a damn any more!'

'What?' Qiao pulled Shi to his feet and looked straight into his eyes, then snapped, 'Just say that again! Where's your confidence in the Party? Your courage? Your sense of responsibility?'

Shi tried to avoid Qiao's eyes which mirrored his thoughts and feelings. He was shocked at himself for being so cowardly. But he would never admit it publicly.

In a mocking tone, Qiao said as if to himself, 'It's ironical really. The

Central Party Committee's determined to modernise our country and now the main obstacles have been removed. All we need is good leaders. Yet look at our cadres. No confidence, no guts! If you ask them to do something, they try to pass the buck or simply refuse with all kinds of excuses. Don't they have any sense of responsibility left as ordinary Party members? I'm like a soldier. Ask me to do something and I'll try my best. There's nothing strange in that, but some people these days take it as seeking the limelight. Perhaps others call me a fool behind my back!'

Shi was hurt again. Seeing his shoulders quivering, Qiao added earnestly, 'Shi, you must come with me, even if I have to drag you there.'

'Listen, giant. . . .' Shi began after a sigh. The familiar nickname immediately warmed Qiao's heart. But Shi resumed his distant tone again, 'So long as you won't regret it, I don't mind. If you think I'm no good, just tell me so. I can go back to the cadre school.'

When the two returned to the meeting room, the members had already reached a decision.

'Qiao will take up his new post tomorrow,' Huo told Shi, 'and you can go there in a couple of days. Have a rest first. If you don't feel quite fit, go to the hospital to have a general check-up.'

Shi Gan nodded and then left.

Huo turned to Qiao and said, 'Someone's anxious to take your place even before you leave!' He then eyed the others and asked, 'Any other recommendations? Better put your cards on the table now and let us see them.'

There was a deathly silence. They all knew Huo's rule: Speak up at a meeting or forget it.

Xu, Huo's deputy, broke the silence by saying, 'Ji Shen of the Electrical Machinery Plant hopes to be transferred to work in the Electrical Appliance Company under the bureau, as he's not in good health.' Following him, some other members made their recommendations.

His eyes gleaming, Huo said angrily, 'Recommending oneself isn't something new. After all, Qiao recommended himself. But your recommendations are completely different. If we accepted them all we'd have fifteen deputies in the bureau. All the six companies under the bureau would have ten or fifteen directors each. I doubt if they'd accept that. If you aren't fit enough to work in the factories, how can you work well in the company? It isn't a rest-house. Or do you think the work here isn't important? All those who need to recuperate can take sick-leave. Go and register in the organisation department. But we won't accept just anyone. We'd rather leave places vacant than appoint parasites at the expense of the country. I like Qiao's style of work. From now on, those who do well will be rewarded and promoted, while those who make serious errors will be penalised and demoted! Some cadres pester their friends to find them new posts when they fail at their own jobs. This only encourages officials to hold on to one job, while seeking a better one. No wonder the workers say that their managers aren't really interested in their work. How can a cadre run a factory well with such a mentality?'

Xu spoke up again. 'Ji Shen is the manager of the Electrical Machinery Plant. Now that we've decided to send Qiao and Shi there, what should he do then?'

'He can be the deputy manager,' Huo said firmly. 'If he does well, he'll be promoted. If he doesn't he'll be demoted until he can find a job he can do. Of course, this is my opinion. We can discuss it.'

Xu whispered to Qiao, 'Things will get worse when you go there.'

Qiao shrugged as if saying, 'I never expected it to be a picnic.'

Assuming Office

I

It was late in the evening when Qiao got home. The air in his room was rather stale, so he opened wide the door and windows. He was dying for a cup of tea, but as there was no hot water in the thermos flask, he had to make do with some cold water. Then sitting at his desk, he selected a book entitled *Metallography* from a stack of books. He drew out a photo, the background of which was Lenin's Mausoleum in Moscow's Red Square. In the foreground stood Qiao and a girl. In his light Western suit, Qiao looked young and very handsome, but faintly ill at ease. The attractive girl beside him was smiling at him sweetly. Gazing at the photo, Qiao suddenly closed his eyes, and buried his head in his hands. The photo slipped from his fingers to the desk. . . .

In 1957 Qiao, already in his final year of study in the Soviet Union, had gone to gain some practical experience in the Leningrad Power Plant as an assistant manager. Tong Zhen, the girl in the photo, was a college student working in the plant on her graduation thesis. She was soon attracted to Qiao, who was handsome, intelligent and good at his work. He refused to tolerate fear, suspicion and flattery. Tong, who was similar, fell in love with him, despite the fact that he was ten years her senior and married. Qiao, too, was very happy to meet another Chinese in a foreign land and treated her as his younger sister, protecting her as if she were still a child. But that was not what she wanted. Sometimes she felt jealousy when she saw him brooding, perhaps missing his wife.

Qiao returned home first and was appointed the manager of the Electrical Machinery Plant, a new enterprise which badly needed technicians. Tong, after her graduation in 1958, returned home to work under Qiao. Tong had a nephew, Xi Wangbei, who happened to be an apprentice in the same plant. By chance he discovered that his aunt was in love with Qiao. Being headstrong and suspicious, Xi began to hate Qiao believing he was trifling with his aunt. Though ten years younger, he regarded himself as his aunt's guardian and kept an eye on her. He went out of his way to prevent her from meeting Qiao when he was alone. Quite a few young men wanted to court her, but Tong sent them away, saying she would never marry. This made Xi even more irritated and so he put all the blame on Qiao. In his eyes, Qiao was a playboy, who was ruining his aunt's life.

Seven years later, the Cultural Revolution started. Xi became the leader of a faction with Qiao as the main target of his attack. Apart from labelling Qiao as a 'capitalist roader', Xi called him a 'womaniser'. To protect his aunt, he never went into details. Some of his men, however, were interested in the romantic angle and magnified the whole affair by making up stories about Tong and Qiao. Tong was greatly hurt. In her eyes, there were not many people like Qiao who were able to run a modern factory. He had enjoyed a high prestige before, but now his reputation was ruined. People did not really hate those who had not followed the Party line, but those who were immoral were always despised. How could she clarify the truth? She blamed herself for making Qiao suffer more than other so-called 'capitalist roaders'. She wrote to tell him that she had decided to commit suicide. But Xi, ever cautious, caught her in time. Since then, Qiao had felt indebted to the two women in his life.

Qiao's wife had been the head of the propaganda department at a university. In spite of the gossip about her husband, she had never doubted him. She died mysteriously when being illegally detained for investigation in early 1968. With bitter regrets, Qiao confessed before the portrait of his late wife that he had once wavered before Tong's passionate words and that he had sometimes felt drawn to her. He made a vow never to speak to Tong again. When his youngest son entered the university, Qiao was left alone, leading the life of a monk, as if deliberately torturing himself to show his faithfulness to his late wife and children.

Even he didn't know what prompted him to ring Tong up and ask her to come over. 'What do you want?' he asked himself in surprise. If he had not volunteered to return to the plant, the affair would have been finished for ever. How could they work together again after all that trouble? Only ten years before, they had been cruelly slandered. Now Qiao realised that Tong was still important to him despite his efforts to forget her. His feelings were so subtle, so complicated, he could not work them out. 'Better take a grip on yourself,' he told himself.

'There's a lot to do tomorrow.' All of a sudden, he sensed someone at his shoulder. He looked up. His heart missed a beat when he saw Tong standing beside him gazing tearfully at the photo. He jumped to his feet and gripped her hands, whispering, 'Tong Zhen! Tong!'

Tong shuddered and withdrew her hands from his ardent hold. Then she turned around, wiped away her tears and made an effort to control herself. Her appearance had changed so much that Qiao was quite shocked. Though only a little over forty, Tong's hair was streaked with gray. Though her eyes were soft and feminine they conveyed a deep bitterness. There was no sign of their former warmth and courage. Qiao's heart ached. This promising and talented woman engineer could have done much. Now there was no sign of the idealistic, energetic girl. Was it only time which had made her age so quickly?

Both of them felt rather awkward. Though Qiao searched for warm yet suitable words to break the silence, in the end he blurted out, 'Tong, why don't you get married?' He hadn't intended to ask this. Even the voice didn't sound like his.

'What do you mean?' she retorted.

He waved his hand as though brushing away all hypocrisy. Suddenly he came closer to her and said, 'Why should I pretend? Tong, let's get married! Tomorrow or the day after tomorrow? Agreed?'

Though she had waited for this moment for twenty years, Tong was thrown off balance by his proposal.

'Isn't it a bit sudden?' she said softly. 'Why the rush?'

Now that the ice was broken, Qiao replied with his usual enthusiasm and strength, 'Look, our hair is already gray. How can you talk about rushing it? We don't need to prepare anything for the wedding. We can just throw a party and announce our marriage, that's all.'

Her face, glowing with happiness, looked younger. 'You know how I feel,' she murmured. 'You decide.'

'So it's settled,' he said joyfully, holding her hand again. 'When I go back to work at the plant tomorrow, I'll tell our friends and relatives that our wedding will take place on the day after tomorrow.'

'Go back to the plant to work?' Tong was startled.

'Yes. The bureau Party committee decided this morning that Shi Gan and I should go back to the plant. You know we're old partners.'

'Oh no! No!' Tong protested automatically. She had imagined being transferred after their wedding to a new factory, where no one would know anything about their past and where they would live in peace. But how would people at the plant talk about Qiao's going back and their marriage? She shuddered at the thought of the gossip and slander. Moreover, Xi, who had been Qiao's most vicious persecutor, was now a deputy manager. How could they co-operate together?

'You're doing very well in the company,' she said unhappily. 'Why do you want to come back?'

'The work in the company doesn't suit me really,' he replied. 'I'm no man for office work.'

'Our plant's a mess. Do you think you can sort things out?'

'Well, if we let all the big factories like ours remain in chaos, modernisation will remain a dream. It'll be rather like commanding a battle during the war, getting the plant into shape! I don't like playing just a minor role. I'm not too old. I want to accomplish something before it's too late.'

Tong's feelings were a mixture of surprise, joy and uneasiness. It had been his sense of responsibility to his work, his ability and his masculinity that had made her love him. Now many years later, though he was still the same, she was asking him to give up his career. She murmured, 'I've never seen a man over fifty with such drive.'

'Drive, like youthfulness, is independent of age. It doesn't only belong to the young, nor does it vanish with age.' He saw how she had aged not only in her appearance but also in her thoughts and feelings. These days many people were fed up with politics. Their psychological wounds seemed the most difficult to heal. He suddenly felt that a big responsibility had been laid on him. Clasping her shoulders like a young man, Qiao said warmly, 'I say, engineer, where are all the plans you kept whispering to me? Don't you remember you wanted to make 600,000, 1,000,000 or 1,500,000 kilowatt generating sets? We even hoped to build the first nuclear power station in our country with a capacity of a million kilowatts. Have you forgotten all that?'

Tong's heart began to thaw.

Qiao continued, 'We must get the latest information from abroad. In the fifties and early sixties, we could keep up to date. But now I know nothing about new developments. By the way, will you teach me English for an hour a day after our marriage?'

Tong nodded, looking straight into his eyes with warmth. She felt secure beside him, more determined and confident. 'Funny, you haven't changed in the least. You're still so idealistic after all you've been through,' she said with a grin.

'How can one alter one's nature?' he chuckled. Not wishing to change the subject, he continued to encourage her, his eyes fixed on the slender woman. 'I was put through the mill – so what? You know the old saying, "Stone whets a sword, difficulties strengthen will-power".'

He asked her to show him around the plant. When she was reluctant he teased her, 'What was the word you cursed me with? I remember, it was 'coarse', wasn't it? Funny, how this 'coarse' man can talk about love? Listen, love is a strong passion. You've longed for it. Now it's here, you don't have to fear it, let alone hide your feelings and suffer for it. I'm only worried that your passion is drying up like your interest in politics.'

'Nonsense!' Tong denied, blushing. 'A woman's love never dries up.' Overwhelmed by emotion, she kissed him passionately.

On their way to the plant, she persuaded him not to marry her right away on the pretext that, for her, her wedding day was of vital importance and that she had paid a lot more for it than other women. She wanted to prepare herself well for it. Qiao agreed.

2

The two of them first entered Workshop No. 8 which was nearest the entrance. The familiar look of the shop floor made every bone in Qiao's body cry out for work. His hands were itching to touch the lathes. Then he thought of the twelve advanced workers whom he had trained, each in charge of a processing section.

'All your advanced workers are in other jobs now,' Tong told him. 'One has become a foreman, another a warehouse-keeper, a janitor, a checker and so on. Don't you remember how four of them condemned you at the criticism meeting, saying you had corrupted them with material incentives? Don't you have any grudges against them?'

'Oh no,' Qiao brushed this aside. 'At those meetings, everybody raised their fists and shouted slogans against me. If I begrudged that, I wouldn't be back here. If those twelve men are no longer pace-setters, then I'll have to train new ones. We must have the most skilful workers and best products.'

While talking to Tong, Qiao walked from lathe to lathe. Nothing pleased him more than feasting his eyes on purring machines turning out top quality products.

Qiao halted before a young man who was casually throwing processed turbine blades on to a pile on the ground, while humming a foreign pop song. Qiao picked up some of the blades to examine them and found that most were defective. Staring at the young worker, he snapped, 'Stop singing!'

Not knowing who Qiao was, the youngster winked at Tong and sang louder:

O mother!
Please keep your cool.
Young people are just loafers!

'Stop it!' Qiao bellowed, his authoritative voice and furious eyes startling the turner. 'Are you a turner or a ragpicker?' he continued. 'I bet you don't know anything about the operating rules!'

Obviously Qiao was an official, and his air of authority silenced the boy. Taking a white handkerchief from Tong, Qiao wiped the lathe. The handkerchief turned black.

'So is this the way you look after your lathe?' Qiao demanded, his eyes fixed on the young man. 'Keep this handkerchief hanging on your lathe until you've cleaned it. Then you can have a white towel.'

Many workers had gathered around them.

'Comrades,' Qiao said to them, 'I'll ask the equipment section to hang a white towel on each of your lathes tomorrow. Let the towel tell in future whether or not you look after your machines well.'

Some of the old workers recognised Qiao and quietly withdrew. Red in the face, the younger turner was too embarrassed to say anything. He nervously hung the black handkerchief on a lever which apparently he never touched. This brought him more trouble.

Qiao, having noticed the dirty, greasy lever, asked, 'What's that handle for?'

'I don't know.'

'But there's a notice explaining how to use it, isn't there?'

'It's in a foreign language. I don't understand it.'

'How long have you been working at this lathe?'

'Six years.'

'And for six years you've never touched that lever?'

The young man nodded. His face twitching in anger, Qiao asked the others around, 'Who can tell him how this works?'

No one replied. Some certainly did not know, while others did not want to further embarrass their young man.

'Will you tell him then, engineer?' Qiao asked Tong.

Tong, to ease the tension, explained to him what it was for and how it worked.

'What's your name?' Qiao asked again.

'Du Bing.'

'I'll never forget you, humming while you work and not greasing your lathe for six years.' Then he changed from a sarcastic tone into a severe one. 'Tell your foreman that this lathe needs overhauling at once. I'm the new manager.'

When Qiao and Tong turned to leave, they heard someone whisper, 'Just your luck, Du Bing. He's our former manager!'

Another said, 'An expert like him, he knows at a glance what's wrong.'

'With bums like him around,' Qiao said angrily, 'even the best equipment we import will be damaged.'

'Do you think he's one of the worst?' Tong asked.

'Well, I find it shocking that not a single person bothered to look into such matters for six years. The cadres are so careless, so irresponsible. As a chief engineer, I must say, you're doing pretty well!' Qiao added, tongue in cheek.

'But if the manager is so negligent, how can you blame people like us?' Tong retorted indignantly.

They were talking like this as they entered Workshop No. 7, where they at once caught sight of a young German testing a boring machine. This visitor to China working night shift caught Qiao's attention. Tong told him that he had been sent by the German firm, Siemens, when snags with an electrical part occurred during assembling. His name was Therl and he was only twenty-three years old. This was his first visit to the East, and he had come via Japan, which was why he was seven days late. Afraid that this might be reported to his firm, he had worked extremely hard and solved the problem within three days instead of the scheduled seven or ten. Though he was an expert and a hard worker, he also liked fun and games.

'Though he's so young, he's able to do the job independently abroad,' Qiao said in admiration. Then he sent Tong to get the foreman in charge of work that day. Before the man could greet him, Qiao said, 'Ask all those under thirty to come here and watch how Therl works. And ask Therl to say something about himself and how he learned his skill. I'm thinking of inviting him to give a talk to all our young workers before he leaves.'

The man did not query Qiao's identity but complied with a smile.

Qiao heard some people murmuring behind him and turned around. They were workers from Workshop No. 8 who had rushed to see him when they had learned that Qiao was the man who had roundly criticised Du Bing.

'You won't learn anything looking at me,' Qiao told them. 'Go and watch that young German over there.' He sent a worker he knew to get all the young workers in his workshop to come too, especially the young turner, Du Bing.

Just as he finished speaking, an old worker pulled him over to a quiet corner and mumbled, 'Do you want a foreigner to set us an example?'

Qiao was startled to see that the speaker was Shi Gan! In his overalls and old blue cap, he looked like a worker. Qiao was delighted to see Shi had started work. He had not changed. Though he had refused to come at first, now that he had agreed he would do his best. His appointment had not yet been announced, but he had come to work.

Shi was sullen, regretting his decision. Earlier that afternoon he had had a look around and talked to a few workers whom he did not know. Because of his injury, he spoke indistinctly, and people thought something must be wrong with him. In this way, he learned a lot that Qiao could not. The workers in this plant were rather confused ideologically. The idol many had worshipped had gone. They had even lost their national pride and faith in socialism. For many years they had been cheated, manipulated and criticised. They'd become demoralised.

Moreover, in this plant, there were three groups of cadres: those who had been cadres before the Cultural Revolution; or during it; or after the downfall of the gang when Ji Shen became the manager. The old people were still hurt, while the young felt resentful. Shi worried that one day they would flare up and clash head-on, causing renewed conflict within the party. There was not only chaos awaiting him and Qiao, but also bitter political rivalries. They were up against a very difficult situation.

Shi was furious with himself for having gotten involved in such a mess. Political struggles had taught him a great deal. Now he seldom became excited or lost control of himself in public, and resented pretentiousness of any kind. With his feelings thus hidden, he believed he could resist any temptation. So how on earth had he been persuaded by Qiao that very morning? He was quite certain that his return would do both of them no good. Qiao would never be a politician. He had started working even before the announcement of his appointment. That was no way for a manager to behave. He did not want to talk to Qiao at this moment. But, surprised to see Tong beside Qiao, he could not help warning him, 'You mustn't get married for at least six months.'

'What do you mean?' Qiao was put out.

Shi told him briefly that the news of the management reshuffle had leaked out and that some were gossiping that Qiao had only come back to marry Tong Zhen.

'All right,' Qiao said shortly, 'I may as well be hanged for a sheep as for a lamb. We'll hold a wedding ceremony in the auditorium tomorrow evening. You'll be our witness.'

Shi whirled to leave in a huff, but Qiao caught him. Then Shi complained, 'Didn't you ask me to give you advice? But when I do you just turn a deaf ear!'

Clenching his teeth, Qiao muttered after a while. 'OK. I'll listen to you. After all, it's a personal thing. But tell me, the decision to reshuffle was made only this morning, how on earth did people learn about it this afternoon?'

'That's nothing unusual. These days, news travels faster on the grapevine than through official channels. Rumors are proved by documents. Right now, the plant Party committee is having an urgent meeting. My instinct tells me it has something to do with our return.' But instantly Shi regretted telling him what he only guessed. Emotion was something harmful. Shi found himself together with Qiao sinking faster into the swamp.

On impulse, Qiao dragged Shi and Tong to the office block. The meeting room on the first floor was brightly lit, with cigarette smoke filtering out of its wide-open windows. Someone was making a speech in a loud voice, talking about the next day's production campaign. This worried Qiao. He asked the other two to wait for him for a moment while he went to make a phone call to Huo Dadao. Then the three of them entered the room.

People were surprised at the sudden appearance of the three gate-crashers. Ji Shen fixed his eyes on Tong, who immediately looked away wishing to escape since she wasn't on the Party committee.

'What's brought you here?' Ji asked, as though he knew nothing about the reshuffle.

'Just having a look,' Qiao said in a loud voice. 'We heard that you were having a discussion on production. We'd like to know what you think.'

'Fine! Fine!'

Ji looked haggard. He had mobile yet inscrutable features. 'There are two items on today's agenda,' he explained. 'One, the suspension of Xi Wangbei at the request of the masses. Two, tomorrow's production campaign. I spent much time and energy on political movements in the past and not enough on production. But all the members of the committee are confident. Once the campaign gets going, things will improve. Comrades, we can be more specific. Qiao and Shi are the former leaders of our plant. Perhaps they can give us some good advice.'

He was an experienced man, composed and steady. He was hoping to impress Qiao with how he conducted a meeting. That very afternoon he had learned of the bureau's decision by telephone, and he bitterly regretted ever having joined the bureau.

It was true that he had been persecuted by the 'Gang of Four' for ten years. But he had not suffered much as he had been appointed the deputy principal of the Municipal Cadre School in the countryside. At that time, when the cadre school was regarded as a good socialist development, Ji realised that it was a safe place in which to lie low, with all its unfortunate prominent people. Being a deputy, he became acquainted with some former high-ranking officials. It would have been very difficult to get in contact with them if it had not been for the school. They had become his subordinates, and felt very grateful to him for making life a little easier for them in terms of accommodation, food, work and holidays. Besides, he found it easy to get on with people, and they, in turn, found him very agreeable. Now, since most of them had been restored to their former posts, Ji had friends in many high places and had become a man of influence himself.

Two years before, he had decided to work in the Electrical Equipment Bureau, fully aware of the importance of this industry for China's modernisation. He only had experience in personnel work and knew nothing about production. In order to get some practical experience, he had asked to work in this Electrical Machinery Plant for a couple of years. Moreover, to be a manager of a big factory was very useful when construction and the economy were being stressed. It would pave the way for him to climb higher. He dreamed of becoming an important cadre in the bureau, where there might be chances to visit other countries. If you had been abroad, your future would be even brighter. Ji worked hard, but being only a bureaucrat and too cautious politically, he did things according to the way the wind blew. Naturally he was slow to act. When a knotty problem occurred, he tried to avoid it. Crafty and sophisticated, he put his individual interests above everything else. But with these values, how could he run a factory well where the problems were practical and specific? In another place he might have muddled along, but certainly not here under the eye of Huo Dadao. He knew that success was not merely a stroke of luck. It depended on ability and struggle. That was why he was banking everything on a new production campaign. If that raised production, he could leave the plant a hero. But that was not all. By dismissing Xi from his post, he would leave a thorny problem for Qiao to solve, which would certainly unseat him in time. Then no one would say Ji was incapable. Shi, however, smelled a rat, and Qiao too saw through Ji's trick.

Everybody at the meeting wondered what Qiao and Shi were up to, appearing so late at night. They were not really interested in the campaign business. Noticing the people's mood, Ji hurried to close the meeting, thinking he could thus achieve his ends. Just as he was clearing his throat to speak, Huo Dadao entered. His arrival caused another stir.

After asking what all the talk was about, Huo, without further ado, announced the bureau Party committee's decision to reshuffle. And finally he added, 'Due to the chief engineer's long absence because of health reasons, the bureau has decided to promote Tong Zhen to be the assistant chief engineer.'

Tong was taken by surprise and felt very nervous. She could not understand why Qiao had not hinted about it.

The announcement of these decisions came like a lightning blow to Ji Shen, who was almost speechless for once. Checking his anger with a great effort, he forced a smile and said, 'Of course I accept the decisions. Both Qiao and Shi are old hands here, and I'm sure they'll do a better job than I.' Then he continued, turning to Qiao and Shi, 'Tomorrow I'll talk things over with you. Have you any opinions about the two decisions we've made at this meeting?'

Instead of speaking, Shi half closed his eyes lest they betray his thoughts.

'I hadn't the faintest idea about the suspension of Comrade Xi,' Qiao said without formality. He could not help eyeing Xi, who was sitting in a corner. By chance he caught Xi's angry glare. Fearing to be distracted, he averted his gaze at once and continued, 'I'm not for the campaign either. Well, Comrade Ji, you're suffering from coronary thrombosis, aren't you? Can you run at top speed five times from the ground floor to the seventh floor of this office block?'

Not knowing what Qiao was driving at, Ji gave a blank smile.

Qiao continued, 'Well, our plant is like you, a man with coronary thrombosis. To make it leap forward will only mean suicide. To fulfil our quota by such campaigns from month to month is no way to run any plant.'

His words struck the right chord, as the committee members had also been wondering why Ji wanted to launch a campaign to coincide with the reshuffle of the leadership. With a sneer Ji struck a match and lit a cigarette. It seemed there was something he wanted to say.

Noticing Ji's expression, Qiao, who had planned to say just a few words to show his attitude towards the decisions, shifted to another subject in a sharp tone, 'I haven't seen any good plays for years,' he said sharply, 'so I can't tell if there are any good new directors around. But in industry, I know there are a number of political directors. Whenever there's a political movement or a problem in work, they call mass meetings, give pep talks and then organise a parade, shouting slogans, holding criticism meetings and launching campaigns. . . . Factories are their stages; the workers their actors and actresses. They direct them at random. They're no more than cheap propagandists. They can never make good managers for a modern socialist country. It's the easiest way to run a factory. No doubt there'll be endless after-effects. Modernisation can never be achieved by a few so-called "campaigns".'

Sensing something, he turned his head a little and found that Shi was winking to make him shut up. Qiao hurriedly finished, 'I think I'd better stop here. Perhaps I've gone a bit too far. By the way, I want to tell you that Tong and I got married two hours ago. Shi was our witness. We didn't want to make a fuss since neither of us is young any more. We'll invite you for a drink later.'

Surprised and delighted at this news, people began to tease Qiao and Tong before the meeting was dismissed.

Only Tong, Shi and Xi, for their own reasons, were greatly annoyed by Qiao's announcement. Tong was the first to walk out of the meeting room in a huff. Without a backward glance at Qiao, she went straight to the entrance of the plant.

Huo, noticing this, nudged Qiao and urged him to follow Tong. After Qiao had gone, Huo stopped the others who wanted to tease the bride by saying, 'He's a smart one, isn't he? I've never heard of marriage first and drinks later. What about going to his home tonight for a few drinks?'

Qiao had caught up with Tong. Her voice shaking, she said, 'Have you gone mad? Don't you know how people will talk tomorrow?'

'That's just what I want,' Qiao explained. 'Now it's out in the open, you'll have no more worries and you can concentrate on your work. Otherwise you'd be nagging at me and tormenting yourself all the time. Even a mere glance at you walking with me would worry you to death. The more suspiciously you acted, the more trouble you'd land yourself in. Then we would be the victims of gossip and rumor again. I'm the manager. You're the assistant chief engineer. How could we co-operate under those circumstances? Now we've made it clear that we're husband and wife. Let those who wish to talk about us talk. They'll soon get bored with it. I made up my mind to announce it right on the spot. There wasn't time to consult you.'

Under the lamp, her eyes glowed. Her anger lessened. This was a day of great significance for her.

Following Huo, Shi, no longer agitated, caught up with them. He gripped Tong's hand and nodded, congratulating her on her happiness.

Some violent emotion seemed to be gripping Tong.

Huo told the two women committee members beside him, 'Take my car and accompany the bride to her room. She may want to dress up. Then escort her to her new home. We'll wait for you there.'

Tong said to Huo, 'Don't bother. We'll go and register first.'

'Will there be a big celebration?' one of them asked.

'Maybe. Anyway, at least there will be some wedding sweets.' Everybody laughed.

Qiao and Tong, looking at Huo with gratitude, could not help smiling.

The Main Role

I

Just imagine, as the curtain rises, gongs and drums are beaten. The music starts and the hero swaggers in but he neither speaks nor sings. How do you think the audience would react?

This was precisely the case with the Heavy Electrical Machinery Plant. It had been a fortnight since Qiao assumed office, but nothing had happened, no instructions, no meetings. He was not even in his office. What was the matter with him? He had never been like this before. It wasn't his style.

He was with the workers all day long. When you wanted him, he was nowhere to be found, yet he'd pop up right in front of you when you didn't need him. No one knew what he was up to. He seemed to have relinquished his authority and let the departments, offices and workshops go to pot. The workers without a leader did whatever they liked. The result was anarchy, and production dropped rapidly.

The bureau's operations centre felt the situation was intolerable. They asked Huo several times to go there and do something abot it. Huo refused to raise a finger. When pressed too hard, he said tartly, 'Don't you worry! Before the tiger springs, it crouches back a little. Don't you know this?'

Shi was anxious and puzzled too. He asked Qiao, 'What are you waiting for? Have you a plan?'

'Oh yes!' Qiao replied readily. 'Our plant is just like a sick man suffering from several diseases. We must find the right remedies to cure them. Before we start, we must make sure our diagnosis is correct.'

Shi darted a glance at Qiao, who looked determined and self-confident.

'I've found out something important during the last two weeks,' Qiao continued cheerfully. 'Our workers and cadres aren't as apathetic as you imagined. Quite a number of them are really concerned about state affairs and our future. They make suggestions to me, argue with me and even criticise me, saying I've let them down. It's not a bad thing to have a short period of confusion. This helps us to separate the sheep from the goats. I've already picked out a few people in my mind, who will play an important role in my plan.' He narrowed his eyes envisaging the plant's future.

'Isn't today your birthday?' Shi asked all of a sudden.

'Birthday? What birthday?' Qiao was puzzled. Leafing through the calendar, he suddenly realised it was. 'Well, well! My birthday today. Fancy you remembering it!'

'Someone asked me if you were going to accept presents and throw a party.'

'Hell, no! But if you'd like to come, I'll offer you a free drink.'

Shi shook his head.

When Qiao got home, dinner was ready. On the table were food and wine. A woman has a good memory for such matters. Though just married, Tong remembered Qiao's birthday very well. Happily, Qiao sat down to eat. But Tong stopped him and said with a smile, 'I've invited Xi to come. Shall we wait for him?'

'Did you invite anybody else?'

'No.'

Obviously she wanted the two to bury the hatchet. Qiao understood his wife's intention, but in fact he couldn't care less that Xi had once attacked him.

Instead of Xi, they were surprised by the arrival of a group of junior cadres from the plant, who had been on the management side before the

Cultural Revolution. While some were still the heads of certain departments, offices or workshops, others were no longer cadres.

'We've come to celebrate your birthday, Old Qiao,' they all greeted him jubilantly.

'Forget it,' Qiao said. 'If you want some wine, there's plenty. But forget about the birthday business. Who told you that?'

One bald-headed man, a former head of administration, said meaningfully, 'Old Qiao, you may have forgotten us, but we haven't forgotten you!'

'Come now! Who says I've forgotten you?'

'Well, haven't you? You've been back for half a month. All of us have been expecting something to happen. You've quite disappointed us. You know Liu, the manager of the Boiler Plant, don't you? The day he returned to his office, he threw a dinner party that evening and invited all his old cadres. What a feast! Of course, it wasn't the food or drink that mattered, but it gave them a chance to air their grievances. The following day, all of them went back to their former posts. Good for Liu! He didn't let his old comrades down!'

This got Qiao's back up, but he made an effort to control himself. After all, this was his new home, not the place for a showdown.

'In the two years since the gang fell, you still haven't let off steam?'

'The gang's followers are still around! Xi will soon be reinstated after only a month's suspension. . . .'

Talk of the devil! Xi suddenly entered and obviously caught the last sentence. Feigning indifference, he nodded to Qiao and sat down facing them. In fact he was ready for a fight. Sensing fireworks, Tong cleverly shifted the topic and led Xi to another room on some pretext.

The guests looked at each other and rose to leave. Their bald-headed leader said sarcastically, 'Oh, I see. The feast isn't for us. No wonder that whizz-kid will be back in his job so soon. You've made it up. Fair enough, you're relatives after all.'

Qiao did not insist on their staying but said coldly, 'Wang, to put it bluntly, all you want is to go back to your old job or, better still, be promoted, right? Don't worry. Our trouble isn't that we have too many cadres in this plant. We need a lot more. Of course, I mean capable people who know how to do their jobs. There'll be an examination tomorrow. I don't think it matters if I tell you now. We've all been a long time in this plant and should know about such things as balanced production or what is standardisation, systematisation and universal specifications.'

The men were flabbergasted. They'd never heard such terms. What shocked them most was that even the cadres had to take the exam.

Someone grumbled in a low voice, 'This is very new, isn't it?'

'What's new about it?' Qiao retorted. 'From now on, no one will be allowed to muddle along whether he is a worker or a cadre. To be frank, I'm most unhappy about the plant and have a lot more to complain about than you. It's time we got down to work.'

After he'd seen them off, he returned to his drink. His expression was angry. When Tong brought him a bowl of rice after he had drunk a few cups of wine, he said to the young man opposite him, 'You know pretty well, Xi, the decision to suspend you was not made by the new Party committee. Shi must have told you that your case has been cleared. Why do you still refuse to work?'

'I want the Party committee to make it clear to all the workers and staff members in the plant why I was suspended from my work. Now the investigation is over. It's been proved that, first, I never raided anybody's home or office; and second, I had no personal connection with the 'Gang of Four'. Why did you pick on me? Just because I was the head of a faction, or because I'm a so-called new cadre? How could you make such a decision based on rumour?'

Seeing him wave his chopsticks with indignation, Qiao thought, 'So now you know what it's like! You slandered others, didn't you?'

As if guessing what was in his mind, Xi turned the conversation, 'I request to work on the shop floor.'

'What?' This was rather unusual. New cadres didn't easily quit their jobs lest people think they fell because they were involved with the gang. But Xi had the guts to ask for it. Was he bluffing? Anyway, Qiao called his bluff by saying, 'Fine! I agree. In fact, respect doesn't come with an appointment. You have to earn it. Many people can be high-fliers. Some through their own efforts, while others are tossed up by the wind. I hope you're not looking for such a wind again.'

Xi sneered. 'I don't know what wind you're talking about! If I were an opportunist, I wouldn't have been suspended from my work. Twenty years ago I was an apprentice. I've been a worker, a group leader, a foreman, and when I was a little over thirty, I became a deputy manager, a 'whizz-kid', as some of them called me. I'm willing to go down to the shop floor instead of holding on to a post to the death like some others. Actually those who were once officials still crave more power and promotion.'

The old cadres blamed Qiao for favoring the young, whereas the new ones insinuated that he was a bureaucrat.

Tong offered Qiao a lot of food, afraid he might lose his temper. But Qiao relaxed, chewing over what Xi had just said.

Xi knew that Qiao would never give him sympathy if he pleaded with him, but might soften if he was tough. A coward would never win his respect. Better to be tough with him.

'When will we Chinese rid ourselves of one-sidedness?' he went on. 'During the Cultural Revolution, nearly all the cadres were attacked and removed from their offices. Now, though we talk about drawing a lesson from it, all new cadres have been dismissed. Of course, there are some followers of the gang among the new cadres, but they are only a handful. Most of them were fooled into believing they were following the Party line. If you're active in one political movement, you'll be a victim in the next. The safest way is to sit on the fence and do nothing. Once a movement starts everybody higher than a foreman is investigated. When a new man takes over the leading position, he puts in his own men and kicks out all the others. This is practiced right down to the small units. People are divided into factions. The cadres spend all their time and energy on fixing people with whom they don't see eye to eye. In work they can't co-operate with each other. If things go on like this, despite all your high-sounding slogans, modernisation will never be achieved.'

Hearing this, Qiao grew quite alert though he said, 'Come off it, Xi. You sound like a theoretician. Our country has suffered enough from too many critics, too much empty talk. What we need are hard-working and selfless people.' He had imagined only the old cadres needed to vent their anger and had never expected such a complaint from a new cadre. It would be extremely damaging if the two forces clashed head-on.

2

Qiao went into action the following day.

First, he had all nine thousand workers and staff sit for the exam and have an appraisal made of their work. All those who were lazy, careless or unqualified were made to form a service team. Those who passed were capable and hard-working. After this, production began to pick up speed. The whole plant was stimulated by the new competitive spirit.

The workers felt that Qiao was a man of action. Once he had decided on something, he would go all out for it. As he had promised, a fine building for a kindergarten was soon completed. He had said that bonuses would be awarded if the production quota was reached, and so in August the workers got them for the first time. All skilled, hard-working people said that there could be no better manager than Qiao. At the same time he was hated by some of the service-team members, who were furious at having to work in it.

He dismissed the one thousand temporary workers who had been engaged in building and transportation. Their work was taken over by the service team. Qiao made a capable man, Li Gan, the head of the finance office, the team leader, and gave some of the temporary workers' wages to this team as a material incentive. Though they suffered no cut in wages, the young workers in it felt insulted and humiliated. Du Bing, for one, felt strongly about it, because his girl-friend had jilted him since he wasn't even a qualified turner. He was miserable and desperate.

But Qiao had other enemies. The worst were those angry cadres who had been sent to the service team. They in turn demanded that all the managers should take the exam too. Unperturbed. Qiao went to the auditorium with a few deputy managers to sit for the exam.

The news soon got around, and the workers, having ended their day-shift, rushed to the hall which was soon packed to overflowing. They fired all sorts of questions at Qiao, who answered with ease. But Ji Shen did badly. When he got everything muddled up, the workers called him 'a superfluous manager'. Enraged, he choked back his anger, inwardly cursing Qiao for laying such a nasty trap to make a fool of him in public.

Ji found being a deputy manager was rather demanding. Moreover, he resented being at the beck and call of others, especially so before the workers. Now that he had failed the exam, jealousy and resentment pushed him to join the opposition. He was Qiao's deputy only in name. His frowning face and his dark eyes seemed to be the source of all trouble in the plant. Wherever there was a problem in production, he had a hand in it. Yet he was too careful to be caught out. Qiao had to be both on guard against him and at the same time solve the problems he caused. He was really a damn nuisance.

So Qiao made up his mind to send Ji to the service team and ask him to take charge of construction, unaware that the service team was already a powder keg and that Ji's appearance would certainly spark off an explosion. It was thoughtful Shi who foresaw the impending trouble. Qiao, however, ignored his warning. Even more surprising, he promoted Xi to be the deputy manager instead of Ji, supervising production. Those who 'were capable were promoted. Qiao followed this rule, regardless of personal likes or dislikes. Xi, a personal enemy of Qiao, had become his assistant.

As Shi predicted, only a few days after Ji's transfer, grumbles in the service team became open protests, threatening to topple Qiao again.

Though Qiao was up to his neck in all sorts of contradictions and problems, he had no time to deal with the movement to topple him. What preoccupied him most was preparing for the next year's produc-tion. He hoped to get the output up to two million kilowatts. But the Power Company did not like the idea. They preferred to import some equipment from abroad. Besides, there were problems such as fuel and raw materials. Qiao decided to do some diplomatic work himself.

Unfortunately he met with an ignominious defeat. He had been ignorant of the gap between his wonderful plan and reality. Disorder and corruption made it impossible for him to reach his goal. He felt at the end of his tether. He needed large rotor forgings, the more the better; but the supplier would not listen to him. He wanted raw materials and fuel, but did not know how to get them. He was unaware of the unwritten rule that in return you had to give something the others needed. It was called mutual exchange. So it wasn't just a matter of clinching a deal. Anyway, Qiao learned something new: that it was not important whether or not a manager knew anything about metallography or mechanics. What was essential was to have a good 'relationship' with others.

3

The first thing Qiao did when he returned was to see Shi Gan. Shi, flustered by his sudden appearance, stuffed some papers into his drawer. But Qiao, concentrating on other things, failed to notice this. They sat down and began talking when Li, the head of the service team, broke in. Seeing Qiao, he exclaimed joyfully, 'Eh, Qiao, you're just the man I'm looking for!'

'What is it?' Qiao asked eagerly.

'The peasants are refusing to let us start building our apartment block. Xi is surrounded by them. There may be a scuffle.'

'But the City Planning Bureau has given the go-ahead. We've paid the money.'

'They want five tractors in addition.'

'The same old story!' Qiao bellowed. 'We're producing electrical machinery. Where in hell's name can we get tractors?'

'But Ji Shen promised them.'

'Shit! Where's Ji? Go and get him.'

'He's been transferred, leaving everything in a mess,' Li complained.

'What?' Qiao turned to look at Shi.

'Three days ago,' Shi explained, 'he came to say goodbye to me in the morning. That same afternoon he went to the Foreign Trade Bureau. He knew a certain big shot there, who pulled some strings to get Ji the job. He didn't even say a word to the Party committee. But his file's with us. So he's still on our pay-roll.'

'He can take his file with him. We won't pay him for doing nothing.' Then he gestured to Li, 'Let's go and have a look.'

They got into a jeep and set off at once. On their way to the new building site, they met Xi racing along on his bike.

'Hey, Xi, what's happening?' Li called out.

'Nothing! It's all settled!' With that, he rode on as if on urgent business.

'Well done!' Li nodded admiringly. 'He's got a good head on his shoulders.' He asked the driver to turn around to catch up with him.

When they were abreast of him, Li shouted, 'What's the hurry? Anything wrong? You know, Qiao's back!'

Xi stopped to greet Qiao and then explained, 'Workshop No. 1 has some problem with the coils.'

Xi thrust the bike at Li and jumped into the jeep. As the jeep started for the plant, Li shouted after it, 'Eh, Qiao, what about my problem?'

Problem after problem! There was no end to them. Since it was almost the end of the year and the workers were busier, problems were more likely to occur. Qiao feared that this new problem might mess up everything.

As they entered the workshop, they saw the foreman pleading with Tong Zhen. Calmly shaking her head, she was not budging. 'What a stubborn mule!' the man thought to himself, his patience beginning to wear thin. She did not raise her voice and she was still smiling. Though she spoke in an even tone, she refused to give an inch on technical questions. Even if you shouted at her, she remained the same, until finally you gave in and listed to her. Suddenly the exasperated man spotted Qiao. Immediately he dashed over to him, thinking he was the only person who could change Tong's mind.

'Qiao,' he groused, 'we were certain to fulfil this year's quota eight days ahead of schedule. We can do even better next year. But we've got a slight problem. You see, the puncture rate of the lower coil of a rotor is no more than one per cent. That's really nothing serious. But Tong insists we rewind the coil. Earlier this year, coils with a puncture rate around thirty or forty per cent were passed. So it's a lot better now.'

'Have you found the cause of it?' Qiao broke in.

'Not yet.'

'Yes, we have!' Tong butted in. 'I've told you twice about it. All I'm asking you to do is to erect a plastic covering and take measures to protect the generators from dust. But you think it's too troublesome.'

'Troublesome?' Qiao said in a mocking tone, 'It's easy to turn out rejects, but aren't they troublesome to the country? What about quality? You did fairly well in the exam. Theory is one thing and practice is another, right? Do it again! No bonus for you and your workers this month.'

The man was upset.

'You don't have to be so harsh, Qiao,' Tong pleaded. 'They're bound to finish the work in time even if they do it again. Why cut their bonus?'

'It has nothing to do with you,' Qiao said coldly without even looking at her. 'Just think of the time and materials wasted because of their carelessness!' Then he and Xi walked out of the workshop.

With a wry smile, the foreman said to Tong, 'The service team wants to smash him, and we do everything possible to support him. I can't understand why he's so hard on us.'

Tong said nothing. She was concerned with the technical side and had no say in such things. All she could do was try to console the depressed man.

Tong bought four tickets for a Beijing opera *The Forsaken Wife* to try to cheer up her husband. The other two were for Xi and his wife. As Xi did not turn up in time, the three of them set off first, leaving a ticket for Xi.

Just as they were about to enter the theater, Li Gan appeared out of the blue. Seeing him in such a flurry, Qiao sensed that something must have gone wrong. He asked the two women to go in first while he followed Li to a quiet place.

'What's up?' Qiao asked quietly. The look of authority in his eyes calmed Li down.

'Some people in the service team are out to make trouble.'

'Who?'

'Du Bing. He's backed by Baldy Wang. They're making a noise about Ji Shen supporting them. Du's been absent for three days, so he's probably in touch with those having the sit-in. He appeared this afternoon and talked with a few of his cronies and then wrote some posters. He said they were going to put them up on the wall of the municipal government building, and even threatened to go on a hunger strike.'

'Are you scared?' Qiao asked, sizing up this clever, capable man.

'Why should I be? It's you they're gunning for.'

'Don't worry about me,' Qiao said with a smile. 'You just stick to the rules. Cut the wages of those who stay away from work without good reason. Of they don't want to work here, fair enough. They can go somewhere else.'

A leader must be firmer than his subordinates. Encouraged, Li grinned, 'Watch out when you go home after the opera. They may mug you on the way. I must go now.'

Qiao found his seat and sat down when the bell for silence rang. Some dignitaries entered and took their seats in the middle of the row in front of Qiao. Ji Shen was one of them. With his sharp eye, he'd already spotted Qiao and Tong. Having sat down, he turned around and nodded to Tong. Then he proffered his hand to Qiao, saying, 'So you're back, Qiao. How are things? A man like you always gets what he wants!'

Qiao just shook his head. He hated to talk loudly in public places.

Ji said condescendingly, 'If you come to our bureau, look me up. I'm always at your disposal.'

Qiao swallowed, feeling disgusted. Why was he so smug? Was it his promotion? Was he mocking?

Indeed, Ji now felt superior to Qiao, of whom he'd been so jealous only a few months previously. He'd never commit himself to boost production the way Qiao did, or throw himself into a political movement. That was madness! To him, modernisation was just another political movement, and Qiao was so stupid as to stake everything on it. He was on the brink of a precipice and could fall any minute. Now the Electrical Machinery Plant was already in a turmoil. Ji was proud of his prudent decision to leave the plant in time. Tonight meeting Qiao in such a situation made him feel on top of the world. He seemed to enjoy the opera, discussing it with the people sitting beside him.

But despite his efforts, Qiao could not concentrate on the performance. He racked his brains to find a good excuse to leave the theater, so as not to disappoint the two women.

Xi groped his way to his seat with the help of an usher's torch. The two women inquired why he was so late and if he had eaten anything. He mumbled a few words, nodding his head. Then casting a sidelong glance at Qiao, he whispered, 'Manager, how can you sit still? Let's get the hell out of here!'

Agreeing, Qiao followed Xi and took his leave. But Tong, running after them, caught them in the lobby.

Xi hastily explained to her, 'I have to talk to him. He has the full support of the Ministry of Machine Building and has got some orders for generators from the Ministry of Electric Power. Our problems now are materials, fuel and the co-operation between the factories concerned. Contracts, documents, and Qiao's firmness aren't enough. This is where the deputy manager should come in.'

Qiao had not expected Xi to be willing to do such a job himself. Since he had failed, he couldn't bring himself to ask a deputy to try. Besides, he doubted whether Xi could succeed. Guessing Qiao's thoughts, Xi was upset.

'Are you leaving tomorrow?' Tong asked. 'Why the hurry?'

'I've just discussed it with the Party secretary. He agrees too. We've sent someone to buy the train tickets. We'll probably leave tonight.' Though Xi talked to Tong, he intended Qiao to hear. 'As a manager of a big factory, Qiao has a fatal weakness. He knows nothing about human relationships. It's different from the war years, or even a few years ago. Unlike robots, men have feelings and thoughts. And it's most difficult to influence men's thinking.' Abruptly turning to Qiao, he went on, 'You know how to run a big modern factory. When there is important business in the bureau or ministry, you should go yourself, because you've a reputation and your words carry greater weight. As for public relations, leave that to us deputy managers or chiefs of departments. If things get out of hand, you can smooth them out. But if you do everything yourself and get into a fix, what can we do?'

'OK,' Qiao said, 'but stop giving me all your fine theories! With you it's always theory before practice. I'm sick of it all.' He asked Xi to accompany the two women, while he went to see Shi.

Tong gazed at her husband's receding figure. She knew that he often covered up his anxiety and weakness and that he secretly tried to overcome them. He never showed a trace of depression or hesitation at home. He had to be tough for he shouldered a heavy load. Now the plant was improving. If he backed out at this moment, the plant would collapse. He must not show softness or fear.

Xi was looking at Qiao's back smiling.

'When you two get together,' Tong complained, 'I'm always afraid you'll come to blows!'

'Never!' Xi put his hand on her arm and said cheerfully, 'Frankly, Aunt, there aren't many people as good as Manager Qiao around. Haven't you noticed how many of our cadres are following his example? They'll do well under Qiao's leadership. I confess I don't exactly like him, but I do admire his guts. Though he has a great power of attraction, I'm resisting him with all my might. I won't give in. He despises cowards.'

He looked at his watch and exclaimed, 'Hell! I'm afraid I have to go too. Really to be his deputy isn't easy!' So saying, he dashed off.

Under a lamp, Shi was carefully reading letters of accusation against Manager Qiao, which had been forwarded from the plant's Party committee, the municipal Party committee and even from the Central Party Committee. He felt a mixture of indignation, fear and shame. All the letters attacked Qiao. Not a single one criticised him, the Party secretary. On the contrary, he was described as a victim of Qiao's despotism, as only a figure-head, a living mummy. It was true that Shi had become very quiet and that quite often he pretended to be deaf, not answering certain questions. He had rather prided himself on his sophistication, but now he regretted it deeply and was angry with himself. He had never meant this behavior of his to blacken Qiao and whitewash himself. Sometimes he had been fired by Qiao's enthusiam, and very often his feelings overcame his common sense. On certain important issues, he sided with Qiao by saying nothing or simply acquiescing. He sometimes thought that if all cadres worked like Qiao, China would soon have a new look and that the Party would recover its vitality. But the letters were like a deluge threatening to swamp Qiao for good. Shi's heart ached. He had no idea what to do with the letters. He feared that Du Bing and his mob would gang up with some hooligans to turn the plant upside-down.

While he was thinking, he heard someone call him. Opening the door, he saw Huo Dadao.

Huo looked around and asked, 'Qiao isn't here?'

'No.'

'Well?' Huo slipped the tea Shi had poured him. 'When I heard he was back, I went to see him right after supper. Unfortunately his door was locked. I guessed he would come here.'

'He and Tong have gone to an opera.'

'Then I'll wait for him. I'm pretty sure he won't sit through it all no matter how good! It's a pity that he has to disappoint Tong again.' Huo chuckled softly.

'But he's a Beijing opera fan.'

'I know. You don't believe me? You want to bet?'

Huo, in high spirits, seemed unaware of Shi's bad mood. 'What he's really keen on is his plant, his work,' he added as if talking to himself. Glancing at the letters on the table, Huo asked indifferently, 'Does he know about these?'

Shi shook his head.

'How was his trip? How is he?'

Shi shook his head again. He was about to say something, when Qiao pushed the door open.

Huo chortled and slapped Shi on the shoulder.

Qiao was puzzled by the laughter.

Shi immediately tried to hide the letters, but Qiao noticed his uneasiness. Walking to the table, he snatched up a letter.

Huo urged Shi to show them all to him.

Having read some of the letters, Qiao was enraged and swore, 'The dirty bastards!'

He paced up and down the room, his left cheek twitching, then went over to Huo, who appeared engrossed in reading a paper. So he turned to Shi and asked, 'So what will you do?'

Shi shot him a glance and answered, 'It's time you left this plant for the bureau. This year's quota will be fulfilled. I'll stay and stick it out. I won't leave while there's trouble.'

'What are you talking about?' Qiao roared. 'You want me to run away? What about the plant?'

'But what about you? If you're disgraced, a lot of people will be hurt. Who else will take up this job?' Shi meant this also for Huo's ear.

Huo looked at them calmly, not uttering a word.

Qiao, pacing up and down, snapped, 'I'm not afraid of dirty slanders. As long as I'm the manager, I'll run the plant my way!'

Shi appealed to Huo, 'What do you think, Huo?'

'A few letters and you're scared out of your wits?' Huo asked quietly. 'Still you're his loyal friend. You tell him to get out first and then you'll follow later, eh? A good idea! I must say you've made great progress.'

Shi's face became very red.

Smiling, Huo turned to Qiao and said, 'Qiao, you've only been back for half a year, and one of your achievements is that you've turned this deaf and dumb fellow into a high-ranking official. We had to drag Shi here to be the Party secretary. Now he wants to be the manager as well! Come, Comrade Shi, there's no need to blush! I'm only speaking the truth. Now you're like a real Party secretary. But one thing I must criticise you for is Ji Shen's transfer. Why did you let him go without first consulting the bureau?'

Shi was very embarrassed. Old as he was, he had never got such a dressing-down from his leaders.

Huo rose to his feet and went over to Qiao. 'You know I like the saying, "Better to die fighting than in your bed!" Please tell me, how do you spend your time?'

'Forty per cent on production, fifty per cent on wrangles and ten per cent on slanders,' was Qiao's prompt reply.

'What a waste of time! You should spend eighty per cent of your time on production and the rest on research.'

He suddenly became very serious, 'Modernisation doesn't mean technique alone. You'll have to offend some people. Of course, it's safest to do nothing, but that's criminal. As for misunderstandings, being wronged, slanders, accusations, sneers, never mind them. Ignore them! If you want to achieve something, demand a free rein. We're racing against time. The curtain has just risen on our modernisation drive. The real drama is yet to follow.'

Seeing their faces brighten up, Huo continued, 'The minister rang me up yesterday and told me that he was very interested in the way you are running the plant. He asked me to tell you to be even bolder. Experienced with some new methods. Gain experience. Know what our problems are. Next spring he wants us to go abroad to have a look. China's modernisation will be realised by Chinese, but we must study the experience of other countries.'

The three men sat down, sipping their tea and chattering. Huo suddenly suggested to Qiao, 'You're good at singing Beijing opera. Sing us an aria.'

'OK.' Qiao drank some tea, lifted his head and began to sing. . . .

SECTION 4
Working outside the Official Economy

19 Britain in the Decade of the Three Economies*
J.I. Gershuny and R.E. Pahl

Editor's Introduction: Underlying most ideas about work experience is the notion of wage-labour and the status of employee linked to an employer by a contract of employment. Such conventional ideas were subject to controversial questioning by the following article by Gershuny and Pahl in 1980. The authors would probably now modify certain of the assumptions in the following article: particularly the implied separate autonomy of each of the 'three economies', and the expectation that the 'black' or 'hidden' economy was likely to continue expanding. However, the article still stands as a pertinent and succinct challenge to the more usual concentration on formal paid jobs. A fuller account of many of the ideas presented here, based on recent research, is given in Ray Pahl, Divisions of Labour *(Blackwell, 1984).*

There are a number of fundamental and radical transformations in the nature of our economic life which will dominate the political agenda during the 1980s. Employment will continue to decline as the de-industrialisation of Britain continues. To quote two very perceptive analysts of industrial society, this could enable us to reduce the length of the working day (Harold Macmillan) and free more people from the 'realm of necessity' (Karl Marx). The decline in the numbers employed in manufacturing may soon be matched by a squeeze in the service sector. High wages and new technology will encourage employers to turn to machines, rather than people, to raise productivity and profits.

But all this only affects the 'formal' economy, as chronicled in official figures of gross national product. The Inland Revenue recently said that 'it was not implausible' that in Britain the 'black' economy (ie. work for money which is not declared for tax) now totals as much as 7½ per cent of GNP. Similarly, Professor Gutmann of the City University of New York makes an estimate for the US of about 10 per cent of GNP. Such work is often more satisfying than routine deskilled employment.

The main type of informal and officially unenumerated work is, of course, that which goes on in and around the home: housework,

* First published in *New Society*, 3 January 1980.

cooking, child care, decorating, gardening and so on. It is significant that there is no single word to describe all this activity (which many economists would claim adds 35 to 40 per cent to GNP). Popular discussion often focuses on the growth of 'fiddling,' and makes false assumptions about its novelty.

People have always fiddled, had perks, worked on the side, and helped a neighbour with 'cheap goods.' This is the way the workers have always survived and, at another level and in a different style, the rich have got richer. (Those in the middle may have missed out.) Attempts by the state to organise, tax and control, have shifted various activities from the formal economy or the domestic economy into the informal economy. Yesterday's 'enterprise' becomes part of today's hidden economy. But the political parties huff and puff about the importance of getting people into employment rather than helping people to do their own work.

Obsession with what can be easily counted leads to false ideas about the British disease and our national performance. The political agenda ignores, or misunderstands, the main economic tendencies in our society. This would not matter much if the 'formal' and 'informal' modes of production maintained a constant inter-relationship over time. If the informal economy grew at the same rate as the formal economy, then the significance of GNP as an indicators of change, would be unaffected by the fact that it only measures formal activity. And if the amount of work done in the two economies rose or fell in parallel, then statistics of formal employment levels would indicate the overall availability of work.

But our thesis is that, on the contrary, the two economies develop at different rates. A consequence of social and technological development is the transfer of particular spheres of production between them.

We must first deal with some definitional problems. We are using the term *informal economy* to cover the following three areas, of which the first two are the most important for our argument:

1. *Household economy:* production, not for money, by members of a household and predominantly for members of that household, of goods or services for which approximate substitutes might otherwise be purchased for money.

2. *Underground, hidden* or *black economy*: production, wholly or partly for money or barter, which should be declared to some official taxation or regulatory authority, but which is wholly or partly concealed.

3. *Communal economy:* production, not for money or barter, by an individual or group, of a commodity that might otherwise be purchasable, and of which the producers are not principal consumers.

Like any economic definitions, these have fuzzy edges. Where, for example, do we place those small businesses which rely heavily on family workers, and are less than absolutely scrupulous in their VAT returns? But the definitions will stand up for our present purpose – which is to demonstrate that there are good reasons for expecting the informal economy to grow at the expense of the formal.

In most of the developed world, the massive increase in material production over the last 150 or 200 years has been associated with technological developments and with an increasing scale in organisation. Now this process is showing clear signs of breaking down. With new technology, production can be cheaper, more efficient and often more convenient when it is carried out on a small scale. Work can be done in the household or in the hidden economy, which once was done only in the formal economy.

The man who finds that it pays him to take a week off work to paint the house, or rebuild the engine in his car, will probably do a better job than if he went to a firm in the formal sector. With sewing machines, power drills and food mixers, we can (if we have the skills) get smart clothes, fine carpentry and gourmet food by working in our own time with our own tools. Technology has created this new freedom.

Technology is not the only driving force. Legal changes also push production from the formal into the informal economy. VAT means that money payments in cash become illegal and unrecorded. Steep rates of personal taxation, obligations to pay high national insurance contributions, and employment protection legislation: all these encourage both casual work 'for cash' and do-it-yourself. Changes in relative prices increase DIY, too. Technical innovation has pushed down the price of goods. But rising wages rates have pushed up the price of services. And the satisfactions of informal work – relative autonomy, self-direction and self-pacing – also encourage its growth.

Seen in this perspective, development is not a one-way progress – from reliance on primary production, through manufacturing production, to a society whose major efforts are devoted to the production of services. Nor is there a simple transition from a society in which economic relationships are based on custom, to a modern society in which an increasing proportion of social relationships are cash-based – ie, converted from generalised to specific exchange. The pattern is less tidy. The diagram shows that, instead of a steady one-way flow of economic activity – whereby things move, over time, from the household to the industrial production system – there is a whole series of little transformations of production (perhaps taking place simultaneously) between the formal economy, the household economy and the underground economy. The direction of flow is determined by the social and technical conditions for the production of particular commodities at particular times. As the diagram shows, this involves six possible flows among three types of economy.

Here are some examples. The washing of clothes and linen, which moved from the wash house at home into the laundry, and then back into the home with the technological help of a washing machine, illustrates the two-way flow between households and the formal economy (1 and 2 in the diagram). The current prevalence of household construction work paid for in cash may indicate a shift from formal to underground, or 'black,' production (3 in the diagram). And if unemployment levels rise, the cost of black work will drop and some jobs, now DIY, will move across (6).

There is much discussion about the 'deskilling' of the workforce in the formal economy. But there may be a re-skilling in the informal one. Some people who in the past might have called in a plumber or a carpenter, are now more ready to try to do the job themselves. 'How-to' books democratise skills in the informal economy. Hiring a cook or a chauffeur has always been a minority pastime. The same is now coming to apply to carpenters and glaziers.

Though we argue for a wide range of different sorts of flow between three types of economy, we wouldn't deny that over the last couple of centuries, the aggregate effect has been an overall shift from household/communal production to formal industrial production. But it may be that the most significant transformation in the future will be from the formal economy to the underground and household economies.

We are both engaged in research work, attempting to explore the implications of this hypothesis. One of us (Gershuny) is analysing published and unpublished data to assess more precisely the growth of informal economic activity. For example, the official Family Expenditure Survey shows that, rather than buying formal transport,

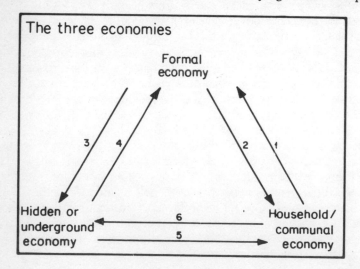

The three economies

Formal economy

3 / 4

2 / 1

Hidden or underground economy

6

5

Household / communal economy

household and entertainment services, the British have increasingly bought *goods* like cars and TV sets – which are used in the informal household production of services.

Another source is the national sample of people's activity patterns, carried out by the BBC Audience Research Department. Re-analysis of the diaries which respondents kept over a number of weeks in 1961 and 1974–75, shows that time spent working for money declined; time devoted to the informal production of services increased.

The other author (Pahl) is exploring the detailed social and economic transactions within and between families in one community. He is trying to document a new kind of rationality, which allocates time and energy between the three economic spheres according to a very subtle calculus. There is employment for which one gets money, and perhaps social satisfaction; and there is work with one's own tools in one's own time, for which one gets much satisfaction and perhaps some money as well.

Work and sociability can get more intertwined in the informal economy than in the formal one. A woman calls on her sister and looks after her child while she has her hair done; she returns with some commodity got through her sister's employment. A man who goes to the pub for a drink and a chat gets suggestions for people who will help him build his house extension.

The whole of everyday life is suffused with contacts, exchanges and reciprocities. Yet the standard economic model is of a marketplace in which you sell your labour for money, and this in turn pays for the goods and services you need. Certainly, that is one option. But, for many people, it is not very satisfactory or rewarding. Any government which assumes that everyone is longing to sell their labour to an employer ought to get closer to the people . . .

20 The Second Economy of the USSR*
Gregory Grossman

Editor's Introduction: The creation of an over-centralised planned economy can give rise to an expanded underground economy linked to the domestic economy. An underground economy (as Gershuny and Pahl indicate, see Chapter 19) exists everywhere whatever the political system, but in Soviet-type societies it can assume significant proportions and shape the day-to-day nature of work experiences in the formal economy. In China, stealing goods or time from the state is called 'eating socialism', a phrase which indicates that economic arrangements, if they are to succeed, must have a moral underpinning.

The standard Western image of the Soviet 'command economy' is one of a state-owned, hierarchically organised, centrally planned and managed, price-controlled and otherwise regimented system, rigidly geared to the goals and priorities of the Soviet leadership, and operating in compliance with a myriad of state-imposed laws, regulations, and directives. However valid this image might be – and, while greatly oversimplified, it is not entirely incorrect – there is another, very significant side to Soviet economic reality, where production and exchange often take place for direct private gain and just as often violate state law in some non-trivial respect. This is the so-called 'second economy,' also referred to by Western observers as 'counter-economy,' 'unofficial economy,' 'parallel market,' and 'private enterprise.' It comprehends a vast and varied set of activities that is attracting ever greater attention from Western scholars. Closely tied to it is widespread corruption of officialdom. Both exist on a large scale in the Soviet Union and in Eastern Europe, and, of course, have many analogies in non-Communist countries, both developed and underdeveloped.

As some scholars define it, the second economy comprises all production and exchange activity that fulfils at least one of the two following tests: (a) being directly for private gain; (b) being in some significant respect in knowing contravention of existing law. So defined, the second economy includes much of the perfectly *legal* private activity which is possible in the USSR. To explain this paradox,

* Abridged version of an article first published in *Problems of Communism*, 26, September/October 1977.

it is important to note that legal private activity, though formally sanctioned and ideologically tolerated, is nevertheless ideologically alien to the Soviet system. Its operating principle are sharply different from those of the 'first' economy. Furthermore, in many cases one cannot practically draw a line between legal and illegal private activity, since the former often serves as a front for the latter and both support one another. In light of this last consideration, and since this article will deal primarily with the illegal and 'semilegal' aspects of the second economy, it may be useful at the outset to describe precisely that private economic activity in the USSR which is legal.

By far the most extensive and best studied part of Soviet legal private economic activity is the 'private plot' – if smaller, the 'garden plot' – in agriculture. The private plot can be cultivated by a peasant household that belongs to a collective farm, by a household with primary employment at a state farm, or, as if often the case, even by one with primary employment outside of agriculture altogether. It has been estimated that in 1974 private agriculture accounted for almost one third of all man-hours expended in agriculture and almost one tenth of all man-hours expended in the whole economy. The land making up the private plots invariably belongs to the state, and the cultivator pays no rent as such. For *kolkhozniki*, or members of collective farms, the plot has lately averaged about three tenths of a hectare (three fourths of an acre), on which not only field crops are grown, but some fowl, smaller livestock, and a strictly limited number of large livestock are usually kept as well. Urban 'garden plots' tend to be even smaller. Still, the approximately 50 million such tiny 'farms,' whose area represents only about 3 percent of the national total of cultivated land, have a gross output which is more than one fourth the gross output of Soviet agriculture. Their contribution to production is especially significant in potatoes, vegetables, fruit, and animal products. Their logical adjuncts are the so-called collective-farm markets, marketplaces where producers sell directly to final consumers and where demand-and-supply relations reign almost supreme.

Although in principle the private plot and the kolkhoz market are legal, they are quite frequently associated with illegalities. For example, limitations on plot area and on livestock holdings may be surreptitiously exceeded; various inputs – particularly fodder, but also fertiliser, water, implements, means of transport, etc. – may be illegally obtained from the 'socialised' sector; and produce may be marketed with the help of middlemen. The collective-farm markets invite violations of the law as well, most notably, the disposal of stolen goods.

Considerable private activity is to be found in the housing sector of the Soviet economy also. By law, the private ownership of housing is allowed only for the owner's occupancy, with some exceptions. And although owner occupancy of houses is not a productive activity in the common sense of the phrase, it is worthy of note that even 60 years after the Russian revolution approximately one half of the Soviet total population, and about one quarter of the urban population, still resides in privately owned housing. What is more, as late as 1975 some 30 percent of all new housing space (measured in square meters) was completed by non-state entities: housing cooperatives, collective farms, and individuals, with the last accounting for the greatest share. Again, while in principle such construction may be legal, there is little doubt that much of it involves the acquisition of materials on the black market, illegal hiring of construction help, unauthorised use of state-owned vehicles, bribery of officials, and other violations of the law.

To complete our list, the law also permits private activity in certain professions, such as those of physician, dentist, teacher, and tutor; in the provision of certain household and repair and personal services, in rural areas only; in a very few (and quite unimportant) crafts and trades; in the prospecting and extraction of some valuable metals, such as gold, by so-called *starateli* (prospectors); in the hunting of some fur-bearing wild animals; and in some other rather exceptional instances. Private prospectors and hunters must surrender the fruits of their efforts exclusively to the state at posted prices. Finally, the sale of used personal objects to other persons is permitted. This, however, opens a loophole for illegal trading.

Other forms of private activity in production or exchange are proscribed. The employment of one individual by another is prohibited, except in the case of household help (which, incidentally, is rather hard to find these days). Any purchase and resale with intent to profit – so-called 'speculation' – is illegal regardless of difference in time or place of purchase and sale. Private possession of foreign currency or of monetary metals is illegal also, such prohibition being common to all countries practicing stringent foreign exchange control. Except for authorised persons, moreover, all transactions with foreigners are against the law. As already mentioned, the plying of nearly all crafts and trades for private gain is prohibited. And, needless to say, the law forbids turning socialist property to private lucrative use; theft from the state and cooperatives, as well as from private persons; bribe-taking by official persons; and bribe-giving, in money or *natura*.

Within the state sector itself, the violation of the innumerable laws, rules, regulations, norms, directives, plans, etc., pertaining to the everyday activity of managers, technicians, workers, clerks, functionaries, administrators, and everyone else, is punishable either by law or by administrative sanction. Nevertheless, despite far-reaching and rigorous prohibitions – and in some measure precisely because of them – and despite the often severe penalties threatening transgressors, the breaking of economic laws and regulations and the passing of bribes are commonplace, everyday phenomena in which virtually the whole population of the USSR is continuously enmeshed, and in which some individuals are involved on a large and at times gigantic scale.

How can this be determined? Readers not conversant with the topic may wonder where one obtains information on 'economic crime' in the USSR. (This Soviet term embraces theft from the state and from cooperatives, bribery, and the whole range of illegal activities involving production and exchange.) Generally speaking, the accumulation of data is no problem whatever in regard to sheer volume. The Soviet press is replete with articles on the theme, mostly in the form of case descriptions of theft, bribery, illegal production and trade, and the like, going into remarkable detail, and often with seeming candor. Similar descriptive information can be found in Soviet juridical literature and in books on such subjects as public order, auditing, 'people's control,' and party activity. How accurate and representative information filtered through Soviet censorship is, however, is another question. Such information contains obvious lacunae. For example, Soviet printed sources rarely mention cases of failure of law enforcement. (Naturally, the most successful illegal activities, those that go undetected, are not publicised at all.) They pass by in silence such crucial problems as corruption of the party *apparat*, of high government officials, and of police and other law enforcement authorities, and they fail to mention, to this author's knowledge, the startling phenomenon of the sale, for high capital sums, of governmental and party posts. Faith in the rectitude of the pillars of the political regime must not be undermined by the press, even though the truth must surely be known by a substantial part of the public. Furthermore, the printed media are typically silent about any shenanigans in the vast defense sector and in the armed forces. They may deliberately distort the facts of individual cases. They rarely print generalising analyses about the second economy or corruption, and, if the authorities dispose of quantitative estimates of the overall extent and incidence of second economy activities or some parts thereof, as they probably do, such never appear in the press. Nonetheless, a researcher can learn a lot from simply reading the newspapers.

Other major sources of data available to the scholar include accounts by foreign correspondents in the USSR, the scholar's own personal contacts and observations in that country, and – of major importance lately – the written and oral testimony of recent emigrants. Of considerable help, too, are similar sources in or from the Communist countries of Eastern Europe, since both the underlying causes of the second economy and its symptoms and manifestations are essentially the same there as in the USSR, even though general conditions, the extent of permitted private activity, and official policies may vary from country to country.

Clearly, then, there are sufficient sources of raw data on the subject to allow the researcher to assert that illegalities exist in all sectors of the Soviet economy. Given this conclusion, it is necessary to examine the forms which these illegal manifestations of the second economy normally assume.

The enormous variety and occasional complexity of illegal and semilegal activities in production and distribution are ensured by the pervasiveness of controls and the massive number of prohibitions in the state and household sectors of the economy, and appear to be limited only by human ingenuity, though, naturally, the most ingenious schemes, being presumably also the more successful ones, tend to escape identification by Soviet authorities and detached observer alike. We will provide a concise summary of the chief forms of relevant activity.

Doubtless the most common economic crime in the USSR is stealing from the state, under which we subsume stealing from all official organisations, including collective farms. All sources agree that it is practised by virtually everyone, takes all possible forms, and varies in scale from the trivial to the regal. All also agree that the public takes it for granted, attaches almost no opprobium to it – and, on the contrary, disapproves of those who do not engaged in it – and sharply distinguishes between stealing from the state and stealing from private individuals. The latter is generally condemned. With some liberty, one might perhaps assert that the right to steal on the job, within certain conventional limits, is an implicit but integral part of the conditions of employment in the Soviet Union. It not only furnishes significant additional income in kind and in money to much of the public, conversely representing a major item of expense for the state, but also provides an important, often indispensable, basis for the second economy. The peasant steals fodder from the kolkhoz to maintain his animals, the worker steals materials and tools with which to ply his trade 'on the side,' the physician steals medicines, the driver steals gasoline and the use of the official car to operate an unofficial taxi; and to all of them income from private activity on the side may be more important than the wage or salary they earn in their official jobs.

An important variant of stealing on the job is the diversion and black-market sale by truck drivers of freight in their custody. This is precisely the source of the apparently considerable amount of building material that enters illegal channels and makes possible much private, kolkhoz, and at times even state-enterprise construction. A more lordly way of stealing, if one is highly placed, is to use the resources of one's own firm or organisation to personal advantage. The Soviet press is full of examples: have the firm build you a summer house (dacha) at little or no cost to yourself, or have it remodel your apartment in town or provide a company car for your wife. Such illegal perquisites – in addition to the legal ones that important officials and managers enjoy – seem often to be taken for granted.

There are also less crude forms of stealing from the state. A very common one consists of the diversion of finished goods, supplies, or materials by enterprise managers themselves. The goods might be recorded in the books as legitimately spoiled or lost in transit, for the books must of course show everything to be in order. But the diverted goods in fact are disposed of on the black market, or, in the case of intermediate materials and parts, used to manufacture items that can then be profitably sold. The proceeds are appropriated, though they may have to be shared with those within and outside the firm who are privy to what has happened.

The aim of those who divert goods is not always private peculation, however; it may be to promote the success of one's firm in terms of official indicators, which, to be sure, could indirectly benefit the operators of the diversion. The diverted goods may be used to barter against needed supplies when these are not available through legitimate channels, to improve the well-being and raise the morale of the firm's rank and file, and so on. An important point which follows from this is that Soviet production statistics may not only be overstated by managers eager to show plan fulfillment in order to earn their bonuses, but may also occasionally be understated, particularly in the light and food-processing industries, where diversion of goods is relatively simple. There is no way, though, for the outside observer to estimate the extent of such understatement by industries and commodities or overall.

Generally speaking, in an economy with pervasive goods shortage such as exist in the Soviet Union, physical or administrative control over goods often confers both the power and the opportunity for economic gain to the individual, be he or she ever so humble in the formal hierarchy. It is clear that many take advantage of this fact. Thus, when goods in high demand arrive in state-owned retail stores, it is common for salespeople to lay them aside for favored customers from which they can expect good tips, if not to preempt the goods themselves for profitable resale. The salesperson usually has to split any gains with his or her supervisor, who most likely again splits his share with the next higher supervisor, and so on up the chain of command. Nevertheless, over time the additional net income gained may easily exceed – sometimes severalfold – the salesperson's salary and legal bonuses, which, perhaps for this very reason, are very modest to begin with. The individual, in fact, may have little choice but to fall in with the system of extralegal gain.

Functionaries in the administrative bureaucracy who handle the allocation of producer goods – and they are very many – and those who are in charge of waiting lists for automobiles, other major consumer durables, and housing also have considerable opportunity for graft and apparently take advantage of it, though how commonly we are unable to say.

Finally, as has already been mentioned, there is widespread speculation in goods which are hard to come by. Given the invariable maldistribution by the state of goods over time and space, and chronic shortages of many items in the USSR, the opportunities for black-market trading for profit are nearly unlimited. The objects of speculation run the gamut from food, through foreign-made clothes purchased from visitors from abroad or in foreign currency (valuta) stores, to precious metals and foreign currency. The speculators may be relatively innocent individuals who pick up a few things on a visit to Moscow for resale to friends at home, or highly professional large-scale operators.

In addition to illicit trade there is illicit production. Although the private practice of nearly all crafts and trades is forbidden, it is far from suppressed. A large number of household repair and building services, typically provided by people 'moonlighting' outside, or even during, working hours; automotive repair; the sewing and tailoring of garments, the moving of furniture and other transport services – these and many others are regular illegal or semilegal features of Soviet life. On a larger scale are the operations of seemingly well organised migratory gangs of builders who contract themselves out, chiefly to collective farms, for specific jobs at preagreed and relatively very high prices. Both individual moonlighters and gangs of workers are referred to as a *shabashniki* (literally: free-time workers).

Lastly, there are the underground entrepreneurs in the full sense of the word: i.e., individuals who promote and organise production on a substantial scale, employ the labor of others, obtain materials and machinery on the black market, and distribute their output widely. They invest their own capital, for underground firms are privately bought and sold at capitalised values that presumably reflect their expected profitability discounted for risk. The products involved are often consumer goods (garments, footwear, household articles, knick-knacks, etc.) but can be producer goods as well. Large-scale private operations such as these commonly take place behind the protective façade of a state-owned factory or a collective farm – naturally, with appropriate payoffs to those who provide the cover – in what might be called crypto-private manner. Another variant of crypto-private (or pseudo-socialist) operation is the following: the enterprise is in fact state-owned and produces the output called for by its plan, but is operated virtually as a private firm by the manager, who pays a fixed sum or a proportion of enterprise revenue to the state and pockets the rest. Naturally, this is most practicable in smaller establishments, especially those producing services with a low material component, so that output cannot be easily controlled as a function of material input.

Illegal activities such as those just summarised are hardly the sole cause of corruption of Soviet officialdom and authorities, but they are surely a major contributing factor. Given the plethora of administrative superiors, controllers, inspectors, auditors, law enforcers, party authorities, expediters, and just plain snoopers that beset every economic activity, legal or illegal, in the Soviet Union, anything done out of line requires the buying off of some and often very many people

*   *   *

In sum, the concept of *kleptocracy*, developed by sociologists with reference to corrupt regimes and bureaucracies in underdeveloped countries, does not seem inapplicable to at least certain portions and regional segments of the Soviet party-government hierarchy.

Certain aspects of the second economy and corruption in the USSR appear to play a particularly important role in shaping the special characteristics of the Soviet *kleptocracy*. Before one tries to estimate the size and ultimate significance of the second economy itself, therefore, some comments about the particularities of the Soviet case seem in order.

Quite apart from the significance of the private plot in furthering illegal private economic activity in the USSR, the collective farm itself plays an important role in this regard. The following are some of the reasons. Formally, it is relatively easy to set up subsidiary enterprises at collective farms. While official policy intends such enterprises either to produce materials or services for the farm's own use or to process its agricultural products, they seem readily turned into fronts for illegal private operations. In fact, some enterprises exist on paper only and serve exclusively front purposes. Furthermore, the farm often can provide illegal undertakings with premises, transport, and labour – all of which are hard to obtain in the city. Finally, the collective farm is subject to less stringent controls than are state-owned enterprises and organisations with regard to conversion of bank money (i.e., deposit balances in the State Bank) into cash. This point is crucial for underground operations which derive revenue from the state sector, because state-owned entities, which may find ways of paying for services rendered with bank money, as a rule dispose of very little currency. Bank money must be converted into currency, however, to pay individuals for their productive contributions, to purchase materials on the black market, to grease the palms of officials where necessary, and to retain a profit for the entrepreneur himself. The collective farm accomplishes this conversion.

Also important to the success of illegal economic activity is the role of persons in direct charge of small means of transport, i.e., truck drivers, taxi drivers, and, lately, owners of private automobiles. The reasons are of course obvious. A good deal of the demand for private automobiles – at high official prices, and even at much higher black-market prices – is generated by the desire to provide transport to the secondary economy, which at once generates the need for nonofficial vehicles and provides the purchasing power necessary to acquire them.

A further aspect of the Soviet case which one can hardly fail to make note of is that alcohol suffuses and penetrates much of the second economy. Vodka – both the illegal 'home brew' (*samogon*) and the state-produced variety, the latter especially since 1972 when restrictions on conditions and hours of sale were tightened – is a major object of black-market trading. It seems likely that a disproportionate fraction of the moderate amounts earned in the second economy or from bribe taking is spent on alcohol (*high* incomes so earned are more likely to be spent on tangible valuables or to be hoarded), thus, incidentally, swelling the coffers of the state treasury. Furthermore, vodka itself occasionally serves as the means of payment of illegal wages or petty bribes. It also functions as a standard of value, in that the price of the *shabashnik's* services is sometimes specified beforehand as so many half-liter bottles of standard vodka, even though the ultimate payment may be the current ruble equivalent thereof.

Last among the special characteristics to be referred to here is that the Soviet second economy has a geographic and regional pattern. Since a significant component of supply on the black-market consists of foreign goods smuggled into the country by merchant-marine crews, port cities such as Leningrad, Riga, and Odessa are obviously major funnels that feed the second economy. The Odessa black market enjoys renown. In fact, illegal private activity and corruption seem especially highly developed in the southern regions of the country, in Transcaucasia, and in Central Asia. Georgia has a reputation second to none in this respect.

How large is the Soviet second economy? So far as its *lawful* component alone is concerned, it is probably rather less than 10 percent of Soviet GNP.

Now, 10 percent of GNP may not be much, but considering the country, it is noteworthy. What is more, the legal private sector produces almost nothing aside from consumer goods (including housing services) and new residential construction. Since household consumption in 1968 claimed only about one half of GNP (at factor cost), the contribution of private value added to household consumption must have been at least 15 percent, and, in regard to household food consumption, perhaps around 25 percent. It is probably still something similar today.

To turn from the legal to the *illegal* private sector (for the moment excluding from consideration illegal activities on socialist account), not even an educated guess of size can be attempted by an outside observer. Perhaps estimates are compiled by one or another institute in the USSR; but even without these one can assert with considerable confidence that illegal private economic activities are a major and extremely widespread phenomenon that for a very large part of the population is, in one form or another, a regular, almost daily, experience. This holds especially if one includes consideration of such common practices as the paying and taking of large tips (really black-market surcharges), petty bribes, and gifts (*prinosheniye*) that are in fact bribes. Moreover, whatever its opinion of large underground operations or more exotic dealings, the public seems to accept petty illegalities as a normal and even inevitable part of making one's way in a refractory and shortage-ridden environment.

21 Hotel Pilferage: a Case Study in Occupational Theft*
Gerald Mars

Introduction

The data to be discussed principally concerns institutionalised pilferage as this was observed in a hotel – one of a number of industrial situations in which I have collected material as a participant observer and one of several where pilferage was widespread. The intention was not, however, specifically to examine pilferage. Observation of and participation in pilferage were by-products of an anthropologist's modified field approach or through working in a number of jobs before receiving formal anthropological training – what can be termed 'retrospective participant observation'. Material on the hotel was in part obtained as a worker and suffers, of course, from the dangers of possible selective recall. As is usual in participant observation, there are dangers too in generalizing from a single case. Inquiry would suggest, however, that the techniques of pilferage found in the hotel have a considerably wider application.

Discussion of the case will compare certain aspects of hotel pilferage with pilferage as this was observed in dock workgangs and which are more fully recorded elsewhere.[1]

In dock work-gangs a regularly hired body of twenty-six men were found organised together to unload cargo. Some work tasks facilitated across to cargo but access alone was insufficient for safe pilferage and hard to be buttressed by the support of other workers in the gang. Support was offered from within the gang by checkers, who would falsify paperwork; by fork drivers who would stack cargo into barriers so supervisors could not see illegitimate activity; and by signallers who acted as look-out men whilst carrying on their normal work. The gang foreman, though formally responsible for hiring, firing and the discipline of his men, had no role in pilferage. Even his formal powers of hiring and firing were considerably modified by the collective action of the gang who could threaten collective restrictions on output if a foreman acted in ways perceived as being against gang interests. If a

* First published in *The Sociology of the Workplace*, edited by Malcolm Warner, Allen & Unwin, 1973, pp. 200–10.

gang found unacceptable new inductees introduced by the foreman, for instance, they would threaten a slow up. A similar result would follow the dropping of a man regarded as integral to the gang. One important criterion for gang membership was a man's participation in and the security of his behaviour in respect of pilferage. This meant not only that he be seen to participate but that he act within the limits on quantity and type of cargo which normally apply. Labour turnover in the gangs was extremely low and the gangs emerge in many respects as typical solidary work groups.[2]

The turnover of waiting staff in hotels, on the other hand, tends to be extremely high – in the case study hotel it approached 30 per cent per year – whilst wages paid by any comparable standards are low. Corporation bus conductors in the same city, for instance, doing a job requiring less skill, averaged approximately 25 per cent more direct take-home pay for about 30 per cent less hours. Both of these factors, high labour turnover and low wages, were used by waiters to justify the industry's institutionalisation of pilferage – the overall term for which, in hotels as in many other places, is the 'the fiddle'. 'Knock off', a common expression among hotel staffs, refers to a sub-type of fiddle, the illicit obtaining of concrete benefits – usually food or artifacts such as cutlery and linen. Present attention, however, is devoted to money fiddles in the hotel's dining-room and lounges, and how this was organised by waiting staff. It should be mentioned that this type of fiddle is not usually obtained at the expense of customers, but at the expense of the hotel – unlike bar fiddles, for instance, which are frequently at the expense of customers. It is distinct too from the theft of guests' personal possessions which is regarded by waiters as deviant and, when it occurs, which is rare, is simply called 'theft'. It is important too to realise that fiddles are regarded as a legitimate entitlement – as part of wages. A typical comment from a very skilful and highly trained waiter on this issue was, 'Who'd work for £12.10s. a week for the hours I put in? No one but a bloody nutcase, I can tell you. Fiddles are a part of wages. The whole issue runs on fiddles, it couldn't work otherwise.'

Data was obtained unsystematically from the staff of a 200-bedroomed hotel in Blackpool, a seaside resort in the north of England. Its dining-room, like those of most hotels, is open to non-residents and it employs twenty waiting staff. I had previously worked in smaller establishments, and these provided essential background knowledge of the technical organisation involved. These experiences, however, were prior to and supplementary to cross-checked information from informants.

The Organisation of Hotel Pilferage

Hotel restaurant organization is basically universal. Food, prepared behind the scenes in kitchens and stillrooms, is taken to dining-rooms and lounges where it is consumed and paid for. The problem for the fiddler is to obtain goods from their source, direct it to his own account, and obtain and pocket the payment at its destination. This means that if three meals are booked out of the kitchen and he receives payment for four he can then pocket the difference. His difficulties in this matter arise partly from the systems of accounting adopted by hotels, partly from the vigilance of higher management and partly because, though a level of pilferage is tolerated by management, this varies at different times and for different people. There is thus a large element of ambiguity and insecurity concerning management's acceptable level at any one time.

Dining-rooms, and restaurants where their scale of operations is large enough, attempt to limit fiddles by the employment of a checker, sometimes called a control clerk. It is the checker's primary job to sit at a desk between the kitchen and the dining room, account for food passing from one to the other, and see this tallies with the waiters' cash receipts. A secondary aspect of his job is to ensure that correct-sized portions are served – Whyte's classic study of restaurants refers only to this secondary task of the checker: he ignores the likelihood of pilferage in his treatment of the role.[3]

Most accounting systems simply involve the waiter's exchange of dockets for food. A waiter takes an order for, say, two meals, writes out a docket, and exchanges this at the kitchen for his meals which he then takes to his customer and for which he receives payment. At the end of the day his cash receipts should tally with his exchange of dockets. The fiddles system hinges on tactics employed by the waiter to get unrecorded food past the checker. How does a waiter beat the checker? In essence the method can be understood by describing its simplest form, which occurs in hotel lounges.

In lounges serving coffee and tea, fiddling is often extremely simple. A waiter receives an order for, say, two coffees. He goes to the kitchen, orders a single coffee, fills in a docket and passes it to the checker. In return he obtains a standard coffee pot, a standard milk jug and one cup and saucer. The problem is to convert this single coffee to two coffees and his first requirement is for extra cups and saucers. These are frequently hidden in strategic areas in or near the lounge. Crockery may be kept behind a flower display, behind curtains, even carried in pockets – anywhere out of direct contact with authority. A waiter's second requirement is for strong enough beverages; coffee and tea ordered for two may be too weak if served to three. This often requires a 'bent' helper in the kitchen who can supply larger quantities than the lesser order would merit or stronger beverages that can more readily be watered. Supplies of extra hot water do not usually cause problems. Bent helpers are usually repaid in beer, rarely in cash.

A third difficulty concerns the dockets. Those a waiter issues to a 'customer (known as a 'punter) and those he passes to the checker are often carbon duplicates so they may more readily tally. There are various ways round this problem:

(a) Writing can be made deliberately ambiguous. For example, fives can be made to look like threes; the customer accepts the five; the clerk accepts the three.
(b) Waiters often have a 'spare' docket book.
(c) If the waiter can retrieve the copy docket passed to the checker's desk after she has received it, this can then be re-used. One method involves the use of a wet tray placed on top of the docket which then sticks to its underside when the tray is moved. Another is to distract the clerk; an accomplice waiter, for instance, can cause an argument. A third involves different varieties of 'bending' the checker, ranging from bribery and flattery to subtle deception.

One very experienced middle-aged waitress with a whimsical turn of humour recounted what happened when she moved to a new job in a coffee lounge. 'I said "six coffees". That shook them. They all looked at me as if I was bloody daft! That way everyone thought I was the most innocent one there was. No one [waiter] had ever ordered more than two coffees in that place.' They thought her innocent because a group of six could very easily have been 'knocked' – whereas groups of two or three are more difficult, it being easier to convert four coffees to six than to convert one coffee to three – yet the gain, two coffees, is the same in each case. Her reputation for naïveté established with the checker, she was then able to fiddle without being suspected.

The more lucrative dining-room fiddles, though following the same basic procedure as to dockets and crockery, are much more complex than are lounge fiddles. These complexities derive from three main sources. In the first place, whereas in lounges most people pay cash, in dining-rooms only non-residents do so; residents have accounts linked to their room number and pay at the end of their stay. It is therefore only through non-residents that fiddles can be obtained. There are two classes of non-residents – those that book meals in advance and those who enter the hotel without prior notice. Tables booked in advance are useless to fiddlers since such bookings are known to the hotel management via the receptionist; it is, therefore, only casual non-resident punters who are good for fiddles. Such punters are called by the generic term 'chance'. Whereas in hotel dining-rooms chance punters are a minority, in restaurants nearly all customers are, of course, chance.

A second distinction between dining-rooms and lounges concerns the systems of accounting which make dining-room fiddling easier. The office of checker exists in both, but the job in dining-rooms would be so complex if all courses of all meals were checked that checking usually applies only to the main courses of meals. If a waiter can 'knock' the main course of a meal he is, therefore, easily able to fiddle the *entire* cost of that meal. Sometimes it is necessary or customary with certain main-course dishes that these be kept in the dining-room if they are to tempt the punter: they therefore bypass the checker. Roast beef on the joint is, for instance, often so displayed. If you are a chance punter where this dish appears on the menu the odds are high that the waiter will feel he 'can certainly recommend the roast beef tonight, sir'!

A third, and the most significant, complication in dining-rooms that is absent from lounges concerns the office of Head Waiter. He is formally responsible for hiring and firing his waiters, overseeing the dining-room and booking in chance punters. These he allocates to their tables and therefore to the waiters who will serve them. The power of a Head Waiter in relation to his waiters is, therefore, considerable and an understanding of his role central to any consideration of dining-room fiddles.

Head Waiters vary as to their 'hardness' or 'softness'. A 'hard' Head Waiter asks for and obtains an accepted upper maximum of 50 per cent of fiddles; a 'soft' Head Waiter, particularly a second or third (deputy) Head Waiter, may receive much less. In return for his kickback a Head Waiter is expected to allocate chance punters, provide services facilitating fiddles and 'cover' any waiter to whom he has allocated a chance party that goes wrong. That is, he must use his office to defend subordinates against higher management. He must, for instance, restrain any tendency of an angry chance punter who has been knocked from complaining on any account to the manager. If this happened and the manager were to check the punter's bill the fiddle would be evident. Managers are usually outside the fiddle system.

Since the supply of chance is limited, its allocation to any one waiter is seen as being at the expense of others. This makes a Head Waiter's job extremely complex: he aims to keep all his waiters happy but cannot do this by a simple rotation of chance among them. Some waiters are cleverer than others at dealing with chance; others are more skilled, have wider experience or longer service, and all these categories merit, or believe they merit, extra increments.

It is this zero sum characteristic of chance, together with the absence of an unambiguous criterion for its allocation, that goes some way to explain why inter-staff squabbles are frequent and why they appear to be an institutionalised characteristic of hotel dining-rooms. This is one reason also why alliances between waiters are uncommon. Though the distracting of checkers is best effected by two waiters operating together, and the sharing of crockery stacks is obviously of mutual benefit, such alliances are relatively uncommon and when they occur are frequently short lived.

Hotel managements are well aware of the institutionalisation of much, at least, of what has been described. On the rare occasions a new and ignorant management has attempted to stop fiddling it has quickly found that staff protest with their feet; this is scarcely surprising when the low level of hotel wages is appreciated.

What managements usually do is to structure hotel situations to *limit* fiddle opportunities rather than aim to eradicate them. One of the ways they do this is by employing checkers, as described above. Another is to structure an opposition of the interests of Head Waiters and Chefs. Chefs are responsible for buying as well as cooking the food consumed in a hotel, and for accounting. Frequently they are given a 'percentage' for extra production out of a given stock and this, therefore, gives them a strong incentive to work closely with the checker to limit fiddles. These controls can on occasion, however, provide a two-edged weapon for management. In one hotel the Chef who received a 'percentage' and the female checker were believed to be in alliance for their own benefit, and were accordingly known as 'Bonnie and Clyde'. In spite of their benefits from this alliance the overall level of fiddles was drastically reduced. The staff, however, including the Head Waiter, left to work elsewhere. More serious for a hotel are situations where a bent Chef and a Head Waiter work in unison. As one waitress explained, 'When that happens it's really diabolical.' Another waitress, after describing the expostulations of a very experienced hotel owner/manager, said, 'Well, you couldn't blame him really – some of them were really diabolical.'

This use of the word 'diabolical', frequently uttered by waiters, refers to a level – whether of money fiddle, bar or knockoff – that is considered too high for safety and likely, therefore, to disturb the *status quo*. There are, however, no group sanctions applied against such 'diabolical' waiters.

It is interesting in this respect to quote the manager concerned in this case as an indication of his acceptance of an institutionalised level of pilferage. He said, 'You wouldn't be worth your weight in salt if you couldn't make a wage for yourself – but Christ! leave me a bit!'

Discussion and implications

Two facilities are found necessary for pilferage to occur. First, and self evidently, men must have or be granted *access* to goods. Second, access alone is rarely sufficient to ensure security in pilferage: for this to be achieved it frequently needs to be backed by the *support* of others. It is in the distribution of these two facilities and the alliances which follow such distribution that a system can be seen.

In the dock, group interests are paramount and individual interests correspondingly mimimal. This is, of course, to large extent derived from the interrelated nature of work tasks that are technically determined. Men inducted into the dock work-gang have to prove – often over considerable periods of time – that they are in all respects 'trustworthy'. Trust in this context means both an assured technical and a social competence as these apply both to legitimate and to illegitimate tasks. It was found that, in their organisation of pilferage, access and support functions in the dock work gang are differentially allocated *within* the group such that no one individual can exert a monopoly over either feature. Control is internal and dispersed; autonomy lies with the group and no one man can act individually without incurring effective group sanctions. In effect it is the group which is seen to exercise social controls. Pilferage is not only organised and effected by the group, but its limits – both of type and of quantity also – are determined and controlled by the group as are also questions concerning output and, to a large extent, recruitment, though this, as in the hotel, is formally the foreman's responsibility.

In hotels the situation is very different. The solidary work group is absent, turnover high, individualism paramount and workers' orientation to their jobs seen as individually instrumental.[4] Yet fiddlers in hotels, as in docks, still require combinations of access and support if fiddling is to be secure. In hotels both access and support, however, are mediated through and monopolised in one role – that of the Head Waiter. Instead of control over both functions being vested in the workers themselves, as in docks, the monopoly of access and support in hotels, located as it is in a single external source, means that control is vested in that source.

We have thus in both situations systems of pilferage facilities that are linked to systems of legitimate work roles. These run in parallel and act in alliance so that access and support roles derived from legitimate tasks work in harness to facilitate non-legitimate tasks. The granting, possession and possibility of the withdrawal of access and support – in a word, the *control* – over essential components in the covert system, however, necessarily involves relationships of power. Thus it is that we are enabled, by appreciating the covert pilferage system, to examine power relationships on a different dimension and with new insights, and to account for factors affecting its incidence that might otherwise be ignored. We can see how power derived from legitimate office, the office of foreman, for instance, may be buttressed or negatived by that office's position relative to a covert socio-technical system. We are particularly able, therefore, to throw a new light on inter-worker relations and on the perennial problems of first-line supervisors in situations where pilferage is institutionalised.

Using this analysis we can appreciate that a waiter is particularly vulnerable to the power of his Head Waiter, *not only* because a Head Waiter has control of hiring and firing but also in that he is able to apply a brake on access or to withdraw essential support in ways quite impossible for a dock foreman. This is so since a Head Waiter's legitimate power derived from his monopoly of access/support both act together to determine his *total* power position *vis-à-vis* subordinates.

Dock foremen, on the other hand, who are also formally responsible for hiring and firing but who find themselves external to the covert socio-technical system, are able only to operate control derived from their (overt) office. In doing this, however, they face a solidary work group whose legitimately derived solidarity is further enhanced by non-legitimate access/support solidarity. In contrast to dock foremen, however, hotel Head Waiters find themselves in a situation where solidaristic tendencies of their subordinates are negatives on both covert *and* on overt levels. The presence of institutionalised pilferage is thus seen to have very different effects on the role of first-line supervisor in the two situations. For the Head Waiter, pilferage buttresses his authority, whilst for the dock foreman its institutionalised presence can only be understood as detracting from his.

In advocating the importance of covert social organisation it is not suggested that the place of institutionalised pilferage in determining work relationships is greater than the place played by other factors (such as class, age, sex or ethnic category) which also contribute to the articulation of roles at work. What is suggested, however, is that the study of covert social organisation based on pilferage is relevant to the interests of industrial sociologists because it *parallels* in the workplace what I have called the overt social organisation. In this the systematic study of pilferage can be rated with studies of work restriction.

What is required in studies of work relationships, it is suggested, is awareness of the importance of the covert and the illegitimate where these appear to be institutionalised. Indeed, we must look with suspicion on studies that ignore or underplay these factors. Whereas this paper has only considered them in brief outline as they influence work groups relations and the role of supervisors, it is considered that the analysis could usefully be extended, particularly to illumine aspects of work socialisation, the control of recruitement by workers, and the linkage of work and non-work. There is thus scope for examining the influence of covert work roles as these articulate with occupational career, life and family cycles.

An understanding of these factors and of changes (and proposed changes) in the workplace which are perceived as disturbing to covert relativities can prove useful in suggesting reasons for unrest in specific situations, particularly where changes to the overt system bring unknown and often unanticipated changes in the covert system.

References

1. G. Mars. 1972. *An Anthropological Study of Longshoremen and of Industrial Relations in the Port of St. John's, Newfoundland, Canada*. Ph.D. Thesis: London University.
—— 1973. In Press. Dock Pilferage: A case Study in Occupational Theft, in *Explorations in Sociology* Series No. 3. Social Control and Deviance (Provisional Title). Ed. Rock, P. and McIntosh, M.: London: Tavistock.
2. Goldthorpe, *et al.* 1968. 'The Affluent Worker: Industrial Attitudes and Behaviour', *Cambridge Studies in Sociology* No. 1, Cambridge University Press.
3. W.F. Whyte. 1948. *Human Relations in the Restaurant Industry*. New York: McGraw-Hill.
4. Goldthorpe, *et al.*, *op. cit.*

22 A Little Larceny Can Do a Lot For Employee Morale*
L.R. Zeitlin

A close friend of mine, an accountant, told me of an experience he had recently when he audited the books of a corporation. It became apparent that the office manager was dipping into petty cash to the extent of about $2,000 a year. He reported this fact to the president. The president responded, 'How much are we paying him?' 'Ten thousand a year,' replied the accountant. 'Then keep quiet about it,' said the president. 'He's worth at least $15,000.'

Employees in American business steal between 8.5- and 10-billion dollars a year. About four billion of this total is theft in cash and merchandise from retail establishments. The remainder is lost through kickbacks, bribery, theft of time, and loss of corporate secrets.

Thefts of merchandise alone amount to approximately five per cent of the yearly sales of American retail establishments, and internal losses outweigh external losses by about three to one. That is, the stores' own employees steal three times as much as do shoplifters.

Monitor. Obviously, business is aware of employee dishonesty. Most retail establishments have some form of internal security system to discourage dishonest employees. Some employ guards at sensitive merchandise-handling points; others require employees to carry company-provided handbags or to leave their coats in company-monitored cloakrooms. Several companies utilise undercover investigators and plainclothes detectives, aided by electronic security measures, to detect thievery on the part of employees.

Despite the precautions taken to minimise 'shrinkage,' employees concoct elaborate schemes to steal and in most cases they get away with it. The ratio of theft incidence to prosecution is lower for this kind of theft than for any other form of grand larceny. For the dishonest employee crime pays. Or does it?

Considering the time and effort involved, the risk of detection and subsequent discharge, and the real (though small) risk of prosecution, the actual return on employee theft is poor. If we divide the total amount of merchandise lost through internal employee theft (about

* First published in *Psychology Today*, June 1971.

three billion dollars a year) by the total number of people employed in retail establishments, the amount stolen per person is approximately $300 a year, or about $1.50 each working day.

Of course, some employees steal a great deal more, others considerably less. But the evidence indicates that well over 75 per cent of all employees participate to some extent in merchandise shrinkage. This theft may range from trivial to important – from taking paper clips or typing paper home for the youngsters' homework to misappropriating substantial amounts of cash or merchandise. The fact remains that in retail establishments internal theft averages out to an unevenly distributed five per cent to eight per cent of the typical employee's salary.

The dishonest employee uses considerable ingenuity. In one case reported in *The Wall Street Journal*, drivers for a retail bakery routinely turned over as many as 4,000 loaves of bread a day to supermarket managers in return for kickbacks. Because retail prices were rising, the bakery couldn't track the cost of thievery onto the retail price of the bread. So, the company began charging drivers the full wholesale price (29c per loaf) for bread unaccounted for. The firm said that it made the move to 'remove indifference among the drivers and create a sense of responsibility.' What it created was a sense of ingenuity. Drivers countered by continuing their illicit sales and replacing the bread so disposed of with day-old bread purchased for 10 cents a loaf from the company's day-old bread store.

Why does the dishonest worker spend so much energy figuring out ways to steal from his employer? One answer is the nature of the job. Most retail jobs are unspeakably repetitive and boring. Advancement usually is limited. The typical retail worker has relatively little freedom of action or decision-making autonomy. If he deals with customers, he must subordinate his own desires to those of the customer. And salaries are low. It is no wonder that in such jobs, employee dissatisfaction is rife and turnover is relatively high.

In order to increase employee work motivation and to decrease turnover, management many choose one of two alternative courses. It can follow the policies described by Frederick Herzberg and other management theorists and enrich the jobs. By providing increased variety of work, opportunity for advancement, and opportunities for individuals to assume responsibility, management can increase the quality of the work situation. Or, if management chooses not to improve low-quality jobs, it can increase worker pay and benefits to the point where, although the job is unpleasant, it is too good to leave.

But management has chosen, largely by default, to reject both approaches, so workers seem to have taken matters into their own hands. When the average retail employee becomes dissatisfied with his job, if he doesn't quit, he starts stealing from his employer. He gets back at the system. In a sense, the intellectual and physical challenges provided by opportunities to steal represent a significant enrichment of the individual's job. He can take matters into his own hands, assume responsibility, make decisions and face challenges. The amount he gets away with is determined solely by his own initiative. He is in business for himself.

In one two-year study, I found job enrichment to be the chief motive behind employee theft in a large Mid-western clothing store. The most convincing evidence came from interviews with 32 persons who had been discharged for stealing. None had been prosecuted, of course, though the personal take had, in at least one case, run to a few thousand dollars.

Eight of the ex-employees admitted that they stole primarily for cash. For the most part they had been young (mean age, 24), and recently hired, working at low-paying jobs in warehousing or stockroom operations. They sold the merchandise directly to friends and associates.

A group of six employees could give no reason other than 'impulse' for their theft. The store had virtually no internal security, and apparently temptation became too much. Job enrichment is an unlikely motive for this group: they were considerably older (mean age, 36) and many held trusted, responsible positions. In fact, the employee with the largest amount of recorded theft – well over $4,000 worth of men's clothing – was a department manager. (Most of the garments were recovered, untouched and unworn, from his rumpus room. Many were ludicrously out of size.) Such seemingly 'pathological' thefts involved little challenge and little planning.

The remaining 18 employees produced surprising responses when I interviewed them sympathetically outside the store context, several months after they had been fired, and assured them that there would be no punitive action. Each of them indicated a sense of satisfaction as 'getting away with it.' Although most of them knew that they were doing wrong, few of them felt any sense of guilt or remorse. A common comment was: 'It's not really hurting anybody – the store can afford it.' In fact, one fellow argued ingeniously that his thefts of men's clothing *benefited* the store, by his being seen around town in the New Look. They often looked upon theft as a condition of employment: 'the store owed it to me,' or 'I felt I deserved to get something additional for my work since I wasn't getting paid enough.' Many of the ex-employees blamed work conditions: boredom, long periods of inactivity, low commissions, supervisors who treated them poorly.

Only rarely did members of this group sell the merchandise. In many cases they gave it as gifts to members of their families and to friends.

Bosses of the discharged employees in all three groups rated them 'good' or better on a performance-review system. They had worked for the store, on the average, considerably longer than the average 'honest' employee. Most were caught by security police who had been hired from the outside because management thought they were losing the merchandise to 'outsiders.' In most cases, the supervisors were honestly surprised – in fact they were convinced only when the security people caught several employees redhanded. It was the store management's bewilderment over the nature of its merchandise thefts that led to my being retained to study the problem.

While it is probable that no job-enrichment or salary increase would have prevented theft by the six persons who stole for impulsive reasons, we can make a fair case that such changes might have minimised theft among the other 26 employees. But would this have paid off for the employer? The average annual theft for all employees in the discharged group amounted to slightly less than $200 a man a year, which is considerably less than the national average. It is hard to see what significant modifications in salary or job responsibility could be made with this small annual investment.

The dishonest worker is enriching his own job in a manner that is very satisfactory (for him). This enrichment is costing management, on the average, $1.50 per worker per day. At this rate, management gets a bargain. By permitting a controlled amount of theft, management can avoid reorganising jobs and raising wages. Management still keeps most business decision-making functions in its own hands and retains workers without increasing salaries and benefits. (I should emphasise that a man who enriches his job by stealing does not suddenly become a 'good' employee, rather, he gives the *appearance* of a good employee so as not to attract attention to his illicit activities. But in many cases this is all that is necessary. Simply *being* there is sufficient for many jobs. It is common knowledge in financial circles that the man with his hand in the till is never absent.)

The important word is *control*. Properly utilised, controlled employee theft can be used as another implement in management's motivational toolbox. As in the case of most motivational tools, costs and conditions of utilisation must be carefully studied. (Ethically, of course, it would be more desirable for management to motivate employees by means other than inviting them into lives of petty crime. It is traditionally considered better to have workers directing their energies toward furthering the course of the business rather than toward satisfying their individual larcenous desires.)

Before deciding to minimise or eliminate employee theft, management should ask itself these four practical questions:

1. How much is employee theft actually costing us?

2. What increase in employee dissatisfaction could we expect if we controlled theft?

3. What increases in employee turnover could we expect?

4. What would it cost to build employee motivation up to a desirable level by conventional means of job enrichment or through higher salaries?

Setting aside ethical and emotional considerations, management may decide that the monetary cost of enforcing honesty is too great. That is, the cost of an effective security system, plus the cost of achieving equivalent employee stability by increasing pay or job quality, is greater than the loss of merchandise due to employee theft. In such a case, a system of controlled larceny may be in order.

In order to set up such a system management would first decide upon the amount of merchandise it could afford to lose. Once it has discovered the tolerable limits of employee theft management would enforce these limits. An effective, informal signalling system would have to be developed to show awareness of employee theft and swift action would have to be taken when the theft exceeded the established limit.

At the same time management would have to maintain a figurehead security system. After all, the major benefit of employee theft is the job enrichment provided by the individual's attempt to beat the system. If all need for precaution is eliminated, then the employee gets no satisfaction from theft. All he gets is a slight addition to his income in merchandise instead of in cash.

Here is an example of implementation in real life of such an informal, controlled-theft job-enrichment approach:

The port authority of a large Eastern city had a great deal of difficulty keeping toll takers on its bridges and tunnels. Back when security was lax, there was much demand for jobs as toll takers. In fact, in the 1930s, one had to offer a bribe (about $1,000) to get even a temporary summer position. But by 1950, an elaborate security system (locked cash boxes, numbered tickets, remote indication of fares, etc.) had made a drastic reduction in employee-theft opportunities. Simultaneously, the turnover of toll takers rose to an unprecedented high. As can be imagined, collecting tolls honestly is an extremely tedious job that offers relatively little opportunity for personal gratification, minimal chance for advancement, and little opportunity to make decisions.

The personnel manager, together with the director of the toll-collecting operation, determined between themselves that the total cost of reducing theft to a minimum was excessive. Admittedly, they saved money in tolls, but personnel turnover cost them more than the amount saved. By this time, the authority knew almost to the penny how much money should be collected per toll booth – as a function of traffic. They determined that they could tolerate toll-taker thefts of $10.00 a week a man.

Although it is no longer possible for individual toll takers to put tolls directly into their pockets, a clever toll taker can figure out ways to collect a portion of the tolls for himself. For example, he can buy a book of commuter tickets and when a traveller pays the full toll in cash, the collector can ring up the price of a ticket and place the difference in his pocket. Of course, this can be done only a few times a day, since a check is run on the distribution of ticket numbers per booth. In fact, the collector must exercise considerable ingenuity to get away with $10 a week.

If the toll taker exceeds the $10 theft limit more than once or twice, the toll-collection manager has an informal system to signal to the collector that he is under suspicion. A brightly painted authority police car parks right in front of the malefactor's toll booth. The toll taker gets the message. Theft drops back to a tolerable level.

Such a system then meets all of the requirements described previously. The managers first determined the cost of absolute enforcement and found that when the turnover costs were included, the price was simply excessive. So, they calculated the allowable amount of theft. The actual theft requires considerable ingenuity on the part of the employee because the authority has some fairly sophisticated procedures for monitoring employees. The employee can steal but it takes work. Finally, they worked out an informal signal to let the employee know when he exceeds tolerable limits. Occasionally, of course, it is necessary to discharge an employee for excessive thefts when he doesn't get the message. This serves to keep the rest 'honest.'

Theft serves as a safety valve for employee frustration. It permits management to avoid the responsibility and cost of job enrichment or salary increases at a relatively low amount of money per man per year. Uncontrolled theft can be disastrous for any business concern but *controlled* theft can be useful. Employee theft, used as a motivational tool, can be an economic benefit to an organisation, if management finds it too costly to meet its traditional responsibility to make jobs rewarding and to pay a living wage.

I do not advocate abandonment of the traditional responsibilities of management, but I suggest that management adopt a more realistic and certainly less hypocritical attitude to business 'honesty' and publicly recognise that there is benefit to be obtained by utilising employee theft as a motivational tool.

23 The Future of Work
Craig R. Littler

During the late 1960s and much of the 1970s, the issues of concern in relation to work centred around job design. There was a broadly based Quality of Working Life movement which argued for the humanisation of work (see Chapter 7). These issues, as we can see from several chapters in this book, remain critical to people's working lives, but during the 1980s the focus of attention has shifted to unemployment, a question which has become entangled with the impact of new technology on work. The most pressing question is that of policy: in the face of chronic unemployment and underemployment in the developed societies, what steps should be taken to provide more work for a broader body of people? I will not attempt to deal with this question here, except to point out that this question leads on to more fundamental questions: is work actually important to the majority of people? Perhaps the impact and rapidity of technological change will alter the name of the game, such that work, and therefore unemployment will take on a different significance. If society cannot provide employment for all the population in the face of rapid technological change affecting all industries, then perhaps we should be concerned not just with a redistribution of work opportunities but also a revaluation of work and leisure and endeavour to increase the status attached to unpaid work.

This argument gains some force from the realisation that the work ethic is socially relative. The ancient Greeks, for example, adopted values which are the precise reverse of our own: for them manual work was debased and debasing and leisure was more valuable than work. Ancient Greece was, of course, a slave society and Anthony notes that:

An ideology of work is redundant when the labour force can be conscripted and coerced at will. In conditions of a freer labour market an ideology has to be developed in order to recruit labour and then in order to motivate it by persuading it that its tasks are necessary or noble. In conditions of a free market and a chronic shortage of labour, the manufacture and communication of an ideology of work becomes a central preoccupation of society . . . the process reaches its highest development in advanced capitalism and in state socialism.

(1977, p. 22)

Perhaps as modern societies move away from labour-intensive industries and as robots line the assembly lines creating a situation of permanent labour surplus, it is time to leave an ideology of work in the attics of the past.

The above argument sounds reasonable on the face of it, but is there any evidence that the significance that people attach to paid work is actually declining? Up to the present (1984), there seems to be very little evidence that this is so. The desire to obtain paid work, whether for economic, social or personal reasons, seems to be deeply ingrained in most members of society. The study by Trevor and White (1983) of Japanese firms operating in Britain concludes that the work ethic seems to be strongly-rooted in the British working class, and that a competent management, which shares the same work discipline as the shop floor, can readily evoke and mobilise enthusiasms (pp. 49–53). Coyle's (1984) study of the experience of redundancy amongst women showed that, regardless of the quality of the work experience, the women exhibited an extraordinary attachment to paid employment. For men, work is an integral part of their daily social relations as men, such that unemployment can precipitate a crisis of identity. For many women, unemployment is experienced as a crisis of autonomy, as a loss of independence for which domestic roles do not offer adequate compensation (ibid., p. 121). At the level of society, there seems to be *more* emphasis, not less, on the work ethic during the 1980s depression, and unemployment still carries the same social stigma as during the years of full employment.

Thus work still occupies a central position in Western societies, and the evidence is very thin that social attitudes towards work or money will change sufficiently over the next decade to persuade large numbers of people, who live in a consumer society and who otherwise would be part of the labour force, that their salvation lies outside of remunerative work (Sackville, 1981).

A different, but related scenario, is the suggestion that the re-distribution of work will be such that the future might consist of a leisured society of part-time workers. However, many technical and professional jobs will continue to demand a degree of knowledge, skills and training that cannot be acquired or retained by a few hours part-time work every week. Therefore the knowledge demands of many skilled occupations will necessitate continued full-time employment, investment of self in those occupations and a continued work ethic. Perhaps, as the CSS Report (1981) suggests, society might be divided into two parts. One group would work long hours at demanding but satisfying work, whilst the second, much larger group would work a few hours each week at some undemanding tasks, perhaps on an optional basis. Thus a new divisive principle of society would be introduced. This would be 'meritocracy' with a vengeance.

Apart from the internal social tensions which such a scenario suggests, there is the probability that, even with good fortune, the Third World countries are likely to remain desperately poor over the next few decades, afflicted by famine and malnutrition. If the developed world turns inwards and solves its employment problems by creating a large, semi-leisured class who can find nothing useful to do with their time amidst a sea of world poverty, then the political repercussions could only be counted in terms of terrorist bombs.

All in all, the scenario of a 'collapse of work' (Jenkins and Sherman, 1979), in which work as we have known it will largely disappear during the next two decades, is not very likely. Indeed such a perspective can be used to distract attention from existing problems. The very real suffering which unemployment still entails at all levels, can somehow be diminished by a futuristic sleight of hand. It is no use giving the man or woman in the dole queue a pamphlet on the changed social situation in the year 2001. As Sinfield (Chapter 16) points out, 'each time unemployment tends to rise, there are suggestions that the stigma of unemployment has been substantially reduced' such that the strains and tensions on the unemployed are in some way lessened. In the 1980s this line of approach has become mixed up with confused ideas about new technology and the age of leisure.

If the conventional concept of paid work is likely to remain central during the next decade, then what is the likely impact of new technology? At one extreme, there are observers who suggest that new technology will result in the unmanned factory and the relocation of office work into the home as most households become 'cabled up'. Again there are grounds for caution: in the early 1960s there was widespread concern about the future impact of technology, particularly information-processing technology, on employment. It was widely predicted that there would be long-term structural unemployment, extensive changes in occupational structures and perhaps a new age of leisure – familiar words! In reality this period of acute concern was followed by a marked lack of interest in such matters in the later 1960s and early 1970s, given that unemployment never threatened to rise above historically modest levels and anybody who took the 'age of leisure' seriously was labelled as a 'drop-out'.

Despite these grounds for caution, and the problems of assessing the time-scale of change, it does seem likely that the new technology of the 1980s will have pervasive and deep effects.

Firstly, the programmability of the new technology combined with cheap data storage creates the potential for the first time of automating not just mass production (a limited area of work) but non-mass production. British industry, which is lagging behind other economies in its take-up and implementation of automation, is still at the beginning of this process, such that it is still too early to measure effects. A survey (PSI, 1984) of 1200 factories showed that microelectronic automation had destroyed about 34,000 jobs in 1982 and 1983 – less than 5 per cent of the total drop in manufacturing employment during that period. However, the authors of the survey underline that the overall figures reflect the relatively limited extent and sophistication of the use of microelectronics in industry to date.

The service sector is especially labour intensive and before 1975 the loss of jobs in manufacturing industry was more than offset by the increasing number of jobs in services. But areas which have been large providers of jobs in the past, such as banking, insurance, communications and distribution, will be radically affected by the revolution in information technology creating a net loss of jobs unless there is a vast, and at present unseeable, increase in demand. Thus the prospects for massive job creation in the near future seem bleak, with a continual contraction of job opportunities in both manufacturing and services resulting from new technology, perhaps not on the dramatic, earth-shattering scale envisaged by some forecasters; just a slow, but cumulative leaking away of human opportunities. The problem of the 1980s and early 1990s will continue to be providing a decent life for millions of people for whom 'the experience of work' is a distant and fractured hope.

References
Anthony, P.D. (1977), *The Ideology of Work*, Tavistock.
Coyle, A. (1984), *Redundant Women*, The Women's Press.
CSS (1981), *New Technology: Society, Employment and Skill*, CSS, London.
Jenkins, C. & Sherman, B. (1979), *The Collapse of Work*, Eyre & Methuen.
PSI (1984), *Microelectronics in Industry: A Report*, PSI, London.
Sackville, R. (1981), 'Summation', in Wilkes, J. (ed.), *The Future of Work*, Allen & Unwin, Sydney.
Trevor, M. & White, M. (1983), *Under Japanese Management*, Heinemann.

Index